Palgrave Studies in European Union Politics
Edited by: **Michelle Egan**, American University USA, **Neill Nugent**, Manchester Metropolitan University, UK, **William Paterson**, University of Birmingham, UK

Editorial Board: **Christopher Hill**, Cambridge, UK, **Simon Hix**, London School of Economics, UK, **Mark Pollack**, Temple University, USA, **Kalypso Nicolaïdis**, Oxford, UK, **Morten Egeberg**, University of Oslo, Norway, **Amy Verdun**, University of Victoria, Canada, **Claudio M. Radaelli**, University of Exeter, UK, **Frank Schimmelfennig**, Swiss Federal Institute of Technology, Switzerland

Palgrave Macmillan is delighted to announce the launch of a new book series on the European Union. Following on the sustained success of the acclaimed *European Union Series*, which essentially publishes research-based textbooks, *Palgrave Studies in European Union Politics* will publish research-driven monographs.

The remit of the series is broadly defined, both in terms of subject and academic discipline. All topics of significance concerning the nature and operation of the European Union potentially fall within the scope of the series. The series is multidisciplinary to reflect the growing importance of the EU as a political and social phenomenon. We will welcome submissions from the areas of political studies, international relations, political economy, public and social policy and sociology.

Titles include:

Ian Bache and Andrew Jordan (*editors*)
THE EUROPEANIZATION OF BRITISH POLITICS

Richard Balme and Brian Bridges (*editors*)
EUROPE–ASIA RELATIONS
Building Multilateralisms

Derek Beach and Colette Mazzucelli (*editors*)
LEADERSHIP IN THE BIG BANGS OF EUROPEAN INTEGRATION

Milena Büchs
NEW GOVERNANCE IN EUROPEAN SOCIAL POLICY
The Open Method of Coordination

Dario Castiglione, Justus Schönlau, Chris Longman, Emanuela Lombardo, Nieves Pérez-Solórzano Borragán and Mirim Aziz
CONSTITUTIONAL POLITICS IN THE EUROPEAN UNION
The Convention Moment and its Aftermath

Morten Egeberg (*editor*)
MULTILEVEL UNION ADMINISTRATION
The Transformation of Executive Politics in Europe

Stefan Gänzle and Allen G. Sens (*editors*)
THE CHANGING POLITICS OF EUROPEAN SECURITY
Europe Alone?

Isabelle Garzon
REFORMING THE COMMON AGRICULTURAL POLICY
History of a Paradigm Change

Heather Grabbe
THE EU'S TRANSFORMATIVE POWER

Katie Verlin Laatikainen and Karen E. Smith (*editors*)
THE EUROPEAN UNION AND THE UNITED NATIONS

Esra LaGro and Knud Erik Jørgensen (*editors*)
TURKEY AND THE EUROPEAN UNION
Prospects for a Difficult Encounter

Paul G. Lewis and Zdenka Mansfeldová (*editors*)
THE EUROPEAN UNION AND PARTY POLITICS IN CENTRAL AND EASTERN EUROPE

Hartmut Mayer and Henri Vogt (*editors*)
A RESPONSIBLE EUROPE?
Ethical Foundations of EU External Affairs

Lauren M. McLaren
IDENTITY, INTERESTS AND ATTITUDES TO EUROPEAN INTEGRATION

Christoph O. Meyer, Ingo Linsenmann and Wolfgang Wessels (*editors*)
ECONOMIC GOVERNMENT OF THE EU
A Balance Sheet of New Modes of Policy Coordination

Frank Schimmelfennig, Stefan Engert and Heiko Knobel
INTERNATIONAL SOCIALIZATION IN EUROPE
European Organizations, Political Conditionality and Democratic Change

Justus Schönlau
DRAFTING THE EU CHARTER

Palgrave Studies in European Union Politics
Series Standing Order ISBN 1–4039–9511–7 (hardback) and
ISBN 1–4039–9512–5 (paperback)

You can receive future titles in this series as they are published by placing a standing order. Please contact your bookseller or, in case of difficulty, write to us at the address below with your name and address, the title of the series and one of the ISBNs quoted above.

Customer Services Department, Macmillan Distribution Ltd, Houndmills, Basingstoke, Hampshire RG21 6XS, England

Europe–Asia Relations

Building Multilateralisms

Edited by

Richard Balme
*Professor, School of Government
Peking University, China*

and

Brian Bridges
*Professor of Politics
Lingnan University, Hong Kong*

Editorial matter, selection and introduction © Richard Balme and Brian Bridges 2008
All remaining chapters © respective authors 2008

All rights reserved. No reproduction, copy or transmission of this publication may be made without written permission.

No paragraph of this publication may be reproduced, copied or transmitted save with written permission or in accordance with the provisions of the Copyright, Designs and Patents Act 1988, or under the terms of any licence permitting limited copying issued by the Copyright Licensing Agency, 90 Tottenham Court Road, London W1T 4LP.

Any person who does any unauthorized act in relation to this publication may be liable to criminal prosecution and civil claims for damages.

The authors have asserted their rights to be identified as the authors of this work in accordance with the Copyright, Designs and Patents Act 1988.

First published 2008 by
PALGRAVE MACMILLAN
Houndmills, Basingstoke, Hampshire RG21 6XS and
175 Fifth Avenue, New York, N.Y. 10010
Companies and representatives throughout the world

PALGRAVE MACMILLAN is the global academic imprint of the Palgrave Macmillan division of St. Martin's Press, LLC and of Palgrave Macmillan Ltd. Macmillan® is a registered trademark in the United States, United Kingdom and other countries. Palgrave is a registered trademark in the European Union and other countries.

ISBN-13: 978–0–230–55067–4   hardback
ISBN-10: 0–230–55067–3   hardback

This book is printed on paper suitable for recycling and made from fully managed and sustained forest sources. Logging, pulping and manufacturing processes are expected to conform to the environmental regulations of the country of origin.

A catalogue record for this book is available from the British Library.

Library of Congress Cataloging-in-Publication Data

Europe-Asia relations : building multilateralisms / edited by Richard
  Balme and Brian Bridges.
       p. cm. — (Palgrave studies in european union politics)
  Includes bibliographical references and index.
  ISBN 0–230–55067–3 (alk. paper)
 1. Europe—Relations—Asia. 2. Asia—Relations—Europe. I. Balme,
  Richard. II. Bridges, Brian, 1948–
  D1065.A78E972 2008
  303.48′2405—dc22
                                              2008000184

10 9 8 7 6 5 4 3 2 1
17 16 15 14 13 12 11 10 09 08

Printed and bound in Great Britain by
CPI Antony Rowe, Chippenham and Eastbourne

Contents

List of Tables, Figures and Box	vii
List of Acronyms	ix
Preface	xiii
Notes on the Contributors	xv

1 Introducing Asia, Europe and the Challenges of
   Globalization 1
   Richard Balme and Brian Bridges

**Part I Inter-Regional Relations in a Globalizing
         Context** **25**

2 Europe–Asia: The Historical Limits of a 'Soft' Relationship 27
   François Godement

3 EU Foreign Policy and Asia 47
   Karen E. Smith

4 The Asia Strategy of the European Union and Asia–EU
   Economic Relations: History and New Developments 66
   Sung-Hoon Park and Heung-Chong Kim

5 EU–ASEAN Relations and Policy-Learning 83
   Yeo Lay Hwee

6 Asian Migrants in Europe: The Need for a Global
   Perspective 103
   Leo Douw

Part II Patterns of Bilateralism **123**

7 A European Strategy Towards China? The Limits of
   Integration in Foreign Policy Making 125
   Richard Balme

8	China's Strategic Thinking: The Role of the European Union *Ting Wai*	145
9	Taiwan and Europe *Czeslaw Tubilewicz*	172
10	From an Issue-specific to a Global Partnership: Japan and the European Union *Machiko Hachiya*	195
11	The European Union and the Korean Conundrum *Brian Bridges*	213
12	India–EU Relations: Building a Strategic Partnership *Ummu Salma Bava*	233

Index of Names — 257

Index of Subjects — 261

List of Tables, Figures and Box

Tables

1.1	Europe–Asia patterns of relations	12
3.1	CFSP decisions (November 1993–August 2006)	56
4.1	Main contents of NAS and country strategy papers adopted by the EU during 1993–96	74
4.2	Destination of EU's exports by region (1995/2001/2005)	76
4.3	Destination of EU15's foreign direct investment by region (1996/1999/2005)	76
6.1	Chinese voluntary associations in Europe (1950s–1990s)	113
8.1	China's trade statistics – exports (in US$ billion)	152
8.2	China's trade statistics – Imports (in US$ billion)	152
8.3	China's total trade with the Western Triad (in US$ billion)	153
8.4	Investments of the EU, US and Japan in China	154
9.1	Taiwan's trade with Europe (including post-Soviet states) (in millions of US dollars)	186
9.2	The EU's trade with Taiwan (in billions of euros from 1 January 1999, in billions of ECU until 31 December 1998)	187
12.1	Overview of the major developments in India–EU relations (1963–2007)	237
12.2	India's exports in % share with different regions of the world (April–March 2001–06)	239
12.3	India's imports in % share with different regions of the world (April–March 2001–06)	239
12.4	India's trade with major trading partners (exports & imports)	240
12.4(a)	India's exports % growth change of total with some main countries (April–March 2001–06)	240
12.4(b)	India's exports % share of total with some main countries (April–March 2001–06)	240
12.4(c)	India's imports % growth change of total with some main countries (April–March 2001–06)	241

12.4(d)	India's imports % share of total with some main countries (April–March 2001–06)	241
12.5	EU's trade with major trading partners (% share)	242
12.5(a)	EU's exports (in million euros)	242
12.5(b)	EU's imports (in million euros)	242

Figures

4.1	Preferential trading arrangements of the EU: a pyramid analysis	68
10.1	Organizational reform of the Ministry of Foreign Affairs, Japan	207

Box

3.1	CFSP Decision-Making Procedures	51

List of Acronyms

ACP	African, Caribbean and Pacific
ADB	Asian Development Bank
AEMM	ASEAN–EC Ministerial Meeting
AFTA	ASEAN Free Trade Area
AIA	ASEAN Investment Area
AIDS	Acquired Immune Deficiency Syndrome
AMED	Asia–Middle East Dialogue
AMM	Aceh Monitoring Mission
APEC	Asia-Pacific Economic Cooperation Forum
APRIS	ASEAN Programme for Regional Integration Support
ARF	ASEAN Regional Forum
ASEAN	Association of South-East Asian Nations
ASEAN-ISIS	ASEAN–Institute of Strategic and International Studies
ASEM	Asia–Europe Meeting
BEM	Big Emerging Market
CAP	Common Agricultural Policy
CCP	Common Commercial Policy
CEEC	Central and East European Countries
CET	Common External Tariff
CFSP	Common Foreign and Security Policy
CSCAP	Council for Security Cooperation in the Asia-Pacific
CSCE	Conference on Security and Cooperation in Europe
CSDP	Common Security and Defence Policy
CSP	Country Strategy Paper
EAEC	East Asian Economic Caucus
EBRD	European Bank for Development and Reconstruction
EC	European Community
ECHO	European Communities Humanitarian Office
ECSC	European Coal and Steel Community
EEA	European Economic Area
EEAS	European External Action Service
EEC	European Economic Community
EFEX	European Financial Expertise Network
EFTA	European Free Trade Area
EID	Economic Integration Division
EIDHR	European Initiative on Democracy and Human Rights

EP	European Parliament
EPC	European Political Cooperation
EPG	Eminent Persons Group
ESDP	European Security and Defence Policy
EU	European Union
EURATOM	European Atomic Energy Community
EVSL	Early Voluntary Sectoral Liberalization
FDI	Foreign Direct Investment
FEALAC	Forum for East Asia and Latin American Cooperation
FIT	French Institute in Taipei
FTA	Free Trade Agreement
GATT	General Agreement on Tariffs and Trade
GCC	Gulf Cooperation Council
GSP	Generalized System of Preferences
IAEA	International Atomic Energy Agency
ICCPR	International Covenant for Civil and Political Rights
ICSECR	International Covenant for Social, Economic and Cultural Rights
IGC	Inter-Governmental Conference
IMF	International Monetary Fund
INTOR	International Next Tokamak Reactor
IPR	Intellectual Property Rights
ISIS	Institutes of International and Strategic Studies
ITER	International Thermonuclear Experimental Reactor
JHA	Justice and Home Affairs
JUSCANZ	Japan, United States, Canada, Australia and New Zealand
KEDO	Korean Peninsula Energy Development Organization
MES	Market Economy Status
MFN	Most Favoured Nation
MoFA	Ministry of Foreign Affairs
NAFTA	North American Free Trade Area
NAS	New Asia Strategy
NATO	North Atlantic Treaty Organization
NGO	Non-Governmental Organization
NIEs	Newly-industrializing economies
NIPs	National Indicative Programmes
NPC	National People's Congress
NPT	(Nuclear) Non-Proliferation Treaty
NTB	Non-tariff barriers
ODA	Official Development Assistance
OECD	Organization for Economic Cooperation and Development

PLA	People's Liberation Army
PRC	People's Republic of China
PSC	Political and Security Committee
QMV	Qualified Majority Voting
QRs	Quantitative restrictions
ROC	Republic of China on Taiwan
SAARC	South Asian Association for Regional Cooperation
SAR	Special Administrative Region
SII	Structural Impediments Initiative
STF	Science and Technology Fellowship
TAFTA	Transatlantic Free Trade Area
TBR	Trade Barriers Regulation
TEP	Transatlantic Economic Partnership
UK	United Kingdom
UN	United Nations
UNCTAD	United Nations Commission for Trade and Development
UNGA	United Nations General Assembly
UNHRC	United Nations' Human Rights Commission
UR	Uruguay Round
USA	United States of America
WEU	Western European Union
WHO	World Health Organization
WMD	Weapons of mass destruction
WTO	World Trade Organization

Preface

In recent years the precept that Europe and Asia should never meet has been proven to be outdated, as flows of people, goods, culture and ideas between the two continents have become ever greater. Nonetheless, the complex nature of this evolving relationship has not been explored as fully as it deserves.

The structure and contents of the chapters in this volume result from a conscious effort to draw in scholars from different disciplines, institutions and countries as the best way to examine this multifaceted relationship. Authors were carefully selected and asked to present the first draft of their papers at an international conference, held at Hong Kong Baptist University on 20–21 May 2005. All of the papers have been revised and updated in the light of discussions at the conference, suggestions from the editors, and, of course, recent developments. Thanks are due not only to the various participants of that conference but also to the Department of Government and International Studies (GIS) and to the Faculty of Social Sciences at Hong Kong Baptist University which proved a gracious host to what became a series of lively discussions. Special thanks also go to the Lee Hysan Foundation, the Consulate-General of France in Hong Kong, the Office of the European Commission in Hong Kong and Macau, Sciences-Po in Paris and its delegation in China, the Hong Kong and Macau Association of European Studies, and the Research Committee of the Hong Kong Baptist University for their financial, logistical and intellectual support of that original conference.

We have benefited from the comments on ideas and drafts from the series editors, and from two anonymous reviewers. Gemma d'Arcy Hughes, Amy Lankester-Owen, Nick Brock and Alison Howson at Palgrave have helped us immensely along the way. We are grateful to William Butcher, Kenneth Chan, Joseph Cheng, Michael DeGolyer, Frank Fu, François Godement, Edmund Kwok, Ng Ching Fai, Thomas Roe, James Tang and Ting Wai, for their support and insights at different stages of the project. In addition to thanking the various contributors for their timely and conscientious revisions to their original papers, we would like to express a joint and special thanks to the supporting staff of the Department of GIS, particularly to Terence Yeung of the European Documentation Centre and to Ada To, for managing the organization of the initial conference. Ada To also provided indefatigable editorial assistance in helping us preparing the final manuscript for publication. This book owes its existence to their quiet professionalism and undoubted generosity. We also thank Bao Peilin and Zhang Hui for their help in compiling the index.

Finally, we would like to thank our wives, Stephanie and Siew Bee, who have had to put up with, and support, our distracted selves as we pulled this volume together.

RICHARD BALME AND BRIAN BRIDGES
BEIJING AND HONG KONG

Notes on the Contributors

Richard Balme is a Professor at Sciences Po, Paris, currently visiting at the School of Government, Peking University. He is Director of the Programme 'Governance and Globalisation' for Sciences Po in China. He has been Head of the Department of Government and International Studies at the Hong Kong Baptist University from 2003 to 2006. He teaches and writes about European politics, globalization and comparative public policy. Among his recent works are (with D. Chabanet) *European Governance and Democracy: Power and Protest in the European Union* (2008).

Brian Bridges is a Professor and Head of the Department of Political Science and Director of the Centre for Asian Pacific Studies at Lingnan University, Hong Kong. He has previously been Head of the East Asia Programme at the Royal Institute of International Affairs in London. He teaches, writes and broadcasts on the politics and international relations of the Asian Pacific region and on Europe's relations with that region.

Leo Douw is a lecturer of Modern Chinese History and Society in the Department of Sociology and Anthropology, Asian Studies Section, at the University of Amsterdam, and in the History Department at the Free University Amsterdam. His research is concerned with the modern history of Chinese economic thought, Chinese transnational entrepreneurship, and Chinese international migration. His publications include: *Qiaoxiang Ties: Interdisciplinary Approaches to 'Cultural Capitalism' in South China* (1999) (editor with Cen Huang and Michael R. Godley); *Rethinking Chinese Transnational Enterprises: Cultural Affinity and Business Strategies* (2001) (editor with Cen Huang and David Ip), and *Conflict and Innovation: Joint Ventures in China* (2006) (editor with Chan Kwok-bun).

François Godement is Professor at Sciences Po, Paris, and President of Asia Centre. He is also co-chair of the European committee of CSCAP (Council for Security Cooperation in the Asia-Pacific) and a co-founder of CAEC (Council for Asia-Europe Cooperation). An outside consultant to the policy planning staff of the French Ministry of Foreign Affairs, he specializes in East Asian international relations and strategy, regional integration and Chinese contemporary affairs. He has also been a consultant to the OECD, the European Union and the World Bank. He is a frequent contributor to the international press on East Asian international relations and strategy.

Machiko Hachiya is an Associate Professor in the Faculty of Law at Kyushu University, Japan. She has been Assistant to the Scientific Counsellor, the Delegation of the Commission of the European Communities, Tokyo (1986–1993). She specializes in EU studies and international politics.

Heung-Chong Kim heads the European Studies programme at the Korea Institute for International Economic Policy (KIEP), Seoul, Korea. His research interests include European economic integration, Europe and East Asia, FTA and trade policy issues, and gender and culture issues. Before joining KIEP, he served as an Honorary Member of Christ Church, University of Oxford and as part of the Chief Advisory Staff to the Deputy Prime Minister and the Minister of Finance and Economy of Korea. He has taught economics and European issues in many universities, including Seoul National University, Yonsei University and Korea University. He was invited as an IV fellow by the State Department of the United States.

Sung-Hoon Park is a Professor in the Graduate School of International Studies at Korea University, Seoul, Korea. He specializes in international economics, with a special interest in international trade, finance and the economics of regional integration.

Karen E. Smith is currently Reader in International Relations and Director of the European Foreign Policy Unit at the London School of Economics and Political Science, London, UK. A specialist on European affairs, she is the editor of *CFSP Forum*, the online bi-monthly newsletter of FORNET, an EU-funded research network on European foreign policy (www.fornet.info).

Ting Wai graduated from the Chinese University of Hong Kong and obtained his PhD in Political Science and International Relations from the University of Paris-X (Nanterre), France. Formerly Research Fellow at the Institute of Southeast Asian Studies, Singapore, he is now Professor at the Department of Government and International Studies, Hong Kong Baptist University. His research interests include the domestic politics and foreign policies of China, and theories of international relations. He has published extensively on Chinese diplomacy, Sino-American relations, Sino-European relations, China and the Korean Peninsula, China and India–Pakistan relations, the proliferation of weapons of mass destruction in Asia, Chinese visions of regional cooperation, Chinese nuclear strategy, Mainland–Hong Kong relations, and the external relations and international status of Hong Kong.

Czeslaw Tubilewicz is Lecturer at the School of History and Politics, the University of Adelaide, Australia. He has authored *Taiwan and Post-Communist Europe: Shopping for Allies* (2007) and edited *Critical Issues in Contemporary China* (2006).

Ummu Salma Bava is Associate Professor and Coordinator of the Netherlands Prime Minister's Grant, Centre for European Studies, School of International Studies, Jawaharlal Nehru University, New Delhi, India. She has carried out extensive research on issues pertaining to European and South Asian security and politics and is fluent in German. Her research interests are in regional integration and organization, European security, transatlantic relations, Indian and German politics and foreign policy, and conflict resolution.

Yeo Lay Hwee is Senior Research Fellow at the Singapore Institute of International Affairs and Honorary Fellow at the Contemporary Europe Research Centre, University of Melbourne, Australia. The focus of her research includes peace and development in ASEAN, ASEAN's external relations (particularly with the European Union), the Asia–Europe Meeting (ASEM) process and comparative regionalism. Prior to joining the SIIA, she had worked in the Ministry of Defence, the Ministry of Information and the Arts, the Institute of Policy Studies, the Danish Institute for International Affairs and she had taught in the University of Macau and the National University of Singapore. She writes and lectures extensively on Asia–Europe relations and on comparative regionalism, and contributes regularly to commentaries and analysis to the newspapers.

1
Introducing Asia, Europe and the Challenges of Globalization

Richard Balme and Brian Bridges

The theme of this volume, contemporary Asia–Europe relations, addresses interactions between what international relations theorists call regions, delineated along geographical lines of continents. Regions are neither territories placed under the sovereignty of political institutions, nor supranational or transnational actors in the strict sense of the term. They consist of wide and complex interactions based on territorial contiguity or relative proximity, established through economic, cultural and political interdependencies, historically developed over time and geographically located across space. They can jointly be understood as patterns of territorial relations encompassing neighbouring states, and as sub-systems of international relations at the global level. Europe and Asia qualify immediately under this definition.

Countries from Europe, for which the enlarged European Union (EU) embodies the more general densification of relations, on one hand, and Asia, which is taken as covering Northeast, Southeast and South Asia on the other hand, share some common cultural and historical heritage, noticeably religious influences, quite proximate values and ways of living, and the legacy of multi-secular territorial conflicts and invasions. They are also engaged not just in raising their own living standards but also in growing economic interdependencies, and increasingly in establishing common institutions such as the EU and the Association of South-East Asian Nations (ASEAN) to develop cooperative policy dialogue and joint policy making. Although both regions display a high degree of internal diversity, economic and political integration is clearly much more advanced in the European than in the Asian case. Nevertheless, both of them exemplify how regional cooperation and integration may develop and, with the help of economic growth and convergence, may possibly contribute to establishing a multipolar world, better equipped to face the challenges of globalization. These are the general perspectives orientating the analysis in this volume. Both Europe and Asia have been praised as potential major actors in the international relations of the twenty-first century, for their potential role in diffusing development and in balancing US hegemony in world security and economic affairs. A decade after the establishment of the first Asia–Europe Meeting in 1996, what are the accomplishments of and prospects for these relations? What is their contribution to the state of international relations, and to the urgent need for governance at the global level? Are they likely to have a significant effect on the course of world affairs?

The chapters in this volume explore these issues in their recent – and in some cases still initial – development. This introduction provides the empirical and theoretical framing for these questions, surveys the findings developed in individual chapters, and proposes a general interpretation of the issues at stake in Asia–Europe relations at the beginning of this new century. We start with a brief historical perspective on Asia–Europe relations, before indicating the new expectations supported by their developments. We then specify how Asia–Europe relations can be approached within the alternative conceptions of international relations rooted in realism, idealism and constructivism. A specific analytical framework is further proposed to account for the political economy of inter-regional relations in the context of globalization, and for its variations according to regions, countries and policy sectors. Finally, the chapter summarizes the findings of the different chapters, and critically reviews the developments and limitations of regionalization and multilateralism in globalization.

A brief historical perspective on Asia–Europe relations

In a long-term perspective, Europe and Asia did not primarily interact as regions, but as states, missions, trade ventures and even individuals pursuing imperial and colonial projects (Godement, 1997; Gregory, 2003; Hobson, 2004). The Portuguese were the first to arrive Asia as traders and then colonizers, but they were by no means the last, as, driven by an amalgam of political, religious, strategic and economic motives, the major European powers competed across Asia. Ironically, it was Japan, which avoided direct colonization but tried to copy the Europeans' imperial ambitions, that helped to precipitate the end of that process of European formal and informal control. Relations between

Europe and Asia, initially established on European trade expansion and conquest, went through different stages of reflux with the decolonization of the British, French, Dutch, Spanish and Portuguese empires. After initially being a Spanish colony, the Philippines obtained independence from the United States (US) in 1946. The United Kingdom (UK) renounced sovereignty over Burma in 1947, India in 1948, Singapore in 1956, Malaysia in 1957, and Hong Kong in 1997. Western settlements in China were expelled when the communists took power in 1949. France officially left Southeast Asia ('Indochine') after the Geneva conference of 1954 following the battle of Dien Bien Phu. Indonesia obtained independence from the Netherlands in 1949, and Portugal left Timor in 1974 and Macao in 1999. The eclipse of the European presence in Asia was paralleled by the growing US engagement in the region as the Cold War deepened (in Taiwan, Korea, and Vietnam). After the People's Republic of China (PRC) joined the United Nations Security Council in 1971 and the end of the Vietnam war in 1975, East–West relations in Asia ceased to be dominated by direct inter-state confrontations, despite the existence of several communist regimes in the region.

At the same time, however, the apparent European 'withdrawal' from Asia was accompanied by a loosening of economic and commercial ties, which meant that the Europeans missed out on some of the new opportunities as, one by one, the Asian states followed the Japanese lead in heading for high-speed economic growth. With the rising development of the Asian economies and with the opening of China and its transition to a more marketized economy, relations between Asian and European countries steadily turned more business-oriented and more cooperative. The collapse of European communism between 1989 and 1991 definitely ended the ideological cycle and corresponding alliances opposing western capitalism to eastern communism. The progress of European integration and the rise of the EU as a major economic power in world affairs, as well as Asian economic development and regional integration have provided opportunities for designing a renewed context for more intense exchanges.

Rising expectations

Consequently, in the early 1990s the Europeans began to think about Asia in a more comprehensive and coherent manner. The realization of the importance of these Asian economies and the relative weakness of the European involvement in the region both economically and politically was the driving force behind European efforts at re-evaluation, which culminated in the European Commission's landmark 'Asia strategy' document in mid-1994 (Camroux and Lechervy, 1996; Park and Kim in this volume). This argued the case for a higher priority to be given to Asia and for more proactive and better-coordinated strategies towards the region.

This shift in European perceptions and policies was reciprocated by an initiative from Singapore, acting on behalf of ASEAN, to establish the first-ever region-to-region dialogue through the Asia–Europe Meeting (ASEM) process. The Asians wanted to reinforce the weakest leg of the Asia–Europe–North American triangle (not least to avoid overdependence on the United States). The first ASEM was held in Bangkok in February 1996 and such summit-level meetings have been held regularly every 18 months since, with various official-level meetings in between. ASEM has continued to focus on three main 'pillars' or areas of relations, namely economic, politico-strategic, and socio-cultural (Gilson, 2002; Yeo, 2004; as well as Chapter 2 in this volume). Although the discussions at the Summits are informal and non-binding, it is possible to see through this developing process a form of institutionalization of dialogue.

At the same time as ASEM was being established, the European Commission was engaged in a series of reviews of the EU's relations with a range of individual Asian states and with ASEAN. A common theme of this series of documents issued through the mid-1990s was the need to engage individual Asian states not just in a commercial sense but also in broader dialogue. The Asian financial crisis of 1997–98 brought temporary disruptions to the economic flows between the two regions and at least some re-evaluations of the 'Asian way' of doing things. But it was not to significantly undermine in the longer run either the European desire to be more engaged in Asia (particularly as China, which survived the financial crisis better than most of its neighbours, continued to grow in economic and political clout) or the Asian desire to have a counterbalance to the United States (particularly as the Bush administration's 'war on terror' provoked some mixed reactions across Asia). A survey conducted across 23 countries in December 2004 by GlobeScan shows that a majority of the respondents (58 per cent) see the possibility that Europe might in the future be more influential than the United States as positive. Asia is more divided on the issue between China (66 per cent as positive), Indonesia (56 per cent), South Korea (53 per cent) and more moderate appreciations in Japan, India and Philippines (35 per cent). The present influence of Europe in world affairs is seen as positive by

68 per cent. Again, Japan (39 per cent) and India (35 per cent) have more moderate appreciations than other Asian countries (77 per cent in China, 76 per cent in Philippines, 71 per cent in Indonesia and South Korea), but positive appreciations always outweigh negative ones. Although the survey does not estimate perceptions of Asia as a whole, available measures about the influence of China are also revealing. China's influence indeed appears more positive than any of the other major powers (48 per cent for China, 38 per cent for the United States and 35 per cent for Russia). Interestingly, European countries have rather contrasted appreciations of China, with a majority seeing it as positive in France (49 per cent), the UK (46 per cent), Italy (42 per cent) and Spain (37 per cent), against a majority as negative in Germany (47 per cent), Poland (33 per cent) and Turkey (36 per cent) (Kull, 2005). The overall increasingly positive images of Europe as well as China compared to the United States and Russia, especially among young generations, therefore coexist with important variations across countries of both regions, and we probably still stand at some distance from achieving common perceptions shared by public opinion at the regional level. Nevertheless mutual expectations seem to be on the rise according to these data.

Europe–Asia relations now face the challenges at the core of globalization, such as controlling the effects of trade liberalization in both regions, securing sustainable patterns of development, managing migration flux, containing global pandemics, and fighting terrorism. They also address the issues of the global power structure, the position and behaviour of the United States in international relations, and the access of developing countries to the global governance structure. Whether Europe and Asia will indeed be able to meet these challenges remains indeed uncertain. The developments of the last two decades, however, suggest a rapid evolution of their relations, which will be highly significant for the impact of globalization on international relations.

Multilateralism, regionalism and theory of international relations

Despite this long history of interactions between Europe and Asia, the diffuseness and distance in these relations may well help to account for the relative neglect of this inter-regional relationship in the academic literature. Nonetheless, as this volume will demonstrate, the contemporary relationship between the European Union and Asia provides ample evidence of the complex and multi-layered nature of the interactions between the two regions, and more generally of the structure of contemporary international relations. At the same time, the patterns of interactions discussed in the following chapters also provide insights into the evolving parameters of the European Union's aspirations for a Common Foreign and Security Policy (CFSP), the developing characteristics of regionalism within the Asian Pacific region, the degree of bilateralism still prevalent in the Europe–Asia relationship, and the extent to which common concerns and issues can act as a basis for cooperative agendas.

The study of international relations has expanded its boundaries over the past decades, now encompassing not just international security issues but also the international political economy, understood as the interaction between markets and institutions at the international level. Within the scope of international relations, however, as the various contributors to this volume demonstrate, it has become in most cases impossible to separate politics (and security) from economics. At the same time, and in part related to this intermingling of the political and economic dimensions, it is also clear that, while states remain the most important actors in international relations, non-state actors such as multinational corporations, non-governmental organizations, and intergovernmental organizations play a growing role. In this context, the role and ability of the EU to be a 'single' actor has come under particular scrutiny.

The development of international relations studies over the past few decades has highlighted a number of perspectives and theories, although it should be borne in mind, as Joshua Goldstein argues, that 'no single theory reliably explains the wide range of international interactions, both conflictual and cooperative' (Goldstein, 2004). If we adopt the approach of realism (and neo-realism) when thinking about Europe–Asia relations, then it implies that states (or governments), primarily power-maximizing and self-interested, remain the most important actors, which result in conflictual or at least competitive circumstances not just within Europe and Asia, but also between the two regions. Such a perspective suggests a weak capacity for foreign policy coordination by the EU, as member states would indeed compete rather than cooperate in external relations. Symmetrically, the prospect for regional integration in Asia would only be limited. It would also mean that Europe–Asia relations after decolonization are predominantly bilateral relations at the country level, without much significance as they do not touch upon the security issues left under the leadership of the United States in both regions. Europe and Asia would remain two loosely-organized areas without many direct relations.

By contrast, liberalism, neo-liberalism and interdependence theorists would see examples of cooperation within the EU and between the European states and their Asian counterparts as showing that international rules and institutions can bring mutual gains to all involved. In providing devices for cooperation and coordination, international organizations would transform politics in a positive-sum game among participants. In such a perspective, the EU potential for external policy is real and is only dependent on the pace of European integration and cultural adaptation of European leaders and citizens to this process. Regional integration in Asia is similarly a function of the intensification of exchanges among Asian countries and of the integration of Asian countries to the world economy. Significant exchanges can be developed at the inter-regional level through dialogue among regional organizations such as the ASEM, adding to bilateral relations at the country level and contributing to the development of multilateral relations at the global level.

Finally constructivism, drawing on sociological constructs, could take the case even further by arguing that EU–Asia contacts help to create norms and values beyond traditional conceptions of national interests. This would produce a significant effect on international relations in Asia, projecting them in a post-modern era where historical issues of state building and regional hegemony would lose significance, to the benefit of public good provisions at the transnational and global levels. In the current context, the EU and Asia would also, through these contacts, develop common visions and be able to promote a multilateral approach to global issues in international organizations, thus contesting the current US practices by promoting different conceptions and an alternative consensus.

Before engaging further in interpretation, it is worth reminding ourselves that Europe and Asia can be contrasted empirically in many aspects. Countries from Western Europe, the European Union and applicant countries have a population of 570 million, against 2,345 million in Asia. More than half the countries with a high human development index (29 out of 55) are European, against only four from Asia (Japan, Hong Kong, Singapore and South Korea). The vast majority of Asian populations live under medium development conditions, with large internal and cross-country variations. The Human Development Index ranges in 2002 from .956 in Norway to .751 in Turkey, and from .938 in Japan to .431 in Timor-Leste (East Timor) (UNDP, 2004). Differences also relate to political dimensions. The overwhelming majority of European countries are consolidated democracies bound together by the institutional framework of the European Union, which acts as a magnet in its own neighbourhood, and with little or no likelihood of resorting to force against each other. By contrast, most Asian countries host political economies in transition, often with competing or conflicting relationships over territory and security, such as in Korea, the Taiwan Strait and Kashmir, or over the past, as between Japan and some of its Asian neighbours. To a large extent, Europe epitomizes the case for post-modern international relations, with cooperative relations established through economic exchange, the development of supranational institutions securing peace among member states, and nascent political identifications beyond the nation-state. Asia, on the other hand, seems to exemplify the permanence of modernism, and sometimes pre-modernism, in international relations, with state and nation building in the making through international rivalries for leadership and conflicts over sovereignty.

Therefore, the EU presence and strategy in Asia provides a good test of the dynamics of international relations, and, as discussed by François Godement in Chapter 2, of the capacity of the 'soft power' of post-modern institutions to take over the classical inter-states rivalries of the Westphalian system. The influence of Europe on the development of Asian international relations will therefore be an important dimension considered in this volume, particularly in comparison with the one exerted by the United States. But, symmetrically, the presence of Asia in Europe, the way it is incorporated within European foreign policies and contributes to their integration should equally be placed under scrutiny. We may not find another United States in Asia, but the rebirth of Asia–Europe relations cleared of the colonial past and structured at a supra-national level may still provide a significant development in the global system of international relations.

Issues of multilateralism and multipolarity in international relations promptly come to mind when EU–Asia relations are considered. The EU portrays itself as a strong advocate of multilateralism, both in a critique of US policies on several issues which appear to undermine multilateral regimes or norms (the Kyoto Protocol or the war in Iraq) and as a defence of multilateral institutions such as the United Nations (UN) or the World Trade Organization (WTO) when they come under attack for policy failure. The idea of a multipolar world is understood equally as an alternative to US unilateralism or hegemony, but also to the concentration of economic and social resources among western countries. As such, multipolarity is part of the conceptual tools of many Asian countries, amongst which China, keen not only to counter-balance US power but also to cast itself as a leading representative of the 'developing world', has become a particularly strong advocate in the post-Cold War era.

The end of the Cold War immediately raised concerns among commentators about the power structure of international relations. Indeed multipolarity, in ensuring a balance of power among competing states, is seen by most realists as a condition for the stability of international relations (Morgenthau, 1948; Aron, 1962; Waltz, 1979). Opponents of this conception argue for the idea of unipolarity, that is hegemony by one power over the others, as the key factor securing cycles of peaceful relations among nations (Gilpin, 1981; Organski and Kugler, 1980; Kugler and Lemke, 1996). The collapse of the Soviet Union may therefore alternatively be understood as the advent of a *Pax Americana* or as the opening of a time of turmoil due to strong imbalances of power. The intensification of relations between Europe and Asia is thus a test to evaluate if international relations are indeed changing towards more uni-polar or multi-polar modes, and if this is a factor of stability or insecurity.

An often-noted irony is that promoting multilateralism is now understood as an instrument to contain or influence US hegemony, while most international organizations and the practice of multilateralism itself were indeed established by the US after the Second World War as institutions to cope with decolonization and the Cold War. Multilateralism refers to behaviours and institutions by which state and non-state actors elaborate rules organizing their relations and define common policies at the international level. Multilateralism can be opposed to unilateralism (state behaviour ignoring or avoiding international rules), and to bilateralism, the traditional practice of inter-states diplomacy prevalent until the early twentieth century. Multilateralism involves a plurality of actors (states, international organizations, non-governmental organizations, and private firms), issues (security, trade, environment, and development) and arenas (international meetings such as ASEM, WTO, Group of Eight, and the UN General Assembly) (Muldoon, Fagot Aviel, Reitano, and Sullivan, 2005). Although under severe criticism for its failure to deliver its own promises of peace and development, and, more recently, for scandals internal to the UN, the system of multilateral institutions is crucial for the development of governance at the global level. It motivates renewed analysis and expectations for 'bottom-up' developments more inclusive of developing countries and civil societies (Cox, 1997).

The development of regional organizations and inter-regional relations definitely plays a part in this development of multilateralism. We will consider if Europe–Asia linkages take primarily bilateral or multilateral forms, and how these relations relate to the changing power structure of the world order. Multilateralism combined to multipolarity may define a more polyarchic and consensual world order, while unilateralism and unipolarity would create a more authoritative structure. But multilateralism may also be combined with unipolarity under a legitimized hegemony, while we should not exclude that current trends sufficiently undermine international rules to establish a kind of multipolar anarchy.

Finally, we will also consider variations across actors and across issues. Countries obviously entertain different relations with multilateral institutions according to their size, wealth and power. Bilateral relations are more likely to prevail among big powerhouses than among others, where mutual gains of pooled cooperation are more apparent, while constraints on their own strategies are less sensitive. On the other hand, issues also present variations in their capacity to be apprehended by multilateral relations. We expect trade, due to the importance of the WTO on public agendas in the last decade and of regional integration in both regions, to offer more relevance to multilateral relations than security, which is still predominantly bilateral. But 'new' security issues, such as nuclear proliferation, migration, climate change, terrorism or pandemics, may also be subject to multilateral developments. Other issues, such as environment or human rights, may obey complementarities rather than competition between bilateral and multilateral arrangements.

As will be seen from the following chapters, the various authors are not wedded to a single theoretical paradigm in analysing the relations between Europe and Asia, but all are convinced that this relationship deserves greater study and explication as its development will be crucial in shaping the twenty-first-century world order. They also acknowledge that bilateral and multilateral relations, realism and liberalism, are not exclusive of each other, but rather are now combining their effects in different settings according to the issues and the actors considered.

Analytical framework: the political economy of Asia–Europe relations

The field of Europe–Asia relations has long been a comparatively understudied one. A number of scholars, in both Europe and Asia, have researched and written on specific bilateral relations between the European Union (or its constituent member countries) and various countries and regions in Asia; for example, there are well-established literatures on Europe's relations with China, Japan and the Association of South-East Asian Nations (ASEAN). But there have been fewer attempts to set these various bilateral relations into the broader context of Europe–Asia relations. However, the upsurge in European governmental and business interest in Asia in the mid-1990s and the creation of ASEM seemed to act as a kind of trigger for these broader studies. Hans Maull, Gerald Segal and Jusuf Wanandi adopted an unconventional editing approach to give a sense of the complexity of the economic, security and political relationships; Brian Bridges and Georg Wiessala provided general surveys which encompassed most parts of Northeast and Southeast Asia; and Christopher Dent undertook a more detailed examination of the economic relationships between Europe and Asia, particularly the more advanced economies of the region (Maull, Segal, and Wanandi, 1998; Bridges, 1999; Dent, 1999; Wiessala, 2002).

More recent scholarship has focused specifically on the evolution and role of ASEM, and the dynamics of inter-regionalism as a separate phenomenon, such as, for example, the volumes by Julie Gilson and Yeo Lay Hwee (Gilson, 2002; Yeo, 2004). Other volumes have adopted more thematic approaches, such as Peter Preston and Julie Gilson's edited volume looking primarily at Europe–Northeast Asia linkages but within a broad political-cultural-economic discourse, and the most recent publication, edited by Zainal Mantaha and Toshiro Tanaka, which looks mainly at the lessons of the regional integration experiences in both regions (Preston and Gilson, 2001; Mantaha and Tanaka, 2005).

Aware of this background of past scholarship, this volume conceives of relationships, in the plural, since it is indeed inappropriate to describe Europe and Asia as entertaining one single relationship. There are, arguably, several levels of analysis: bilateral links between individual European and individual Asian states; links between the EU as an organization and individual Asian states or sub-regional organizations such as ASEAN; and links between the EU and Asia-wide regional organizations, such as the ASEAN Regional Forum, or through the ASEM format. This complexity of levels of interaction, coupled with the various political, strategic, economic and sociocultural dimensions, do not make it easy to draw one simplified picture of the linkages, actors and processes involved in Europe–Asia relations. The following Table 1.1 however, does offer a framework for conceptualizing these relations as a matrix defined by the power of actors and by the scope of issues considered.

From a political economy perspective, the power of actors in international relations refers to the concentration of economic, political, strategic and knowledge resources and capacities (Strange, 1988). The present US hegemony in world affairs is based precisely on its leadership in all areas of the political economy structure. When Asia and Europe are considered, a number of other major powerhouses, such as the United

Table 1.1 Europe–Asia patterns of relations

Issues	Political/security	Economic
Actors		
Small powers (both European and Asian)	*Multilateralism prevalent* – Diplomatic relations with each other (except Taiwan) – Apart from FPDA**, no direct security agreements – Reliance on multilateral organizations (UN), for security concerns – Reliance on inter-regional meetings for political dialogue	*Inter-regionalism prevalent* – Reliance on regional organizations (EU and ASEAN) – Multilateral arrangements (WTO) – Inter-regional Dialogue (ASEM)
Major powers*	*Bilateralism prevalent* – Bilateral links (such as 'strategic partnerships') – Engagement in political and security fields	*Joint multilateralism and bilateralism* – Regional asymmetries: For Asians, bilateral links more important than inter-regional; for Europeans, EU prevails over bilateral relations – Sectoral asymmetries: market access agreements established through multilateral relations; trade and investment promotion based on competitive bilateral relations.

Notes:
*Major powers are defined as China, India and Japan in Asia and France, Germany and the United Kingdom (UK) in Europe. All other states (and territories) fall under the small powers category.
**FPDA is the Five-Power Defence Arrangement linking the United Kingdom with Malaysia, Singapore, Australia and New Zealand.

Kingdom, France, Germany, China, Japan and India, also play key roles in structuring international relations at the global and at the regional levels. The European Union is now a direct economic competitor to the United States, and a key actor in trade relations, but without equivalent strategic and political capacities. The economic power of Japan and Germany tends to compensate for their lack of strategic resources to enhance their political status, while on the other hand, the nuclear power of India and China, coupled with economic growth, provides them with a rising political influence. The power of actors matters, as regional and multilateral institutions primarily offer small powers the opportunity to voice their interests and to compensate for the asymmetries of resources in the international arena. On the other hand, major powers have less direct incentives to regionalism and multilateralism, as their interests are more likely to be constrained by binding agreements.

The scope and nature of issues is the second dimension to be considered to analyse international relations in the contemporary context. Domestic issues (e.g. taxation, welfare provision, national legislation), on the one hand, can be contrasted with the clearly global ones, such as climate change or the control of pandemics, on the other. Multilateralism is more likely to prevail for obvious transnational and global issues than for local or national ones. Many issues, such as migration, human rights, intellectual property rights, environment protection, competition policy and trade, are nevertheless cross-cutting borders, at the juncture of home affairs and international issues, and are therefore often subject to international controversies and conflicts of interests between international norms and state sovereignty. The emergence and consolidation of multilateralism requires not only that mutual gains are to be expected by most, if not all parties, but also that these gains are perceptible in a time-span able to motivate governments' action, and that they are not outweighed by concentrated losses on specific constituencies threatening governments' longevity. This is why trade, where the mutual benefit of sustained economic growth is quickly perceptible and shared by large segments of the governments' constituencies, has been an area of intense regional integration and multilateralism. Whereas environmental protection, indeed a more stringent issue, produces only concentrated costs in the short term and delayed benefits in the long run.

In short, multilateral arrangements are more likely among small powers for transnational issues with short- or mid-term positive effects. Considering economic exchanges, in the last three decades Europe–Asia relations have been deeply affected by economic development. European countries now face not only strong competitors in their export industries, but also considerable market opportunities in Asia. Incentives for economic cooperation are therefore on the rise, and states tend to cooperate to negotiate market access through agreements established at the global (WTO) or inter-regional level (ASEM). The EU, with its competencies over trade, nevertheless acts in a much more coordinated manner than Asia, and deals directly with major economic powers such as Japan, Korea, China or India. When trade promotion is considered, national interests and North–South rather than East–West cleavages still prevail.

For instance, Japan, France and Germany most often act as competitors in gaining industrial contracts in China. Inter-regionalism in the economic field is both selective and asymmetrical.

Turning to security and political issues, it should be noted that 'small' powers do not interact directly with each other at the inter-regional level, apart from the diplomatic relations necessary to ordinary consular activities. Taiwan presents an exceptional case of active diplomacy aimed at small European countries, but overall it proved unsuccessful as even the Vatican is expected to recognize the PRC in the near future. For small powers, security concerns and sovereignty issues in both regions (the Korean peninsula, the Taiwan Strait and Kashmir in Asia, the Balkans in Europe, Islamic terrorism in both) can only be addressed in international organizations and forums such as the UN and ASEM. Major powers, on the other hand, rely on more direct bilateral dialogue and tend to develop political relations such as a 'strategic partnership'. Interestingly, in line with the evolution of threats on international stability after the end of the Cold War, 'strategic' in the diplomatic language increasingly refers to a claim of cooperation in general political and security issues (terrorism, nuclear proliferation, human rights, and environment) rather than to specific security agreements and coalitions.

Through the following chapters, we endeavour to highlight some of the key features of these complex interactions between the two regions and their component countries and peoples.

Structure and content of the book

This volume consists of two main sections. The first section discusses some of the key issues in EU–Asia relations from a multilateral and inter-regional perspective, covering Europe's external relations mechanisms, European policies towards Asia and Asian regional organizations such as ASEAN (the Association of South-East Asian Nations), Asian responses and the broad economic, social and political dimensions of the relationship. The second section examines key 'bilateral' relationships between Europe and Greater China, Japan, the Korean peninsula, and India.

In Chapter 2 François Godement offers an overview of the EU–Asia relationship, particularly by comparing the context of EU–Asia relations today with the situation at the time of the first Asia–Europe Meeting (ASEM) a decade earlier. After identifying four major trends – Europe's self-centred policy making, its greater external force projection, new regional architecture in Asia, and the return of US power – this chapter calls for a more creative adaptation of the EU's policies towards Asia, by capitalizing on its 'soft power' capabilities. Following this, in Chapter 3 Karen E. Smith analyses the current institutional and decision-making framework for making EU foreign policy, including the interaction with First Pillar institutions and procedures in the external relations areas. She assesses the changes to that framework proposed in the draft constitutional treaty and discusses how these changes might affect policy coherence and flexibility. She particularly discusses how these various developments might impact on policy making towards Asia. In Chapter 4 Sung-Hoon Park and Heung-Chong Kim chart the changing landscape of EU's approach towards East Asia, analyse the background factors, and discuss new developments, primarily in terms of the economic relationship between the EU, its member countries and Asia. With a particular focus on the development of ASEM, the chapter discusses how Asian countries should respond to the challenges of trying to find a balanced approach between regionalism and multilateralism. The EU and ASEAN first developed their links for economic reasons, but the political elements have become stronger over time. Chapter 5, by Yeo Lay Hwee, discusses the development of this relationship and explores how the two regional actors have adapted their behaviour to meet these changes and each other's evolving expectations. Finally, Chapter 6 by Leo Douw contributes to an understanding of the human security aspects of Europe–Asia relations. By drawing on detailed examination of migration flows, this chapter argues that, from the vantage point of Europe, Asian migration has recently shifted from being a marginal phenomenon to one that has taken centre stage, not so much in terms of absolute numbers, but because migration has increasingly come to influence state building and policy formation at the regional and inter-regional levels, and thereby influences the quality of international relations and supranational governance.

Turning to patterns of bilateralism, the EU and China celebrated 30 years of official relations in 2005. While trade relations are booming, the established 'strategic partnership' seems now to characterize EU–China relations in the post-September 11 context, but how durable is this and what will be the implications of these developments? Chapter 7 by Richard Balme analyses the conditions under which a strategy towards China was able to be developed among EU member states and institutions, its impact upon Chinese authorities, and its implications beyond Sino-European relations, not least for the differences in EU and US approaches to China. It reviews issues such as the arms embargo, textile quotas and human rights dialogues to estimate prospective developments between Europe and China. While China endeavours to sustain a favourable regional security environment in the post-Cold War world, Ting Wai argues in Chapter 8 that China is simultaneously looking to reach out beyond the Asian Pacific, in particular to Europe. By examining Chinese perspectives on the evolving economic and political-security relations with the EU, this chapter shows the ambivalence of China, which values its new-found relationship with Europe, not least because of shared concerns about the US role in global affairs, but is also wary of the EU's own ambitions. In Chapter 9 Czeslaw Tubilewicz examines Taiwan's political and economic relations with Europe, including both West and East Central Europe, arguing that primarily through the pursuit of economic diplomacy in the post-Cold War period, Taiwan has been able to expand relations with the older EU member states and win new friends amongst the reforming East European states. Chapter 10, by Machiko Hachiya, addresses the multifaceted nature of the EU–Japan relationship, both political and economic, and, by drawing on case studies, such as the Kyoto Protocol and the ITER project, demonstrates how the relationship is developing and deepening. The EU's relationship with South Korea has been well-established, though primarily driven by economic considerations, but in the course of the last decade North Korea has been an increasing focus of EU concern. In Chapter 11 Brian Bridges analyses the dynamics of the EU's relations with both Koreas and discusses the ways in which political and strategic issues have risen in importance. Finally, although a long-standing relationship, the EU's links with India have only become really active in the past decade. Chapter 12, by Ummu Salma Bava, analyses not only the substantial economic exchanges, which are at the heart of the relationship, but also the increasingly important political and strategic partnership. She also contrasts the EU–India relationship with the EU–China one.

Dynamics of globalization: fragmented multilateralism and the return of bilateral relations

This last section offers a survey of results to be drawn from the following chapters in light of the analytical framework presented above. They are reviewed according to the main questions we selected.

The integration of EU policy in Asia

The relationships between Europe and Asia, of course, relate specifically to the ongoing debates about the competence of the EU in terms of external relations. Although the European Commission and the revolving EU 'troika' of three countries do act for the whole EU in many aspects of international affairs, in particular in the economic dimension, the member states continue to resist giving up their sovereignty in other aspects of external relations, particularly in the political and security fields. As Karen E. Smith demonstrates in Chapter 3, the CFSP, a unique concept in international relations, remains, for all its slow evolution towards greater consistency, an area of tension between the desire to act collectively and at the same time to retain a high degree of national control over foreign policy making.

The evolution of the EU's and the constituent member countries' policies towards Asia therefore provide an interesting and informative series of case studies allowing us to test how far it is possible to talk of implementing a 'European foreign policy'. The convergence of interests amongst the Europeans on economic policy issues, such as trade, aid, investment and technology, may not be as complete as some within the EU would hope, but undoubtedly such convergence does exist. Nevertheless, for the areas of political and strategic relations, the divergences of view still remain apparent. In the aftermath of the debacle in European policy making towards Iraq in 2002–03, when significant fissures between different European states were readily visible, policies towards Asia can be examined to test whether or not such differences were specific to that one issue or whether they represent more fundamental divergences over the conception and implementation of a CFSP for the EU. As several of the chapters demonstrate, there are still differences in the political and security policy sphere, although the divisions between EU member states do not cut in the same way as over the Iraq issue and differ from issue to issue. For example, on the issue of whether or not to recognize North Korea France finds itself out of line with other EU member countries (see Brian Bridges' chapter), whereas on the issue of whether or not to lift the ban on arms sales to China several EU members, led by France, are in favour but others led by Sweden are against (see the chapters by Ting Wai and Richard Balme). European diplomacies in Asia, therefore, do not always coincide and do not follow clear lines of cleavages since the end of the Cold War.

Regional integration in Asia

For Asia, of course, the level of integration is still different from that of the EU. The 'ASEAN model' of cooperation, consensus and dialogue is being slowly diffused throughout the Asian region, mostly notably through the multilateral regional organizations such as the ASEAN

Regional Forum, which has a security focus, and the ASEAN + 3 (which puts the ten ASEAN members together with China, Japan and South Korea to talk mostly about socioeconomic issues), but two problems remain. First, 'Asia' is much less clearly defined in institutional terms than 'Europe'. The ASEM process has institutionalized one definition of 'Asia', and, as has been argued by Julie Gilson, has helped to 'create a sense of identity among a group which previously had no such group formation' (Gilson, 2002, p. 64). But inclusion raises almost as many questions about exclusion, such as the membership of such a club of major South Asian states, such as India and Pakistan, or territories such as Taiwan and Hong Kong, which at the very least in the economic sense are important partners of European states. Both the first-ever 'East Asian Summit', held in Malaysia in mid-December 2005, and the second one, in Manila in January 2007, failed to fully resolve these membership issues. While believing in the virtues of regionalism and multilateral cooperation, the Europeans have tended to watch from the sidelines as these developments have occurred in the Asian region. Although the EU is now considered as the 'paramount' European regional organization, European integration itself also developed along a range of competing regional organizations with often-overlapping or cross-cutting memberships, such as the Council of Europe, the West European Union and the Conference for Security and Cooperation in Europe (now the Organization for Security and Cooperation in Europe) (Larat, 2003). So it is not surprising that Asia, with a much shorter history of regional multilateralist thinking, is still in a state of fluidity over its identity as expressed in terms of regional organizational limits.

Secondly, how far are ASEAN and other nascent Asian regional organizations willing or able to replicate the EU model of integration? Although the 1997–98 Asian financial crisis and other regional problems did prompt re-evaluations of the objectives and modalities of the Asian cooperation processes, as argued by François Godement in Chapter 2 and Yeo Lay Hwee in Chapter 5, neither ASEAN nor any other regional organizations are ready or prepared to follow the EU's path of regional integration, particularly as the socioeconomic and political differences within even regional organizations such as ASEAN constrain a common policy approach. In terms of both economic and political-security policy making, therefore, Asian states – or, at least, the smaller ones – prefer a process of consensus building to create a common position, but that lowest common denominator approach is, despite the well-noticed difficulties on the European side, far from the dynamics and aspirations of the EU's CFSP. As a result, Yeo suggests, the EU side has developed an approach that aims at a 'coalition of the willing', working with those Asian states which are most open to closer partnership.

Patterns of bilateral relations

This limited regional identity and capacity for collective action on the Asian side means that, despite the EU–ASEAN dialogue and the ASEM process, bilateralism remains a strong component of European and Asian interactions with each other. Bilateralism can be examined at two levels: between individual European countries and individual Asian countries, and between individual Asian countries and the EU.

All of the EU member states have diplomatic relations with the states normally included in definitions of Asia, except for North Korea, which is not yet recognized by France, and, more importantly, for Taiwan, which, as Czeslaw Tubilewicz shows in Chapter 9, remains an anomaly, recognized only by one west European state (the Vatican) and relying instead on 'flexible', economic-based diplomacy to maintain and even slowly upgrade its de facto representation across the EU. However, although the smaller states on each side have developed trade and investment linkages with each other and with the larger powers on both sides to varying degrees, their formal security links remain almost non-existent. Malaysia and Singapore, through a vestige of past Commonwealth links, are involved in a consultative security arrangement with the United Kingdom, but this is an exception that proves the rule. The smaller Asian states have had mixed success in developing links with the EU; South Korea has a framework agreement with the EU, the ASEAN countries collectively (but not individually) have a regular dialogue, but Taiwan has failed to secure any substantive dialogue.

For the major Asian states the situation is clearly different. Japan has long been a point of EU interest and interaction. As Machiko Hachiya shows in Chapter 10, the EU–Japanese Joint Declaration of 1991 was intended to broaden the EU–Japanese relationship away from its strong, though at times contentious, economic dimension towards creating an equal partnership on global issues; indeed, on some specific issues there has been very intense interactions. While the shadow of the United States still falls deeply across Japanese policy making, the slow but steady progress in creating a thicker institutionalization of the relationship with the EU is an important component of Japan's greater self-assuredness in the international system. Nonetheless, it is tempting to argue that at the same time as it has been encouraging Japan to greater involvement in international affairs, the EU has also become increasingly interested over the past decade, partly at the expense of Japan, in the two new rising powers of Asia: China and India.

As both Richard Balme and Ting Wai demonstrate in their chapters, the EU–China relationship has become multifaceted: a strong economic relationship, with growing trade and investment linkages (albeit some aspects such as Chinese textile exports to the EU are becoming as controversial as the much earlier Japanese export 'surges' to Europe), but also a political dialogue which is broadening to cover not just human rights but a whole range of issues of global importance. The EU approaches China in a mode of 'constructive engagement' with what it sees as a major strategic partner, while China also sees value in developing closer contacts with the EU, not least when the European approach to international affairs seems more favourable to China's interests than the US approach.

India has risen rapidly in the EU's perspective. As an emerging driver of the new economic globalization, India is developing a strong economic relationship with the EU, but, as Ummu Salma Bava demonstrates in Chapter 12, it was the launch of the EU–India strategic partnership in 2004 which attested to the new importance given to political and strategic issues in the relationship. Paradoxically, given the long historical linkage of one EU member country (the United Kingdom) with India, the EU–India relationship seems to be the 'newest' key Asian relationship for Europe, primarily because India itself has only recently become more active both economically and politically in the global arena. China now seems pre-eminent in EU–Asia relations, but potentially India could come to be a rival for European attention.

Policy variations and multilayered relations

Much of the interaction between the two regions has been dominated by commercial imperatives, as demonstrated in several of the chapters but mostly clearly in the contribution of Sung-Hoon Park and Heung-Chong Kim. Political and security dimensions have been relatively secondary and it should not be forgotten that there is another interface: the sociocultural. This has always been seen as less central to the relationship, yet, arguably, it is the face-to-face contacts of students, tourists, businessmen and others that help to shape the relationship at the societal level and give reality to the rhetoric of politicians about better relations between countries and regions. Indeed, the importance of this dimension has been recognized specifically by the efforts of ASEM to promote this so-called third pillar. Historically, of course, it was Europeans who travelled to and often settled in Asia, but in more recent times the flows of people from Asia to Europe have increased significantly. As Leo Douw argues in Chapter 6, using primarily the case of significant and recent increases in Chinese emigrating to Europe, Asian human flows to Europe can be beneficial to both the sending and the receiving countries. Migration, and more broadly human security, typify the new types of issues on the international agenda on which greater dialogue between Europeans and Asians can only be helpful. It is clear that issues such as nuclear non-proliferation, terrorism, global warming and pandemics cannot be solved by one country, or even one region, alone. In the increasingly globalized and interdependent world regional and inter-regional cooperation is essential.

Resisting unipolarity?

This brings us back to the relationship between multilateralism, regionalism and multipolarity. It is rather premature to draw definitive conclusions with regard to the dominant pattern of international relations in the early twenty-first century, as many of its features are still unstable. A number of characteristics highlighted by the chapters collected in this volume are nevertheless worth noticing. First, developing relations between Europe and Asia, in some cases referred to as a 'honeymoon', do not so far overshadow the importance of the United States to both regions. If these relations are conceived as triangular, it is clear that the Europe–US and Asia–US sides refer to more intense relations than along the Europe–Asia dimension. This fact demonstrates the US leadership in all major aspects of the international political economy, with the exception of trade, where the EU is a competitor of comparable importance. Consequently, the intensification of diplomacy between Europe and Asia is mainly reactive to this imbalance in world power. The current situation fits more with the idea of tempered unipolarity than of balanced multipolarity. Secondly, the general trend, however, supported by economic development in Asia, progress in regional integration, and growing criticism of US foreign policy, seems to favour the role of other poles like Europe and Asia in the medium term, and significant developments have occurred since the 1990s in this respect as reported in this volume.

Thirdly, the net effect in Asia of European proclaimed 'soft power' is indeed impossible to assess independently of other diplomacies and from the domestic or regional dynamics of political change. Significantly, however, what matters is that Asian and European countries, with the noticeable exceptions of North Korea and Myanmar, are engaged in economic agreements and political dialogues, are supportive of the same international institutions, and overall cooperate to deal with common issues more than they compete in zero-sum games. Euro-Asian diplomacy has contributed to this achievement and to the advent of this new area of relations between the two regions.

Fourthly and finally, short-term prospects for further developments of indicated trends seem rather limited. A significant step forward in global multilateralism would require a significant change in the attitude of the United States, as well as real political dynamics within the UN. Trade liberalization, one of the engines of multilateralism through WTO, seems to miss the political consensus necessary to develop further, as exemplified by failure of the Cancun meeting in 2003 and the more than limited achievements in Hong Kong in December 2005. Finally, regionalism, despite substantial developments in Asia (as shown by the move to the East Asian Summit in Malaysia in 2005), entered into a crisis in Europe with the rejection of the Constitutional Treaty by France and by the Netherlands in May and June 2005. Both the institutions and policies of the EU are indeed contested by large segments of public opinion, and government preferences are likely to be more protectionist and more domestic oriented, to the detriment of governance capacities at the transnational and global levels. History is not written in advance. But serious political and institutional challenges limit prospective developments for multilateralism and inter-regionalism in the short and medium term.

References

Aron, Raymond, *Paix et Guerre entre les nations* (Paris: Calmann-Levy, 1962).
Bridges, Brian, *Europe and the Challenge of the Asia Pacific* (Cheltenham: Edward Elgar, 1999).
Camroux, David, and Lechervy, Christian, 'Close Encounter of a Third Kind?: the Inaugural Asia-Europe Meeting of March 1996', *Pacific Review*, 9(3), 442–53.
Cox, Robert (ed.), *The New Realism: Perspectives on Multilateralism and World Order* (London: Macmillan; Tokyo: United Nations University Press, 1997).
Dent, Christopher, *The European Union and East Asia: An Economic Relationship* (London: Routledge, 1999).
Gilpin, R., *War and Change in World Politics* (Cambridge: Cambridge University Press, 1981).
Gilson, Julie, *Asia Meets Europe* (Cheltenham: Edward Elgar, 2002).
Godement, François, *The New Asian Renaissance: From Colonialism to the Post-Cold War* (London: Routledge, 1997).
Goldstein, Joshua, *International Relations*, 5th edn (New York: Longman, 2004).
Gregory, John S., *The West and China since 1500* (London: Palgrave Macmillan, 2003).

Hobson, John M., *The Eastern Origins of Western Civilization* (Cambridge: Cambridge University Press, 2004).
Kugler, J., and Lemke, D. (eds), *Parity and War* (Ann Arbor: Michigan University Press, 1996).
Kull, Steven, 'L'Europe et la France dans le monde selon l'opinion internationale', in *Les Cahiers du Débat* (Paris: Fondation pour l'innovation politique, May 2005).
Larat, Fabrice, *Histoire Politique de l'Intégration Européenne* (Paris: La Documentation Francaise, 2003).
Mantaha, Zainal, and Tanaka, Toshiro (eds), *Enlarging European Union and Asia* (Singapore: ASEF, 2005).
Maull, Hanns, Segal, Gerald, and Wanandi, Jusuf (eds), *Europe and the Asia Pacific* (London: Routledge, 1998).
Morgenthau, Hans, *Politics among Nations* (New York: McGraw Hill, 1948).
Muldoon, James, Fagot Aviel, Joann, Reitano, Richard, and Sullivan, Earl (eds), *Multilateral Diplomacy and the United Nations Today* (Cambridge, MA Westview Press, 2005).
Organski, A.F.K., and Kugler, J., *The War Ledger* (Chicago: Chicago University Press, 1980).
Preston, Peter, and Gilson, Julie (eds), *The European Union and East Asia* (Cheltenham: Edward Elgar, 2001).
Strange, Susan, *States and Markets: An Introduction to International Political Economy* (London: Pinter, 1988).
United Nations Development Programme (UNDP), *Human Development Report 2004* (New York: UNDP, 2004).
Waltz, Kenneth, *Theory of International Politics* (New York: Mcgraw Hill, 1979).
Wiessala, Georg, *The European Union and Asian Countries* (London: Sheffield Academic Press, 2002).
Yeo, Lay Hwee, *Asia and Europe: the Development and Different Dimensions of ASEM* (London: Routledge, 2004).

Part I
Inter-Regional Relations in a Globalizing Context

2
Europe–Asia: The Historical Limits of a 'Soft' Relationship

François Godement

It has now been more than a decade since Europe–Asia relations took off with some fanfare, as the first Asia–Europe Meeting (ASEM) convened in Bangkok in March 1996. Until that event, Europe–Asian relations, historically dependent on the relationships of the colonial era, had paled in the post-colonial period. Not only had the United States, during the Roosevelt era of the Second World War and its aftermath, effectively displaced the Old World as the leading western presence in East and Southeast Asia, but it had also inherited the Wilsonian policy of favouring independence over colonial ties. Partly to fight Japan, partly out of genuine belief, the United States created lasting relationships with many of Asia's new elites after the Second World War, while these very same elites sought to distance themselves from the old colonial powers. It is therefore useful to gauge the progress in the Asia–Europe relationship by the same yardstick we might apply to the relationship that exists between Asia and the United States.

After nearly five decades of Cold War, the Asia-Pacific – a hyphenated geographical definition of Asia which in itself proclaims the primacy of the new link created across the Pacific with the United States – remained indeed primarily a locus of American influence. Since the second half of the 1980s, economic interaction across the Pacific has exceeded transatlantic exchanges. The end of the Soviet Union has diminished the value of the transatlantic relationship or at least encouraged a mutation towards more debate among the 'old' allies. Many American strategists therefore believe that the new transpacific relationship had already superseded the old transatlantic bonds.

Furthermore, during the first postwar decades, Europe's institutional region-building process was focused primarily on economic integration and economic instruments rather than on political institutions, including a common foreign and security policy which only appeared on the stage as a result of the 1992 Maastricht Treaty. This added to Asians' perceptions of the growing irrelevance of Europe. The new Asia – including a China in transition from Maoism to a market economy – was torn between economic policies firmly led by the nation-state, and a new market liberalization and push towards free trade: these changes hardly included a move towards region-wide economic institutions. For the rest of Asia, security was provided by bilateral and usually asymmetric alliances with the United States. Scepticism towards supranational institutions was not confined to regionalism: Asia, after all, was not a major participant in the United Nations (UN) or the International Monetary Fund (IMF), save for Japanese financial contributions to the former. A global wave of capital market liberalization and a regional reluctance to approach sensitive or divisive topics such as political or security issues all combined to make Europe and the European Union (EU) an unappealing model to Asians. This reluctance went far beyond the 'bureaucracy' for which the European process was famous: newly founded post-colonial states, divided nations, and historical adversaries without true reconciliation could not see the advantages of the European building process, while they lamented its ponderous course and its opacity to outsiders.

A renewed Europe–Asia relationship was not borne therefore out of a strategic sense by either Asians or Europeans that this was a priority in their own international environment. Rather, Europeans had been struck in the early 1990s by the so-called 'Asian miracle', and were coming to the realization that their own economic interests in Asia required a toning down of criticism towards Asian political and social issues and instead paying more attention towards a satisfactory political relationship (Maull, Segal and Wanandi, 1998; European Commission, 1994).

For Asians, Europe–Asia relations were not only the 'missing link' in the tripolar global economy, but also a growing liability as Asian exports expanded globally (Hänggi, 1999). On the first issue, Asian initiatives towards Europe were influenced by the need to avoid complete dependency on an exclusive relationship with the United States, which was seen as being either very demanding in terms of trade liberalization, or fickle from the strategic point of view in the post-Cold War world, where the United States had far less need for some of its Asian allies. On the one hand, it would provide a complement and perhaps, at times, an alternative to the relationship with the United States, which had dominated the Asia-Pacific and were now often seen as economically selfish and politically too demanding, or at least prone to sudden mood changes in that field of relationship. 'Keeping the United States honestly international' was how one observer aptly summed up the rationale for the relationship (Segal, 1996, p. 118). With its accent on domestic economic issues, its push for trade liberalization and its demands on human rights as well as its reduced military and strategic footprint in Asia, the Clinton administration in the 1990s opened new uncertainties throughout the region. To some extent, Asians began to hedge their relationship with the United States by opening new channels to Europe. This was soft power balancing on the part of Asians and especially South-East Asians, as they would later also practice it with China (Ikenberry and Mastanduno, 2003).

But, on the other hand, there was also a preventive move by Asians in the direction of Europe. The prospect of a single market and currency coupled with Europe's economic and social woes – including the cost of absorbing Eastern Europe – raised the spectre of a possible 'closed regionalism', which would be detrimental to Asian economic interests.[1] 'Fortress Europe' – (usually without the historical reference to Joseph Goebbels, the Nazi propagandist, who had coined the phrase during the Second World War) – was how Europe was seen by its Asian partners in the wake of the Maastricht Treaty. The move by Asians to upgrade relations with Europe grew out of the sense that it represented a hedge against exclusive US influence and its growing demands in the area of trade and economic liberalization. But it was also influenced by the very real possibility that a Europe absorbed by the travails of its own reunification after the fall of European communism, and facing severe economic adjustments, might possibly close its doors to the flow of goods from Asia and the economic challenge it represented. Like South Asia, although less strongly so, South-East Asia's foreign trade with Europe was more important than with the United States, and free access to the European market was therefore important to regional economies.

True, Europe's process of unification and its resultant regional peace and stability also impressed many Asians. Although they perceived Europe as a weak political actor in Asia, they nonetheless held a vision of an imminently strong Europe, where a future unified currency coupled with institutional reforms heralded a European-wide unity and quasi-government. Europe would then become a formidable economic partner, grudgingly granting access to its own markets for outsiders, building up a reserve currency and in many ways becoming another United States. Asians were impressed by the strength of the European construction process, so alien to the international meanderings in their own region. They also decried, however, the European bureaucratic rigidity, the reputed prevalence of rules over consensus, or give and take, as well as the value requirements inherent in a democratic international system that could easily take upon itself to become a lesson-giver to others. Asians therefore both welcomed and feared the advent of Europe.

Not surprisingly, therefore, it was one of Asia's smallest nation-states, but one which possessed the highest foreign trade to gross domestic product (GDP) ratio, Singapore, which played a key role in forging a renewed Asia–Europe relationship. It advanced the idea of an Asia–Europe Meeting between heads of states and governments in both regions. A natural advocate of free trade and a consummate practitioner of power balancing and geopolitical hedging, Lee Kwan Yew, the then Singaporean prime minister, had also forged in the preceding years the theme of Asian values, in practice a neo-Confucian-tinted ideology of political and social conservatism, to help the region resist the political demands of liberalization pushed by a Democratic administration and Congress in the United States. But this was no strategic estrangement from the United States, nor would Singapore's insistence on openness in regional integration and its push for a Europe–Asia relationship be exclusive of increased trade and economic ties with the United States. In fact, Singapore would later seek to join the North American Free Trade Area (NAFTA), and in March 2005 it signed, at the same time as Chile, a free trade agreement with the United States that mirrors most NAFTA provisions. There is nothing more alien to the culture of Singapore's leaders than the notion of an exclusive relationship. The proposal and concept for ASEM was made to France in 1994; Japan on the Asian side and Helmut Kohl's Germany were initially reluctant, but both contributed importantly to the first meeting in March 1996 (Gilson, 1999).

Singaporeans, and after them other Asians, sought as much to keep the road to Europe open as to balance some of the overbearing requests that the United States could press on Asia. They therefore saw the ASEM as a mirror event to APEC, the Asia–Pacific Economic Cooperation forum, which had started formally in 1989. In fact, the first ASEM gathering in Bangkok in May 1996 was staged and choreographed with APEC as a role model (Camroux and Lechervy, 1996). Heads of states and governments met with much prepared informality; the diplomatic language of the Asian way – voluntary cooperation and consensus – was prevalent. A recurring quarrel between Indonesia and Portugal over the former's handling of Timor was dealt with nicely in the antechambers of the meeting. European heads of states and governments – as well as the European Commission – now thought that the Asian miracle was too important to entertain public controversies over human rights. From the first ASEM Summit, one important aspect was the encouragement of a business roundtable whose focus was on the financing of large-scale

Asian infrastructure projects (energy, transport). Their Asian counterparts, who had fretted over the previous years over the risk of a 'Fortress Europe' which would enforce closed regionalism after the Maastricht Treaty, wanted a high-level dialogue that would guarantee access to European markets for Asian goods, without the controversies over social rights that were, in their eyes, a thin excuse for protectionism. Retrospectively, neither of these positive developments has materialized completely. The Asian financial crisis of 1997 opened a decade of underspending in much of emerging Asia – except China – on infrastructure. And for the same reason, participation by Europeans at many ministerial meetings, and their implementation of initiatives, would also abate. Rather, the event may be seen as recognition by Europe of Asia as a potential case of regionalism, which required special recognition on the part of Europeans (Hänggi, Roloff and Rüland, 2006).

In this politically symbolic sense, the founding of ASEM also represented a European offer to Asia that promised to best what the United States had brought into APEC and the other Asia-Pacific multilateral fora of the late 1980s and early 1990s. First, Europeans recognized *de facto* the existence of an Asia that was distinct from the Asia-Pacific entity, yet no less significant as a region. An Asian institutional grouping had been taboo since the end of the Second World War and Japanese military dominance. In spite of East and Southeast Asian economic growth, and the weakening of the US economy at the end of the Cold War, a hyphenated Asia-Pacific was the accepted format for the region. Two countries, Japan and Australia, which had most to lose from a purely Asian regional development, had outdone each other to conceive and promote APEC, with the United States enjoying the chance of benevolently endorsing the new institutional arrangement. Cast as a heretic or a villain, Malaysian Prime Minister Mohammad Mahathir had aimed at creating an East Asian Economic Caucus (EAEC), a purely Asian grouping, but this was politically unacceptable and probably economically unsound as well: transpacific economic relations were on the rise in every aspect.

Suddenly, the East Asian grouping which had been excluded from debate came into existence as a result of ASEM. It was certainly weakly coordinated on the Asian side, and ASEM's accomplishments would prove to be limited in actual scope, but the symbolic card handed to Asia was essential. Characteristically, a Europe that had only a weak offer to make to Asia had made a concession that went beyond what the United States was willing to grant its Asian partners. It doubled that concession with a decisive change in tone towards Asian governments: although security issues, political dialogue and human rights goals were high on the list of priorities of the first Asia paper of the European Commission and on the agenda of the first ASEM Summit, the tone of the meeting itself heralded a change of posture. This was also the first collective international venture outside Europe by its constituent governments and regional institutions, and the aim was to compete with the United States in terms of international relations and sophisticated influence.

Much of this was emulation and competition rather than contradiction (Takashi, 1997). The EU and its member states were not going beyond what the United States had accepted across the Pacific: they merely emulated the rhetoric of the Clinton administration which had begun to tone down its human rights advocacy, especially towards China, and to substitute a globalist, win–win, free market approach to the Asia-Pacific rather than the more protectionist sentiments of previous years. Chinese President Jiang Zemin's and Indonesian President Suharto's attendance at the first APEC Summit in Seattle in November 1993 had already been gingerly secured. Europe now ran the risk of being isolated as a lesson-giver in the political arena and a sanction-prone actor in the field of trading relations. Perhaps for this reason, American policy makers hardly reacted to the advent of ASEM, judging that it was playing catch-up rather than conflicting with existing relationships (Bobrow, 1998).

Europe's new policy towards Asia happened on the eve of Asia's worst financial and economic crisis since the Second World War. Much of what had been envisaged in the first ASEM Meeting or in its hallways, including the creation of a second-track process for European and Asian businessmen, would not be implemented very concretely over the subsequent years. Europe, a net capital creditor and even more so during the high interest and low growth years after Maastricht, had envisaged a mutually profitable partnership to help Asia build its infrastructures. Symbolically, the Bangkok ASEM Summit had even launched a Europe–Asia railway plan that would go the way of all such grandiose projects after the financial crisis of 1997–98. One collective aim of these policies was the achievement of a trade balance between Europe and Asia, when Asian trade surpluses, even originating in low-income emerging economies, were becoming a preoccupation. European public opinions now saw Asia more as an opportunity than as an economic threat, and in fact it remains striking, to this day, that Asia–Europe events such as ASEM Summits have attracted far less opposition from anti-globalization movements than other global or inter-regional summits.

It is worth recalling these new beginnings of the Asia–Europe relationship because so much has happened since, in both regions and globally, as to render obsolete the philosophy and instruments on which the relationship was based. Perhaps the main legacy of the first years of the ASEM process is indeed the indirect legitimacy it bestowed on Asian regionalism as defined by what is now the ASEAN+3 format of ASEAN and China, Japan and South Korea (Stubbs, 2002). The financial crisis made it hard for Asians to build on this legacy – a first summit meeting of the leaders of East Asia in December 1997 ended in *non sequitur* speeches about the raging financial storm.

A decade of changes

A summary of what has changed could cover the following points:

Europe's self-centred process

In 1995, Asians were worried about the possibility of a 'closed' Europe, and had already noted the degree of self-absorption of European leaders and institutions in the post-1989 and pre-Maastricht period. ASEM was a collective turn towards the outside world – at some risk to the overloaded agenda of European leaders. Since 1995, Europe has again turned inwards for a number of reasons. Chief among these is simply the expansion of the European Union itself. The debates around the institutional reforms, from the Nice and Amsterdam Treaties to the new Constitutional Treaty and its derailed ratification process in 2005, add a second layer of concern.

Other arms of the European Union have indeed expanded their competence and areas of influence, and that is also the case for the foreign and security policy, but it is increasingly focused on neighbouring regions and has tended to be reactive on issues rather than proactive, particularly in respect of Asia. Moreover, the Iraq crisis and its legacy remain as much an intra-European source of debate and a permanent search for common ground as it is a global issue. The debate on the eventual lifting of the embargo regarding arms transfers to China in 2004–05 also achieved mixed results. After an initial clash between the advocates and opponents of lifting the ban, a European Summit resolution in December 2004 pointed to the goal of lifting the embargo. There is every indication, however, that this agreement was premature and not thought through. Then, a rewritten, and reportedly more technical, Code of Conduct on arms exports in general was almost agreed on. Almost, but not quite. The debate over the embargo has led to renewed tension across the Atlantic, apart from Iraq. And Europeans find themselves in the uncomfortable position, after having prematurely reached a conclusion, of not choosing any outcome. The resulting indecision hampers the credibility of Europe's common foreign and security policy.

The supranational level and member states

A case can be made, of course, that in spite of this process Europeans have been increasingly engaged with the outside world. This is the case for official development assistance (ODA) disbursements – given Japan's lowered budgets, European ODA is by far the world's largest source. Its contribution to developing Asia is itself as high as Japan's, and twice the level of US aid. It is also the case in respect of European involvement in peacekeeping or other UN-sanctioned operations: with more than 15,000 soldiers engaged in outside operations, including in Afghanistan and East Timor, Europeans have been important contributors. They have also been, together with the ASEAN (Association of South-East Asian Nations) contribution, the brokers of an agreed disarmament in Aceh between the former rebels of Gam and the Indonesian military. If the Iraqi contingents of the United Kingdom and other European countries are factored in, Europe is indeed a second pillar of security and intervention internationally.

Most of these policies, however, are decided at the national level, and they possess little collective coherence. A symptom of this trend can be found in the European reaction to the December 2004 tsunami in Southeast Asia: the amounts donated by various European countries have set records, and indeed a competitive drive for charity occurred among European governments. Several navies were present on the spot in the Indian Ocean after the disaster, and ECHO, the European humanitarian aid agency, has been very active. Seen by locals, however, this mobilization is hardly as visible: the sum of the whole does not equal its contents. This is partly a problem of public diplomacy, partly a structural issue: in 1991, European aid to a resurrected Cambodia was also granted piecemeal by European national governments and thereby lost much of its political efficiency. Amounts of European ODA allotted to each country in Southeast Asia vary considerably from one member state to another, with former colonial ties being the main predictor on the actual level of aid extended bilaterally. For some, to criticize this situation is tantamount to misreading the true nature of the European project, an association of sovereign member states with only limited supranational areas of competence. For others, it signals a long road ahead to build an effective European policy. One of the key innovations of the Constitutional Treaty signed by member states in 2004 was to create a European

Minister of Foreign Affairs. These aspects of the treaty are likely to be salvaged, after the failure to ratify by France and the Netherlands in 2005. Unless words are mistaken, this means that the second, more ambitious perspective should be the yardstick from which future developments are judged.

The regional architecture of the Asia-Pacific

In 1995, the Asia-Pacific was dominated by perceptions of the Asian miracle and of the integrative path to regionalism. Growth was transnational, predicated on FDI and the advent of free trade and 'win–win'. Even if Japan's economic supremacy was levelling off, this merely rebalanced a regional economy where Japan's push had been pervasive. The ascent of the so-called 'Tigers' and 'Dragons' did not create a new factor in the power equation, except perhaps in contributing some momentum towards regional construction. To Europeanists, the rise of a regional process centred on ASEAN and its experience could be likened to the 'Benelux' model for Europe, where a group of small countries had been more European than the larger states with their sovereignty to defend.

By contrast, the more recent rise of China has offset the regional balance. Trade pact initiatives, foreign direct investment (FDI) flows, triangular trade and technological innovation all focus on China as the essential dynamo for Asia. This is a relative, rather than an absolute trend, and therefore both Japan's and Southeast Asia's economies have not receded as a result; they have just been cut down to a more modest size: in proportion for Southeast Asia, in prospect for Japan. The simultaneous process of an extended rise in China's military budgets is very impressive, although China has seldom taken major new provocative initiatives: it merely applies a strategy of calculated pressure and irritants on territorial issues, while providing general reassurance at other points in time. By virtue of its sheer size and dynamism, however, little can happen in terms of major regional construction issues if China is not interested and involved (Gill and Huang, 2006). Whether it is multilateral security, monetary agreements or issues of shared political values, China is more of a restraining force than a dynamo for regional construction, even though its economic growth now drives much of the region. Conversely, of course, Japan may be described as adopting a more defensive posture on many issues – especially as far as they concern history – as a result of uncertainty about its future status in the region.

In 1995 Asia was reaping the benefits of regional détente, after what some now call a 'golden age' of relationships among the main powers of the region (Vogel, Yuan and Tanaka, 2002). Many problems were certainly unresolved, but they were conveniently forgotten or at least tucked away under the rug, with transnational economic forces reshaping the region. Today, the power equation of the region is in doubt, and mutual suspicions have risen as a result of these doubts. In 1995 Europeans were concerned with the extraordinary lead that the United States possessed in relation with the region, and with the influence that flowed from its security role. Multilateral relations within the region, and extending to other countries or groups of countries, appeared as a soft supplement to hard security and political relationships, which remained provided by the United States (Pempel, 2005). Even if the mantle of security alliances still applies to Asia, there is much that is happening today among the major Asian actors – the race for energy resources, territorial conflicts, conflicts about historical posture, overall competition for regional leadership – which is not covered directly by these security alliances. In 1995, Europe was becoming a region where reasons for unity prevailed over causes for conflict. Today, the geopolitical balance of power and potential conflicts have to be taken into consideration by outside powers.

The come-back of American power

America never left the region, as Europe did after the end of the colonial era. But American influence was on the wane for almost two decades throughout Asia, even though economic and human ties never stopped increasing across the Pacific shores. The 1980s had left the United States with a huge budget deficit and a productivity slowdown that allowed Asia to think it could 'catch up', while it also complained about the mercenary instinct in some US policies. The 1990s saw the unravelling of some political ties forged with close allies of the region: some of these ties were with security states now judged obsolete since the end of the Cold War, others were eroded by economic competition. It was from a feeling of benign neglect or complacency on the part of the region's main guarantor that policies looking towards Europe were forged.

That legacy was over by 2005, even though the United States has not returned to its former posture and maintains a safe distance from involvement in the region's many potential conflicts. But from the Korean peninsula to Taiwan over unfinished conflicts from the twentieth century, from Southeast to Central Asia over conflicts of the twenty-first century symbolized by extreme terrorism, the United States is more deeply engaged than at any moment since 1975. Its network of global coalitions has also included Asia. Japan and South Korea – the latter in spite of a reluctant public opinion – Australia and also rising India have forged new ties to the United States, with strong practical implications. Neutralist or non-involved rhetorics notwithstanding, the countries of Southeast Asia have also on the whole reinforced their relationships with the United States. A former opponent such as Vietnam has become increasingly dependent on the US economy. It is now apparent that North Korea's strategic gamble is to obtain an iron-cast security guarantee for the future from Washington, the power it fears most, and therefore also acknowledges most.

Over non-security matters – such as trade policy and environmental choices – there can be coalitions in the region that go against the United States. On security issues, it is out of the question for all. Regarding the Middle East and Iraq issues, the region has been caught in a schizophrenic trap: it criticizes the choices made by the United States, but has to bank on their ultimate success, if only for the sake of energy resources and the future of sea-lane security. Only China, the rising power of Asia, retains a more cryptic attitude, combining an attitude of 'peaceful rise' with fundamental reservations that could one day fuel a more fundamental competition with the United States. Even so, most Chinese interests and strategic options are still located in the Asian neighbourhood, and it is highly unlikely that these neighbours would wilfully leave the shadow of a distant hegemon for binding ties with an uncomfortably close master. In principle, the return of American power is a hard security trend, not a diplomatic embrace of the region's potential multilateralism. In some cases, such as after the December 2004 tsunami, the American military factor can be put to highly practical – and highly visible – 'soft power' use.

Critically, one never equates US Asia policy and its overall relationship to the region with the uneven fate of APEC. The machinery of APEC Summits has endured, and it has functioned as a clearing house for trade liberalization projects, but APEC has never taken an institutional role in the region-building process. A critical occasion was lost at the time of the East Asian financial crisis, when traditional financial organizations such as the IMF, the World Bank and the Asian Development Bank (ADB) proved much more effective, if not successful. Subsequent trade developments have happened well outside the framework of APEC. At several moments in APEC's early history, the United States had wanted to create a security agenda for APEC – something that was roundly resisted by most other members: it is under that implicit condition that Taiwan has been able to participate officially in APEC meetings, an inclusiveness that has never been actively sought by Europeans. APEC's only involvement with security issues came in the aftermath of the September 11 attacks, when counter-terrorism created the backdrop for a unanimous APEC Summit in Shanghai in November 2001.

Yet the United States has never merged its policies towards the region with the APEC agenda. It has therefore been able to distinguish between the ideal world of regionalism under construction, and the real world of power relationships and coalitions. Asians, too, have increasingly reverted to bilateral relationships for their two most important sectoral issues, trade and security.

The combination of these four major trends creates the necessity for some creative adaptation of Europe's policies towards Asia. These changes are both in content – Europe's strategic choices, its offer to Asia – and in form – the nature of Europe's collective presence throughout the region and its communication towards Asians. The two aspects, however, are closely linked and overlap at some points.

Adapting Europe's policies

Europe's strategy in Asia

Europeans share with Americans an almost identical degree of economic involvement with the region. Yet they often seem to draw different conclusions from that situation, just as they have often made different strategic judgements about the relative merits of possession *versus* access to worldwide energy resources. Each major European economy, and also the EU as a whole, has a larger degree of dependency on international trade than the United States, but trading partners are also more dispersed. For a long time, European trade relations with Asia were not a key concern. The US interaction with Asia, while on a par with European involvement for trade and investment, involves far more services, financial and monetary interactions. Sourcing from Asia and production and market integration with Asian suppliers are also larger from a US perspective and in fact dominate both some traditional sectors of consumer goods and the 'new economy'. Recycling of surplus trade dollars into the American financial markets is indeed essential. The US security role is often viewed as an insurance policy that pays for itself thanks to host countries. Europeans, on the other hand, feel less involved by their partnerships in the region and do not feel tied by a security alliance and its eventual costs. The difference is more historical than conceptual, and is also due to America's lack of involvement with its European partners in any Asia-Pacific process. The Korean War was perhaps the only exception to this rule, while most Europeans did not support the Vietnam

War. Recent cases of European involvement in security affairs are either extensions of the Korean peninsula division, or the result of single peace keeping and/or humanitarian operations in Southeast Asia. In the political arena, Europeans have developed no special relationships with the region's more mature democratic states, notwithstanding some attention being paid to Japan.

The different economic perspectives are narrowing, however, especially as EU–China trade increases at a speed that matches the US–China trade growth. In 2005, the EU–China trade deficit (viewed from EU statistics) widened to more than €106 billion, or nearly 5 per cent of the EU's entire external trade (Eurostat, European Union, February 2007), while the same figures for the United States are $202 billion and 6 per cent (US–China Business Council). Since the surplus financial flow back into European capital markets and currency reserves is much lower than towards the United States, it is clear that Europe is acquiring an external deficit with China that is on the scale of America's: in 2005, the suddenly hardened perceptions of many Europeans in respect of Chinese textile exports to the EU have much to do with this trend. Other statistics show that Chinese exports often displace other Asian exports, with the overall level of European trade deficit more stable as a whole. Yet China–EU trade relations could become a sensitive political issue.

Yet Europeans have, on the whole, been less vocally protectionist in defence of many of their sectoral economic interests than have Americans. European policies in Asia are diverse, and include a large degree of economic assistance that is not necessarily tied to other policy prospects (Boisseau du Rocher and Fort, 2005). They have also bid to participate in Asian security affairs, for example when Europe sought to be represented as such at the ASEAN Regional Forum and decided on participation in KEDO (Korean Peninsula Energy Development Organization), the energy substitution scheme for North Korea launched in 1996. EU policy papers include a large list of standards which Europe seeks to help disseminate in its relationship with Asia, but these are exclusive of any strategic goal or partnership. In fact, a misunderstanding about the adjective 'strategic' is always possible, as may be the case with China today (Dejean de la Batie, 2002). For the European Commission, a strategic partnership is one that matters and that has many sectoral implications, but this does not necessarily translate into agreement on all issues or a security relationship. The word could almost be mistaken for a business 'action plan'. For China, the word retains obvious overtones that imply broad agreement and comprehensive alliance with strong political ties.

Post-modern policy?...

Europe is therefore faced with important choices. Perhaps its policy towards other regions, and particularly towards an Asia which is only at the beginning of the curve towards regional integration, reflects the post-modern nature of Europe's institutional project. In this case, what Europe has to offer Asia is essentially constituted by a set of values, multilateral rules, and what is generally considered as 'soft power': development and humanitarian assistance, peacekeeping, environmental policies, but also counter-proliferation and disarmament policies. To some extent, better trade policies, generally associated with free trade, are consistent with these principles. But they also overlap with sectoral and national interests, and it is certainly noteworthy that Europe, whose most active tool of institutional integration remains in the area of foreign trade, has nonetheless lagged behind in its capacity to propose free trade pacts to the Asian region (Avila, 2003) – or to respond to various offers brought up within the region. These negotiations only started in 2006 with countries such as India and Thailand, after it became evident that larger negotiations of the World Trade Organization's Doha round were becoming bogged down.

The choice of a multilateral and 'soft' approach is not wholly inconsistent with realist interest. Many soft policy options, conflict avoidance schemes and in general an emphasis on the governance of international relations have also been promoted by Asian countries. They were the foundation on which the initial core for Asian regionalism, ASEAN, was built, and also the rationale for many of Japan's postwar policies. They also serve today to balance the self-interest of the United States, and to ensure that China's 'peaceful rise' remains just that: peaceful. This could be termed soft power balancing, as opposed to a multipolar approach that immediately raises huge security concerns. None of these policies, however, will genuinely lead to practical results if they are not accepted by either China or the United States – or preferably by both. Europe is a facilitator or a stimulus to others, not the source of a new order.

... or classic policy?

The catch with this approach, however, is that it is not entirely consistent with the nature of the European system, which is made of several strata. It is not only the values and principles outlined by a post-modern agenda that have become European features. National interest has also been carried to the European level, particularly in terms of trading and non-proliferation policies. Furthermore, national interests and policies are still around in Europe, and in fact could sometimes be described as even more affirmed than in the past. Thus, governments sometimes 'kick upstairs' thorny issues of their external relationships – a primary example in recent years is as often as not the human rights issue – while they pursue trade and economic diplomacy on their own. Some particularistic policies or special relationships are entirely predictable, as is the case for the UK's special relationship with Commonwealth countries and its defence pact with four Asian/Australasian states. Legacies of the colonial era, as noted above, abound and justify a special role for France and the Netherlands in their former colonial areas, while Portugal has undoubtedly played a large role on East Timor. New division lines appear – such as the pro- and anti-nuclear energy camps – and these divisions hamper a unified energy policy approach to Asia, in spite of a European Council resolution on energy security adopted in the spring of 2007 (European Council, 2007). Issues such as the lifting of the arms embargo to China do rest on different perceptions, but they also contain a dose of diverging interests, since countries with a traditional arms export basis are more favourable to lifting the embargo than countries without arms industries.

In practice, therefore, outlining a unified European 'soft policy' runs the risk of letting European nation-states practice more traditional foreign policies for themselves, and eventually clash over competitive interests. Defining and applying a common foreign policy and strategy towards Asia is a harder goal, but one which would both strengthen Europe's unification and make it more influential in Asia.

Asia will not choose for Europe

Unlike relations between Europe as a region and single Asian countries – such as China, India or Japan – the Asia–Europe relationship as a whole is not managed equally on both sides (Acharya, 2006). In spite of the ambiguities and multiple layers of European policy, there is no counterpart in Asia that would answer to the European Commission, Council or, of course, Parliament. No regional grouping, even be it ASEAN with its long existence, has generated the governance and capacity to negotiate with the EU. One might add, of course, that the EU has undertaken so many complex tasks at the same time that, while the Asian side of the relationship is often ill-organized or covered with a thin veneer of consensus, it is the European side which appears to be overloaded. Proactive agendas in Asia still pertain to national issues – so that one could easily describe, for example, what are the Chinese requirements for a European China policy, but much less so for the whole of Asia. Significantly, China's first official policy statement in October 2005 regarding the EU had almost nothing to say about Asia as a region. Indeed, viewed from China, this is still a bilateral relationship with a new European partner. ASEAN itself is in a different position – and at times seems to have built new regional capacities inspired by the European experience or at least egged on by some of its lessons. An instance of the first is the drafting of an ASEAN charter,[2] launched at the eleventh ASEAN Summit in Kuala Lumpur in December 2005: it is often represented, and sometimes by ASEAN officious sources themselves, as a 'Constitution for ten countries'.[3] In the second category: engaging Burma/Myanmar while seeking to influence political outcomes in Yangon was and remains linked to the necessities of inter-regional dialogue with the EU. The transformation of ASEAN from a league of sovereign nations into a more interventionist institution has stopped recently, and is probably derailed by the occurrence of a military coup and government in Thailand, one of the founding countries of ASEAN. Thus, the balance shifts back and forth towards democracy among ASEAN members: if one counts Singapore as an apostle of good governance, and therefore in the democratic camp, there are now four democracies among ASEAN members, with others at least experiencing a degree of voting process. Yet ASEAN countries seem to have retreated into the management of their domestic problems and political transitions, and their external agenda is dominated by the shadow of China's influence and the games of band-wagoning or power balancing that this situation requires.

For better or for worse, Asia therefore has no stated agenda to press on Europe. Those who have been more intent on developing a relationship with Europe are often doing so in order to free themselves from regional constraints, and as a complementary relationship to the United States: Japan, South Korea and Singapore are cases in point, with Singapore often taking on a self-declared role as the spokesman for other ASEAN states – while developing its own capacity as an intermediary in all international economic relations.

Conclusion: defining an Asia policy as a way to create a European identity

There are many limitations which can be placed on Asian regional construction. Indeed, there is no shortage of cynics who portray Asia's future as Europe's past, or as a return to what they think were tributary relationships with the Middle Kingdom. Realists point to the economic imperative implicit in almost all Asian foreign strategies. Yet this is the only region apart from Europe that has made repeated, if particularistic efforts at regionalism. Mercosur, NAFTA, the Shanghai Cooperation

Organization, the Organization of African Unity and the League of Arab States are *ad hoc* groupings with varying functions. ASEAN, ASEAN+3, the ASEAN Regional Forum, the new East Asian Summit, APEC and ASEM are interlocking developments. Defining a European policy towards Asia has proven difficult, because the target region is evenly split between realist interests and conflicts on the one hand, and a recurring constructivist approach which is particularly prevalent among ASEAN policy elites. The single issue of China's rise will have a decisive role in this respect: regional norms and problem-settling procedures are necessary to harness China's future power into a positive direction. On the other hand, China's choices regarding the region will also define its future structure.

Europe, which has raised its foreign and security ambitions since a decade ago, has probably arrived at the end of a cycle in its policy towards Asia. Using regional and inter-regional dialogues and institutions as mirrors (ASEM as a mirror to APEC, EU as a harbinger of East Asian regionalism) (Berkofsky, 2005) has served well for the building of symbolic and diplomatic ties and for overcoming the mutual suspicions of the past. In some cases, the dialogues become prisoners of their own rules: it is, for example, outrageous that the Myanmar issue, as important as it is, can derail EU cooperation with ASEAN and the ASEAN Regional Forum. Constructive engagement – over human rights with China and even North Korea – has its limits and becomes a self-fuelling activity limited to professional participants to these dialogues. Just as in other areas of European construction, relations should again become project-driven, rather than meeting-driven.

Europeans should also begin to form common data resources, pools of expertise and common analyses on Asian strategic, political and economic issues: what exists massively at the level of the federal government in the United States needs to be built up in Brussels and Strasbourg, as well as in many member states.

Fundamentally, Europe will face a choice of strategy. It can leave most of the hard strategy and security contribution to the United States, hopefully complemented some time in the future by a regional multilateral system. That is indeed what present trends regarding the European contribution in those areas indicate. It means that European policies and influence will be focused on soft issues and economic interests, in essence made possible by the geostrategic balance maintained in the region by the United States. This, however, will limit Europe's role and its potential partnership in many politically sensitive areas, where the United States possesses immense leverage over allies and potential competitors alike. A 'soft policy' Europe is a natural complement of a 'hard policy' United States – and may be appreciated by Asians for the complementarity without risk that it brings to the region. Such a vision is definitely multilateral, but not multipolar: it implies that Europe, eschewing power politics but loyal to its primary alliance, does not undercut the prevailing security architecture, but only acts at its margin, for conflict-reduction or prevention purposes for instance. Ironically, this policy choice is akin to taking a 'postwar Japan' option on Europe's policy towards Asia: it is consistent with the definition of Europe as a new international form coexisting with nation-states, and largely avoiding the issue of power.

The other choice is much harder to make, yet it is more interesting for future European influence. Strategic implications – starting with Eurasian and transatlantic debate on these issues – and contributions to Asian security, deepening relations with the region's governments and enlarging the scope of these relations with the new or transitional democracies that have appeared throughout Asia, would enhance Europe's future influence. It would also give more leverage to European and member state policies with Asia's main actors, China, India and Japan.

It is a very tall order, however. European institutions, even after some solution is found to the issue of the Constitutional Treaty, may not be so ready for joint strategic action in out-of-zone areas. The present involvement, under North Atlantic Treaty Organization (NATO) command, of several European nations in Afghanistan may already have tested to the limit their will to engage. Member states differ in their degree of acceptance and cooperation within the alliance, and new tensions arising from Asia policy – of which the arms embargo has been a good example – could make more difficult the harmonization among Europeans.

Overall, it might therefore seem preferable that Europe continue along path number one – the soft policy approach – while combining some national policies or special situations that would allow to start on path number two. Different national policies would provide some emulation as well as stimulate constructive engagement; special situations could bring Europeans together in key projects or task force mode. Providing more security in some areas – such as maritime safety – and contributing to crisis resolution in others – such as the Korean peninsula – is nothing revolutionary for European policy makers: in fact, Europeans at the national level were already engaged in some of these developments 15 years ago. A renewal of this engagement with a better sense of strategic issues would serve well the interests of Euro-Asian relations and the multilateral system as a whole.

Notes

1. Fred C. Bergsten actually makes the historical reference to the closed economic zone created in Central Europe by Nazi Germany in the 1930s in *Open Regionalism*, Working Paper 97-3 (Washington: Institute of International Economics, 1997).
2. Kuala Lumpur Declaration on the Establishment of the ASEAN Charter, Kuala Lumpur, 12 December 2005. (http://www.aseansec.org/18030.htm).
3. Website: http://www.12thaseansummit.org.ph.

References

Acharya, A., 'Europe and Asia: Reflections on a Tale of Two Regionalisms', in B. Fort and D. Webber (eds), *Regional Integration in East Asia and Europe: Convergence or Divergence?* (London: Routledge, 2006), pp. 312–21.

Avila, J.L., 'EU Enlargement and the Rise of Asian FTAs: Implications for Asia–Europe Relations', *Asia–Europe Journal*, 1 (2003), 213–22.

Bergsten, F.C., *Open Regionalism*, Working Paper 97-3 (Washington: Institute of International Economics, 1997).

Berkofsky, A., *Comparing EU and Asian Integration Processes – The EU a Role model for Asia?*, European Policy Centre, Issue Paper No. 22, Brussels (2005).

Bobrow, D.B., 'The US and Asem: Why the Hegemon did not Bark', CGSR Working Paper No. 17/98 (Coventry: Warwick University, November 1998).

Boisseau du Rocher, S., and Fort, B. (eds), *Paths to Regionalization: Comparing Experiences in Europe and East Asia* (Singapore: Marshall Cavendish, 2005).

Camroux, D., and Lechervy, C., '"Close Encounter of a Third Kind?" the Inaugural Asia–Europe Meeting of March 1996', *The Pacific Review*, 9(3) (1996), 442–53.

Dejean de la Batie, H., *La politique chinoise de l'Union neuropéenne*, Policy Paper No. 1 (Paris: Centre Asie Ifri, April 2002).

European Commission, *Towards a New Asia Strategy*, COM (94) 314 final, Brussels (13 July 1994).

European Council, Presidency Conclusions (8–9 March 2007).

Gill, B., and Huang, Y., 'Sources and limits of China's Soft Power', *Survival*, 48(2) (Summer 2006), 17–36.

Gilson, J., 'Japan's Role in the Asia–Europe Meeting: Establishing an Interregional or Intraregional Agenda?', *Asian Survey*, 39(5) (September–October 1999), 736–52.

Hänggi, H., *ASEM and the Construction of a new Triad* (Geneva: Graduate Institute of International Studies, April 1999).

Hänggi, H., Roloff, R., and Rüland, J. (eds), *Interregionalism and International Relations* (London: Routledge, 2006).

Ikenberry, J.G., and Mastanduno, M. (eds), *International Relations Theory and the Asia-Pacific* (New York: Columbia University Press, 2003).

Maull, H.W., Segal, G., and Wanandi, J. (eds), *Europe and the Asia-Pacific* (New York: Routledge, 1998).

Pempel, T.J., *Remapping East Asia: the Construction of a Region* (Ithaca: Cornell University Press, 2005).

Segal, G., 'Thinking Strategically About ASEM: The Subsidiarity Question', in *Europe–Asia: Strengthening the Informal Dialogue*, Project directed by François Godement, *Cahier de l'Ifri* no. 19 (Paris: IFRI, 1996).

Stubbs, R., 'ASEAN Plus Three: Emerging East Asian Regionalism?', *Asian Survey*, 42(3) (May–June 2002), 440–55.

Takashi, S., 'Outline of ASEM: A Regional Forum as a Jealousy Driven Mechanism', *Journal of Japanese Trade and Industry*, 16(5) (1997), 8–11.

Vogel, E.Z., Yuan, M., and Tanaka, A. (eds), *The Golden Triangle of the US–China–Japan Relationship 1972–1989* (Cambridge, MA: Harvard University Asia Center, 2002).

3
EU Foreign Policy and Asia
Karen E. Smith

The EU is by far the world's most successful case of multilateralism. Its distinctive framework for cooperation and integration even extends to foreign and defence policy, traditionally seen to lie at the heart of 'national sovereignty'. The EU member states have long declared that the EU will formulate and implement a common foreign and security policy, they have set up mechanisms to try to do this, and they have periodically reformed those mechanisms to make them more effective and efficient (often in response to quite spectacular failures to act collectively). The Common Foreign and Security Policy (CFSP) is unique in international relations: in no other setting have states worked as closely together to try to achieve a collective stance on such a wide range of foreign and security policy issues.

But the CFSP is 'voluntary': while there is a hardening expectation that member states will act constructively to further their common interests and pursue common policies, foreign policy remains an area of intergovernmental cooperation. It is *not* an area where the member states have ceded authority for policy making to central, supranational institutions. There is an obvious tension between the urge to act collectively and the protection of the EU member states' sovereignty in the area of foreign policy. Observers have argued that over time the CFSP has been 'institutionalized' and 'legalized' (Smith, 2001, 2004). It is, however, debatable the extent to which this has resulted in more common policies and less pursuit of national foreign policy interests: slow change there has certainly been, but not such that the 'capabilities–expectations gap' (Hill, 1993) can be said to have been filled, perhaps because expectations that the EU will be an effective, influential international actor tend to be too high.

This chapter first briefly traces the evolution of the framework for making EU foreign policy, from European Political Cooperation (EPC), set up in 1970, to its replacement from 1993, the Common Foreign and Security Policy (CFSP), through to the 2007–08 'reform treaty' (under negotiation at the time of writing), which incorporates the foreign and security provisions of the defunct 2004 draft constitutional treaty. The chapter does not discuss the EU's frameworks for making trade and other foreign economic policy (of particular importance for the EU's relations with Asia but covered elsewhere in this volume); the emphasis here lies squarely on the development of the overtly political side of the EU's foreign relations.

The rest of the chapter then analyses the extent to which this framework has been used by EU member states to conduct political relations vis-à-vis Asian states, on a bilateral (that is, with individual Asian countries), regional (with particular regional groupings) or multilateral (with Asian countries in general) basis. While EU political activity towards Asia has increased over the past decade, it is still quite low compared to the EU's relations with many other areas of the world. Economic relations predominate (and here both the EU and the individual EU member states play a strong role, the latter sometimes to the detriment of collective EU action), but the relative absence of EU political relations with Asia is also due to the marginalization of this area of the world in most EU member states' foreign policies. The EU's relatively weak political role has resulted not because it has been crowded out by the EU member states' foreign policies, but because neither at the national nor at the collective level is 'Europe' heavily involved in political relations with Asia. There have been periodic disagreements among the member states over political relations with Asia – as over whether to lift the arms embargo on China. Nonetheless it is the low-key nature of EU–Asia political relations that is striking.

The evolution of the CFSP

Although the roots of European integration can be found in a unique resolution of the 'German problem', or the preponderance of German power – and are therefore profoundly security-related – the integration process itself was initially limited to economic sectors. But in 1970, awareness of the political implications of the European Community's growing economic power prompted the member states to set up a framework known as European Political Cooperation (EPC) for cooperation on foreign affairs.

EPC was separate from the Community and based on intergovernmental principles, namely unanimous voting. Its goals were modest: regular consultation, coordination of national positions, and, where possible, common action – though this was usually limited to a declaration, issued in reaction to external events. But it did foster a reflex to consult among the member states whenever an international problem arose (de Schoutheete, 1980, p. 118). Furthermore, the foreign ministers periodically reformed EPC procedures by, for example, involving more officials in the mechanism (Nuttall, 1992).

The dynamism of the Single European Market at the end of the 1980s and then the end of the Cold War created internal and external expectations that the Community would take on a greater international role. Discussions on deepening integration, launched in response to German unification in 1990, expanded to include reform of EPC, which was considered inadequate for the 'new world order'. In the Maastricht Treaty, which entered into force in November 1993, the CFSP replaced EPC (Nuttall, 2000).

Maastricht created three separate pillars – the European Community (EC), CFSP and Justice and Home Affairs (JHA). The CFSP's provisions were intended to improve on those of EPC in several ways. First, the European Commission could propose actions, alongside the member states. This would help to ensure consistency of action by the Community and CFSP pillars. The vast majority of CFSP proposals are still initiated by the member states, illustrating the extent to which the Commission is *not* a driving force in the CFSP (Nuttall, 2000, pp. 256–7) – though in practice, comprehensive approaches towards third countries, combining EC, CFSP and even JHA matters, have become the norm. Secondly, two new procedures were added to the traditional instrument of a declaration: the Council can agree a Common Position or a Joint Action, the latter signalling that the EU was actually doing something (spending money, for example). Thirdly, qualified majority voting (QMV) was slipped into decision-making: the Council could decide, by unanimity, that further decisions on a Joint Action would be taken by QMV (though QMV has never actually been used). However, the CFSP was still represented externally mostly through the presidency. There was thus no single 'EU phone number' for third countries to call to ask what the EU's position was on international issues.

The real innovation of CFSP was that it covered defence. EPC had not discussed defence issues at all; that was NATO's job. Yet at the end of the Cold War the US was withdrawing its troops from Europe, and the Europeans were expected to contribute to international peacekeeping missions. The member states were (and still are) divided over issues such as the relationship of a European defence structure to NATO (several do not wish to jeopardize NATO's pre-eminent role in European security), and to the EU (several member states oppose any moves to turn the EU into an alliance). But they could agree to discuss defence, and under the Maastricht Treaty, the Union could request the Western European Union (WEU) to implement EU decisions that have defence implications.[1]

In the meantime, the WEU decided that rather than provide for collective defence, it would engage in humanitarian and rescue, peacekeeping and crisis management tasks (the Petersberg Tasks). To undertake these, the WEU would almost certainly have to rely on NATO facilities and resources and arrangements to allow this were formalized in 1996. But in the end, EU/WEU action still depended on member state agreement – and in fact, the WEU was rarely asked to do much by the EU.

Disappointment with Maastricht contributed to a more substantial revision of the CFSP provisions in the Amsterdam Treaty, which entered into force in May 1999. Unanimous voting was to become less the rule and more the exception, though in practice unanimity remains the decision-making mode of choice. The Amsterdam procedures are still in use (see Box 3.1).

The Amsterdam Treaty created the post of the High Representative for the CFSP to help formulate, prepare and implement policy decisions. The intention was to give the CFSP more continuity in its international representation, providing a 'single phone number' for third countries' representatives to call. But the High Representative cannot speak on behalf of the EU if the member states do not have an agreed position. Javier Solana, a former Spanish foreign minister and NATO Secretary-General, was appointed High Representative in 1999. Solana has generally been perceived to be a success – though he has been left out of some discussions among the putative *directoire* of the three big member states. He was sidelined during the Iraq discussions in early 2003 and the initial diplomatic manoeuvres by France, Germany and the UK vis-à-vis Iran in 2003–04.

Following Amsterdam, the member states set up a small Policy Planning and Early Warning Unit within the Council Secretariat. The Policy Unit and the creation of Solana's post are steps in what David Allen called 'Brusselization': foreign policy issues are more and more discussed and decided in Brussels, by officials based in Brussels (Allen, 1998, pp. 50, 54). One observer argues that Brusselization is 'diminishing the roles of the Member States and of intergovernmentalism', and represents a new form of governance of the CFSP (Müller-Brandeck-Bocquet, 2002, p. 261).

Box 3.1: CFSP Decision-Making Procedures

The European Council agrees **Common Strategies**, by unanimity, in areas where the member states have interests in common. A Common Strategy sets out the EU's objectives, duration and means to be made available to carry it out. The Council of foreign ministers implements Common Strategies by agreeing **Joint Actions** and **Common Positions**; in so doing, it votes by qualified majority voting.

The Council may also approve Joint Actions and Common Positions separately. In this case, the Council votes by unanimity, although it may decide unanimously to implement a Joint Action by qualified majority voting. **Joint Actions** address specific situations where operational action by the EU is considered to be required. **Common Positions** define the EU's approach to a particular matter of geographical or thematic nature. The Council may also issue declarations and confidential demarches.

A member state can oppose the use of qualified majority voting for reasons of important national interests (the **national interest brake**), and qualified majority voting does not apply to decisions having military implications. One or more member states (up to a limit) can abstain from voting on a decision, without blocking it (the **constructive abstention** clause). But they must accept that the decision commits the Union and agree not to take action likely to conflict with it.

The Commission shares the right of initiative with the member states, but does not have a vote.

After the Amsterdam Treaty was agreed, radical change occurred swiftly in the security and defence dimensions. In late 1998, the new UK Prime Minister, Tony Blair, agreed the St Malo initiative with France, the other major military power in Western Europe. They declared that the EU itself (not through the WEU) must be willing and able to respond to international crises by undertaking autonomous action, backed up by credible military forces. There are clearly differences in the British and French visions: for Britain, the EU can act when NATO does not wish to do so; for France, NATO does not have such a primary role. But for the time being, the two countries can at least agree to develop the EU's military capacities (Howorth, 2001; Deighton, 2002).

Surprisingly, even the neutral EU member states were willing to go along with this. In December 1999, the Helsinki European Council set the famous headline goal: by 2003, the EU must be able to deploy within 60 days and sustain for at least one year military forces of up to 50,000–60,000 persons capable of the full range of Petersberg Tasks. In addition, largely at the behest of the neutral member states, the EU is acquiring capabilities to intervene with civilian means: the EU can send police forces to strengthen local policing in third countries, and can conduct 'rule of law' missions, deploying lawyers, prosecutors, judges and prison officials to train local personnel and provide expertise. Since these decisions, the EU has embarked on 19 mostly small-scale missions – one of which has been in Asia (with others in Europe, the Middle East, and Africa).

To provide direction to EU military operations, the Helsinki European Council set up new bodies within the Council: a Political and Security Committee (PSC); a Military Committee; and a Military Staff – all based in Brussels. The PSC consists of ambassadors from the member states, and meets at least twice a week. Its tasks include: helping to formulate policies and monitoring their implementation; coordinating CFSP working groups; and leading political dialogue with third countries. Some observers have argued that there is increasing socialization among participants and that consensus is becoming easier to reach in the PSC. Furthermore, the PSC can concentrate on policy 'substance' rather than on institutional questions. Thus the creation of the PSC may prove to be a very important step towards fostering more common foreign policy making.

So in the early twenty-first century there was a rapidly developing CFSP and European Security and Defence Policy (ESDP), with increasing Brusselization and institutionalization. However, intergovernmentalism was still the dominant decision-making mode, and doubts remained about how deeply the member states were committed to forging common policies, particularly where these might clash with national interests.

In 2000 and 2001, general dissatisfaction with the Nice Treaty, looming enlargement, and public discontent with the EU led to discussions of future reform among EU leaders. In December 2001, the Laeken European Council set up a Convention on the Future of Europe to address these various challenges, including 'how to develop the Union into a stabilizing factor and a model in the new, multipolar world'.

In contrast to intergovernmental conferences (IGCs), which traditionally amend the EU's treaties, the Convention consisted not only of member states' representatives, but also of national parliamentarians, members of the European Parliament, Commission officials, and representatives of the acceding countries. For most of 2002 and the first half of 2003, the Convention prepared a final document to be presented to an IGC, which became popularly known as the draft constitution. The IGC, which met in the second half of 2003 but could not agree on the draft in December 2003, eventually succeeded in mustering agreement by June 2004. After the French and Dutch rejected it in referenda in the spring of 2005, the draft constitution was set aide. In June 2007, the member states agreed to include most of the constitution's provisions, including on foreign relations, in a new 'reform treaty' (still under negotiation at the time of writing).

The outcome of this (rather tortured) negotiating process gives us a good idea of the extent to which the member states were willing to reform the CFSP/ESDP – even as they squabbled, publicly and bitterly, over Iraq. Several of these reforms have already been implemented. After the Madrid bombings in March 2004, the member states agreed to assume the obligations of a solidarity clause, which kicks in after a terrorist attack or natural or man-made disaster. The 'Petersberg tasks' have been extended to include joint disarmament operations, military advice and assistance tasks, conflict prevention and post-conflict stabilization. The European Defence Agency has been launched, to coordinate defence procurement policy and research and development. And member states have set up battle groups, combat units of about 1,500 soldiers which could be deployed rapidly to undertake Petersberg tasks, particularly in response to a request from the UN.

Two important reforms cannot be implemented until the reform treaty is ratified. The constitution provided for an EU foreign minister, to try to reduce the 'problems' caused by the pillar division between the Community and CFSP pillars; the reform treaty renames the post as High Representative of the Union for Foreign Affairs and Security Policy. The idea is for one person to do the job of High Representative for the CFSP *and* the job of External Relations Commissioner, and therefore be able to unite the EU's diplomatic, economic and military capabilities in pursuit of more coherent policy. Furthermore, a European External Action Service (EEAS) will be created, to bring together Commission and Council officials, and national diplomats, into an EU diplomatic service, to assist the new High Representative.

What would the reform treaty not change? There is virtually no extension of QMV in the CFSP,[2] and none at all for defence policy. The division between the CFSP/ESDP and the rest of the EU remains, though it is considerably fuzzier than ever before (Nuttall, 2004). Neither the European Parliament nor national parliaments saw an increase in their powers to scrutinize or contribute to decision-making in foreign and defence policy.

In conclusion, in tracing the evolution of foreign policy cooperation between the EU member states over the last 35+ years, three trends in particular can be highlighted:

- the trend towards 'Brusselization', or locating CFSP decision-makers in Brussels itself rather than national capitals;
- the search for stable and coherent leadership of the CFSP, accompanied by a tendency for a *directoire* to form on significant issues; and
- the extension of the EU's policy instruments, to include most notably armed force.

The next sections of this chapter examine the extent to which this strengthening of the CFSP has been accompanied by the geographic expansion of EU foreign policy activity to Asia.

Political relations between the EU and Asia

The Cold War history of relations between 'Europe' and 'Asia' is one marked particularly by the decline of European political influence in Asia. In this period, 'Europe' could not compete with American hegemony in Asia, and political and economic relations between the two regions diminished. A prime example of this is that Asian countries were left out of the European Community's premier relationship with developing countries, the Lomé Convention (which lasted from 1975 to 2000).

The exception to weak European–Asian links was the EC's relationship with the Association of South-East Asian Nations (ASEAN). This is in fact one of the EC's oldest formal relationships with a regional grouping, dating back to a ministerial meeting in 1978. Alongside an economic cooperation agreement between the two organizations (dating from 1980), the EC and ASEAN have also engaged in a regular 'political dialogue' of officials at several levels (up to that of foreign ministers). The Community was attracted to ASEAN not only for economic reasons (though boosting trade was clearly of interest to both sides), but also because ASEAN represented an attempt to use regional cooperation to foster stability and security in the region – remarkably similar to the Community's underlying rationale (Nuttall, 1992, p. 289). Promoting cooperation among countries in other regions has long been a key EU policy objective – and the relationship with ASEAN is an early example of this.

Otherwise, the political relationship between Europe and Asia was quite limited – despite the fact that the geographical 'reach' of European Political Cooperation (measured in declarations issued) was fairly wide, given the numerous Cold War crises around the world. Asia did not occupy much of EPC's agenda, although there was a flurry of activity from the late 1970s as the member states proposed peaceful solutions to the Soviet invasion of Afghanistan, and expressed concerns about the crises stemming from Vietnam's invasion of Cambodia (Regelsberger, 1988).

The end of the Cold War did bring about renewed European interest in Asia – though, as indicated earlier, this has been predominantly economic (and therefore not necessarily always cooperative in nature). It also began a period in which the European Union increasingly incorporated into its foreign relations concerns about the state of human rights protection and democracy in third countries around the world (European Council, 1991; Council of the European Union, 2001). As discussed further below, this in turn has complicated its relations with Asia – though compared to some areas of the world (such as Central, Eastern and South-Eastern Europe, or Africa), in relations with Asia, such 'ethical' concerns have been less prominent.

There are several ways to gauge the strength and depth of EU–Asia political relations, by looking at the place of 'Asia' in CFSP/ESDP decisions, CFSP declarations, the European Security Strategy, and Council agendas. As Table 3.1 illustrates, CFSP priorities have been quite apparently the Eastern neighbourhood and Africa. Only three CFSP common strategies have been agreed – and all dealt with the neighbourhood (Russia, Ukraine, the Mediterranean). Since the Maastricht Treaty entered into force, a little over 8 per cent of all CFSP decisions have dealt with Asia, though most of the activity has occurred in the period since 1999. Most of the decisions involved sanctions on Burma/Myanmar, with Afghanistan and Indonesia more recent preoccupations.

Given the still–nascent character of the EU–Asian political relationship, it is quite surprising that in September 2005 the EU went well 'out of area' and agreed to send an ESDP mission to the province of Aceh (Indonesia) to monitor the implementation of a peace agreement between the Indonesian government and the Free Aceh Movement (Council of the European Union, 2005a).[5] The Aceh Monitoring Mission (AMM) followed a peace initiative led by former Finnish President Martti Ahtisaari, so the EU's involvement did not come entirely out of the blue. Nonetheless, it is a striking example of a civilian ESDP mission taking place far from Europe – a clear case of global EU activism.[6]

Table 3.1 CFSP decisions (November 1993–August 2006)

Area/country	Maastricht Treaty in force, November 1993–April 1999			Since Amsterdam entered into force, May 1999–August 2006			Grand totals
	Common positions	Joint actions	Others	Common positions	Joint actions	Others[3]	
Asia							
Afghanistan	3			6	9		
Burma	7			15			
Indonesia/Aceh				1	4	4	
KEDO	1	1		2			
East Timor	1			1			
Central Asia					2		
Uzbekistan				1			
Sub-total	12 (16.44% of CPs)	1 (1.28% of JAs)		26 (13.68% of CPs)	15 (6.98% of JAs)	4 (2.9% of others)	58 (8.23%)
Africa	22 (30.14%)	10 (12.82%)	3 (27.27%)	61 (32.11%)	33 (15.35%)	13 (9.42%)	142 (20.14%)
Security/ESDP[4]	6 (8.22%)	26 (33.33%)	2 (18.18%)	32 (16.84%)	39 (18.14%)	55 (39.85%)	160 (22.69%)
Eastern Neighbourhood	26 (25.62%)	34 (43.59%)	5 (45.45%)	56 (29.47%)	105 (48.84%)	62 (44.93%)	288 (40.85%)
Latin America	3 (4.11%)						3 (0.42%)
Middle East and Mediterranean	3 (4.11%)	6 (7.69%)	1 (9.09%)	12 (6.32%)	23 (10.7%)	3 (2.17%)	48 (6.81%)
Miscellaneous	1 (1.37%)	1 (1.28%)		3 (1.58%)		1 (0.81%)	6 (0.85%)
Total	73	78	11	190	215	138	705

Source: Council of the European Union (2006a).

Table 3.1 does not include the hundred or so CFSP declarations issued each year (some of which relate to Asia). Declarations, however, are not necessarily a sign of EU political strength: just as happened in EPC, CFSP declarations are often issued in reaction to external events, and may constitute the only EU 'involvement' in those events. While the dramatic events in Nepal between 2004 and 2006 (including the dissolution of the monarchy) prompted a robust declaratory response from CFSP (the EC was already involved in funding development projects and promoting human rights and democracy there), other situations have not. For example, in the midst of considerable tensions between India and Pakistan in May 2002 (tensions which could ultimately have led even to a nuclear conflict), the EU issued only one anodyne CFSP declaration on the situation, calling for a reduction in tensions between the two countries. In Thailand the September 2006 coup and its aftermath has generated only one presidency declaration on behalf of CFSP. Likewise, developments in North Korea's nuclear weapons programme do generate a CFSP declaratory response, but the EU's role is quite marginal – neither it nor any EU member state is in the group of countries negotiating with North Korea.[7] Thus CFSP declarations give us an indication that the EU may be more interested in Asia than the record of formal CFSP decisions shows, but not at a very deep level.

CFSP declarations illustrate the short-term reaction of the EU to important developments in international affairs. But there is also a much longer-term process at work, and here Table 3.1 also fails us. It does not capture the declarations issued by regular meetings of the EU–ASEAN dialogue or the Asia–Europe Meeting (ASEM, a forum created in 1996, involving EU and ASEAN member states, Japan, China and South Korea), or the declarations from the EU's bilateral meetings with Asia countries. Since 2000 in particular, the EU has strengthened its bilateral relations with key Asian partners, holding regular summits (at head of state level) with China, Japan and India. These institutionalized partnerships illustrate best the EU's growing – though still nascent – involvement with Asia (see next section).

Asia's relatively low-key place in the EU's foreign political relations is also reflected in the December 2003 European Security Strategy (European Council, 2003). The European Security Strategy declares that the EU has three core strategic objectives: addressing security threats (terrorism; proliferation of WMD; regional conflicts: state failure: and organized crime); enhancing security in the EU's neighbourhood; and creating an international order based on 'effective multilateralism', which entails upholding international law and strengthening the United Nations.

Asia is not terribly visible in this document, though the conflicts and tensions in Afghanistan and the Korean peninsula are noted, and ASEAN is mentioned as contributing to global order. The policy prescriptions state that the EU will seek strategic partnerships with individual Asian countries – Japan, China and India – though, curiously, not with regional groupings.

The agendas of External Relations Council meetings, and the programmes of recent and upcoming presidencies, provide yet another indication of Asia's low-profile place in the EU's foreign political relations. The neighbourhood (relations with the Balkans, Russia, Ukraine, and the Mediterranean; events in the Middle East) and large issues such as terrorism or anti-proliferation tend to dominate these agendas. Asia is by no means absent: not only is the EU consistently concerned about developments in places such as North Korea and Afghanistan, but it also consistently pushes along the long-term strengthening and institutionalization of relations with ASEAN and core partners such as Japan, China and India (Council of the European Union, 2005b, 2006b, 2006c).

Asia's relative marginalization reflects a number of factors: sheer geographical distance (combined with the need to stabilize the EU's periphery); the primacy of economic interests (and the fear of economic competition) in the EU's relations with Asia; the bare fact that since the end of European colonialism in Asia, European influence has never been great, particularly in comparison to that of the USA; the difficulty of engaging with many Asian partners on political and security issues of importance to the EU (human rights, democracy, East Timor, etc.); and divisions – not to mention conflicts and discord – within Asia itself.

Nonetheless, since the end of the Cold War, the EU's interest in Asia has undeniably grown – and equipped with a stronger foreign policy-making framework, it has been strengthening its political relations with the region. The drive to enhance the EU's political relationship with Asia is quite diffuse, widely shared by the member states, but, in turn, not strongly pushed by any one of them in particular. Interest in developing the relationship stems not just from a perceived need to address particular political issues, but also from a desire to establish institutionalized relations with rising powers and other Asian countries. It does not seem to stem from recent EU enlargements, as the 1995 and 2004 enlargements of the EU did not bring in member states with extensive interests in Asia (though in the past enlargement has tended to expand the EU's geographical interests). Some observers have argued that numerous actors within the EU wish it to become a global actor – and that 'in order to play such a global role in the world, it is necessary that the EU increases its "actorness" and attains the qualities of an actor that is capable of making more autonomous foreign policy decisions' (Söderbaum, Stålgren and Langenhove, 2005, p. 371). Certainly it appears that the strengthening of the CFSP (and ESDP) has been accompanied by more activity in geographically distant areas, as far as Asia. Asia cannot be ignored if the EU is to be a global actor, which means the EU must engage with the opportunities and problems (including those related to security) in the region.

Regionalism, multilateralism and bilateralism in EU–Asia political relations

As the editors note in their introduction, the EU–Asia relationship is 'multilayered'. The EU's relations with Asia are a mix of both 'regionalism' (in the sense that the EU deals with other regional groupings) and bilateralism (in the sense that the EU is developing relations with individual countries), with some multilateralism (broad Europe–Asia consultations) – notably in the context of ASEM. But in the last five years or so, bilateralism has become more prominent in EU–Asia relations. This partly reflects the challenges the EU faces in developing relations with ASEAN (not to mention the South Asian Association for Regional Cooperation, or SAARC) and within ASEM, and partly an apparent acknowledgement by the EU that it needs to deal with the 'rising powers'.

The long-established EU–ASEAN relationship has been rocky. Two issues in particular have caused problems: East Timor (particularly after Portugal's accession to the European Community in 1986, and the massacres in Dili in 1991) and Burma/Myanmar. Because of the East Timor issue, Portugal blocked the revision of the EC–ASEAN agreement. But when a new, democratically-elected government in Indonesia allowed East Timor to become an independent state, one obstacle to closer EU–ASEAN relations was removed.

The remaining obstacle has, however, been highly problematic. Since 1990, the EU has imposed diplomatic and economic sanctions on Burma, after the military government refused to recognize the results of elections (won overwhelmingly by the democratic opposition led by Aung San Suu Kyi). Over the following years, the sanctions have been progressively tightened (though they still exclude a trade embargo or total ban on investment). When ASEAN enlarged to include Burma, Cambodia and Laos in 1997, the EU refused to allow Burma to accede to the EC–ASEAN agreement and suspended dialogue with ASEAN. In the meantime, in 1996, the Asia–Europe meeting (ASEM) was launched, with the EU and most ASEAN member states (but not Burma, Cambodia and Laos), Japan, China, and South Korea. ASEM was a convenient way to get around the tricky issue of dialogue with Southeast Asian states, since it excluded Burma. With the resolution of the East Timor issue, the EU tried to minimize the Burmese problem: in July 2000, it agreed to resume meetings with ASEAN even if they included Burma. But the EU has not been able to convince ASEAN to back its negative measures on Burma. Although some ASEAN states and even, on occasion, ASEAN and ASEM foreign ministers have called on Burma to release Suu Kyi from detention, the tendency has been for ASEAN to concentrate instead on gently encouraging the military regime to reform.[8]

As a result, relations between the EU and ASEAN continue to be rocky, and have also affected ASEM. For example, controversy swirled around the bi-annual ASEM Summit, scheduled for 8–9 October 2004 in Hanoi. The EU sought to include its ten new member states in the meeting; ASEAN refused to allow this unless the EU allowed its three new members (including Burma) to participate. In September, EU foreign ministers agreed that Burma could attend the Summit, but they also imposed additional sanctions on that country. The 2004 ASEM Summit, however, did not address Suu Kyi's detention (Council of the European Union, 2004a, paragraph 4.7), despite the more visible role given to considerations of human rights and democracy in the EU's foreign relations.

The Asian side of ASEM itself is also not entirely coherent – primarily, but not solely, reflecting Chinese–Japanese tensions. These two countries have different visions of Asian regionalism, with China pushing for an East Asian Community of ASEAN plus China, Japan and South Korea, and Japan preferring a wider group embracing Australia, New Zealand, and India (which would thus help balance Chinese influence). The EU's relations with another grouping, SAARC, are virtually non-existent – because SAARC itself hardly functions collectively. Weak regionalism in Asia complicates matters in EU–Asia relations – even before we add into the mixture differences over issues such as the promotion of human rights and democracy.

Since 2000, the EU has been developing 'strategic partnerships' with individual Asian countries – Japan, China, and India (and soon South Korea). These entail regular summits at head of state level. The EU has relatively few such high-level partnerships; the others are with the USA, Canada, Russia, Ukraine and Brazil. The bilateral relationship with Japan began in 1991, with a joint declaration on relations – though for the most part that relationship is dominated by various economic issues. There is a clear intention to develop political cooperation, but this is, again, still nascent (Solana, 2006).

Relations with China have developed rapidly, despite the continuation of the EU arms embargo on that country (imposed after the Tiananmen Square massacre in 1989). Summit meetings began in 1998 (lower-level political dialogue began in 1994), and the Council has recently committed the EU to developing an even stronger 'comprehensive strategic partnership' with China (as declared in Council of the European Union, 2006b). Annual summits with India began in 2000, and again here, there is a desire to develop a 'strategic partnership' and enhance the political relationship with that country as well (Council of the European Union, 2004b).

The development of stronger bilateral links with Asian 'powers' is striking. There might be a slight whiff of 'soft balancing' here: the EU could be positioning itself to take advantage of a more multipolar world. But it has to be reiterated that on several core issues the EU and its key Asian partner – particularly China and India – find it hard to agree, and thus it can hardly be claimed that the EU is lining up with large Asian countries to 'balance' the US. Human rights is one area of disagreement – and this is not just about the tensions with China over human rights (despite the EU–China human rights dialogue, begun in 1996). It is about the importance countries give to human rights more generally – in Asia and beyond. Neither India nor China is keen on the 'responsibility to protect' doctrine (though this was agreed by the UN Summit in September 2005), and the EU and these two countries have quite different conceptions of sovereignty. The EU has failed to convince China and India to back negative measures against the Burmese regime – in fact, those two countries appear now to be competing for influence there (Leonard, 2007, p. 43). Likewise, neither China nor India share the same enthusiasm as the EU regarding 'effective multilateralism'. As Georg Wiessala notes, in Asia 'the Europeans were often faced with very divergent concepts of "democracy", "civil liberties" or "tradition", and with different mentalities, negotiating styles, priorities and tactics, in spite of a semblance of commonality on the surface' (Wiessala, 2002, p. 163). And we should also not forget the sensitive nature of relations between the Asian powers themselves. All of these differences present challenges to the development of the EU's relations with key Asian states.

Japan would seem to be a more obvious natural partner for the EU in seeking to boost multilateralism (in a form acceptable to the EU). And there is an established framework for EU consultations with Japan at the UN – though these are consultations with 'JUSCANZ' (Japan, US,

Canada, Australia and New Zealand). But one of the problems posed by the intergovernmental set-up for EU foreign policy cooperation is that intra-EU negotiations take up much time and energy. The EU member states are involved in an intensive mechanism for coordinating their positions at the UN, but this leaves little time for 'outreach' to key partners at the UN. So, for example, in 2003 in New York there were only 12 meetings with JUSCANZ, plus two with Japan, one each with ASEAN, India and China. This contrasts with the additional 12 meetings with the US alone and 16 with EFTA members (Norway, Switzerland, Iceland, Liechtenstein). But even so, these meetings with 'third countries' are small percentage of the thousand or so coordination meetings in all – most of these meetings involve only EU states (European Union, 2003). With a more determined effort on the part of the EU to reach out to like-minded partners at the UN, however, this could change, and EU–Japan relations could strengthen still further. But this requires further strengthening of the CFSP framework; implementing the post of the new High Representative might help, but probably even more useful would be the creation of the EU External Action Service.

Conclusion

Does reforming the EU's institutions and decision-making rules makes it a more effective and cohesive international actor? Reformed procedures and institutions have allowed for quicker decision-making and implementation (though this does depend on member state will to act collectively in the first place), and for more coordinated and consistent policy making towards particular areas of the world. The strengthening of the framework for foreign policy cooperation and the extension of the EU's 'toolbox' of available foreign policy instruments have gone hand in hand with a geographical widening of the EU's political relations. With respect to Asia, EU political relations are still underdeveloped, particularly when compared to the EU's extensive activities in its periphery. But there is nonetheless a serious attempt by the EU to create frameworks for the institutionalization of EU–Asia relations, as well as growing CFSP/ESDP activity in the region. There are still limits to these developments – posed by external constraints (including different visions regarding the promotion of democracy and human rights) and the internal constraints of the EU's intergovernmental procedures for making foreign policy.

The EU's evolution as a global actor and the growth in its foreign policy activity in Asia does not mean that it is contributing to building

Karen E. Smith 63

multilateralism in Asia. Alongside the development of EU relations with ASEAN, the EU is trying to build 'strategic partnerships' with large Asian countries. ASEM does bring in three of those countries (China, Japan, and South Korea) into an inter-regional relationship with the EU, but the EU is still seeking to develop wide-ranging bilateral relations with key states. As the EU, albeit haltingly, becomes more of a cohesive global actor, it seeks out other global players. If regional groupings cannot match the EU's cohesiveness, then it will deal with countries bilaterally. This may boost the EU's pursuit of its own political, security and economic interests – and its global reach, but does not necessarily contribute to more multilateralism in Asia itself.

Furthermore, EU–Asia relations do not appear (yet) to be contributing to strengthening multilateralism at the global level – there are simply too many differences in the approaches to 'global governance' between the two sides. At best, then, we can conclude that the political relationships between the EU and Asia (as a whole) or Asian countries (in particular) have much room for growth.

Notes

1. The WEU was created in 1954 (after the European Defence Community was rejected by the French National Assembly) on the basis of the 1948 Brussels Treaty of mutual defence between Belgium, France, Luxembourg, the Netherlands and the UK. West Germany and Italy joined the WEU in 1954. But its core function – defence – was carried out by NATO, and it lay largely dormant for 30 years. In 1984, the seven members revived the WEU, as a forum in which they could discuss defence issues without a US presence. At the time, the WEU did not include Denmark, Greece or Ireland, long opposed to discussing defence issues within EPC. Denmark was also granted an opt-out from the Maastricht defence provisions.
2. The proposed reform treaty would subject to QMV decisions adopted on a proposal from the new High Representative minister made at the request of the European Council; the Nice Treaty had already extended QMV to decisions on appointing special envoys.
3. Includes decisions such as Common Strategies.
4. The 'ESDP' section of 'Actes Juridiques' contained several decisions that appeared elsewhere under geographical categories; these were not double counted (158 decisions are listed; 23 are not double counted). Of the remaining 135 decisions listed, only 37 were not geographically specific.
5. The Aceh Monitoring Mission included personnel from ASEAN countries, Norway and Switzerland: of 226 personnel, 130 come from EU member states. The AMM was concluded in December 2006, and generally considered to be a success.

6. In the case of Afghanistan, however, the Belgian presidency in the fall of 2001 did suggest that the EU contribute military forces to what became the International Stabilization Force but the other member states – particularly the large ones – refused to go along with an 'EU force' (and at that stage, the Helsinki ESDP process was still quite young).
7. Furthermore, the EU member states were unable to reach a collective stance on diplomatic recognition of the North Korean regime – and went their separate ways. See General Affairs Council (2000) and Chapter 11 of this volume.
8. For example, in October 2003, the ASEAN Summit did not criticize Suu Kyi's detention, and even 'welcomed the recent positive developments in Myanmar... *The Leaders also agree that sanctions are not helpful in promoting peace and stability essential for democracy to take root*' (ASEAN, 2003, paragraph 25; emphasis added).

References

Allen, David, ' "Who Speaks for Europe?" The Search for an Effective and Coherent External Policy', in John Peterson and Helene Sjursen (eds), *A Common Foreign Policy for Europe?* (London: Routledge, 1998).
ASEAN, 'Press Statement by the Chairperson of the 9th ASEAN Summit and the 7th ASEAN + 3 Summit', Bali, Indonesia, 7 October 2003. http://www.aseansec.org/15260.htm
Council of the European Union, 'Council Conclusions on the European Union's Role in Promoting Human Rights and Democratization in Third Countries', Luxembourg, 25 June 2001.
Council of the European Union, 'Chairman's Statement of the Fifth Asia–Europe Meeting, Hanoi, 8–9 October 2004', Document No. 12895/04 (Presse 280), Brussels, 10 October 2004a.
Council of the European Union, 'Fifth India–EU Summit, The Hague, 8 November 2004: Joint Press Statement', Press Release No. 14431/04, 8 November 2004b.
Council of the European Union, 'Joint Action 2005/643/CFSP of 9 September 2005 on the European Union Monitoring Mission in Aceh (Indonesia) (Aceh Monitoring Mission – AMM)', in *Official Journal of the European Union* L234, 10 September 2005a.
Council of the European Union, 'Operational Programme of the Council for 2006 submitted by the incoming Austrian and Finnish Presidencies', Document No. 16065/05, 22 December 2005b.
Council of the European Union, 'Actes Juridiques PESC: Liste Thématique', Brussels, 3 August 2006a. http://www.consilium.europa.eu/uedocs/cmsUpload/ACTES_JURIDIQUES-2006-Continuing-updating.pdf accessed 29 September 2006.
Council of the European Union, 'External Relations Council Meeting', Press Release No. 16291/06, 11–12 December 2006b.
Council of the European Union, '18-month Programme of the German, Portuguese and Slovenian Presidencies', Document No. 17079/06, 21 December 2006c.

Deighton, Anne, 'The European Security and Defence Policy', *Journal of Common Market Studies*, 40(4) (2002), 719–41.
de Schoutheete, Philippe, *La Coopération Politique Européenne* (Brussels: Editions Labor, 1980).
European Council, 'Declaration on Human Rights', *EC Bulletin*, No. 6, Luxembourg (1991).
European Council, 'A Secure Europe in a Better World: European Security Strategy', Brussels, 12 December 2003.
European Union, 'Total of Meetings New York Liaison Office, Greek Presidency and Italian Presidency', mimeo (2003).
General Affairs Council, 'Conclusions on European Union Lines of Action Towards North Korea', Press Release No. 1343/00 (Presse 435), (20 November 2000).
Hill, Christopher, 'The Capability–Expectations Gap, or Conceptualizing Europe's International Role', *Journal of Common Market Studies*, 31(3) (1993), 305–28.
Howorth, Jolyon, 'European Defence and the Changing Politics of the EU: Hanging Together or Hanging Separately?', *Journal of Common Market Studies*, 39(4) (2001), 765–89.
Leonard, Mark, *Divided World: the Struggle for Primacy in 2020* (London: Centre for European Reform, 2007).
Müller-Brandeck-Bocquet, Gisela, 'The New CFSP and ESDP Decision-Making System of the European Union', *European Foreign Affairs Review*, 7(3) (2002), 257–82.
Nuttall, Simon, *European Political Co-operation* (Oxford: Clarendon Press, 1992).
Nuttall, Simon, *European Foreign Policy* (Oxford: Oxford University Press, 2000).
Nuttall, Simon, 'On Fuzzy Pillars: Criteria for the Continued Existence of Pillars in the Draft Constitution', *CFSP Forum*, 2(3) (May 2004), 4–7.
Regelsberger, Elfriede, 'Chronology of European Political Cooperation', in Alfred Pijpers, Elfriede Regelsberger, and Wolfgang Wessels (eds), *European Political Cooperation in the 1980s: A Common Foreign Policy for Europe?* (Dordrecht: Martinus Nijhoff, 1988).
Smith, Michael E., 'The Legalization of EU Foreign Policy', *Journal of Common Market Studies*, Vol. 39 (1) (2001), 79–104.
Smith, Michael E., *Europe's Foreign and Security Policy: The Institutionalization of Cooperation* (Cambridge: Cambridge University Press, 2004).
Söderbaum, Frederik, Stålgren, Patrika, and Langenhove, Luk van, 'The EU as a Global Actor and the Dynamics of Interregionalism: A Comparative Analysis', *Journal of European Integration*, 27(3) (2005), 249–62.
Solana, Javier, 'The EU's Strategic Partnership with Japan', speech at Keio University, Tokyo (24 April 2006).
Wiessala, Georg, *The European Union and Asian Countries* (London: Sheffield Academic Press, 2002).

4
The Asia Strategy of the European Union and Asia–EU Economic Relations: History and New Developments

Sung-Hoon Park and Heung-Chong Kim

Introduction

The relationship between Asia and Europe can be termed ambivalent: on the one hand, the two continents have been maintaining a long-standing relationship, ever since Marco Polo 'discovered' Asia. On the other hand, some Asian countries had been colonies of their European counterparts until at least the end of the Second World War. These characteristics in the relationship of the two continents have undergone substantial changes after the Second World War, most of which were found in the context of the ebb of European influence in Asia through Asian countries' independence from their European empires, and Asia's growing ignorance of Europe.

The period between the end of the Second World War and the beginning of the 1990s had been characterized by the two following factors: the dominance of the United States, which Europe was either unwilling or unable to challenge, and Asia's orientation to the United States as a destination for their products. Asia–Europe relations during this period had, therefore, been largely shaped by bilateral country-to-country negotiations, leading to a relatively low degree of congruence and weak focus from a European perspective.

However, at the beginning of the 1990s, there seemed to be several coincidental developments that led to a greater European consciousness of the necessity to develop a common strategy of European countries towards Asia. Having successfully completed the Single Market programme, Europe was in a position to devote the necessary energy and resources to the pursuit of more active external relations, and there is evidence to suggest that this was done with a high priority being given to Asia. Asia had been regarded as the most dynamic economic region with the potential for becoming the centre of world economic growth, and thus Asia's strategic value had been increasing continually since the mid-1980s. It was at this point that Europe began rediscovering Asia as a serious partner of cooperation.

The first official Asia Strategy of the European Union (EU) was adopted in 1994. During the period 1993–96, the European Union presented a number of strategic concepts to strengthen political and economic ties with East Asia, before its attention was redirected to other Asian countries: beginning with the adoption of the Korea Strategy in 1993, the EU successively adopted strategic policies towards Asia (1994), China (1995) and Japan (1995), as well as Southeast Asia (1996). This series of strategic concepts led on to the launch of the Asia–Europe Meeting (ASEM) in 1996, which has had six summit meetings since its inception.

The purpose of this chapter is to review the trend of the EU's strengthened strategic approach towards East Asia primarily in the economic dimension, to analyse its background factors, and to discuss recently-observed developments.

EU's preferential trading regime and East Asia

Characteristics and hierarchy of EU's external economic relations

External economic relations of the EU, which are conducted mainly through the Common Commercial Policy (CCP), have several defining features. Among them, the sole competence of the European Commission for conducting the CCP and an extensive use of Article XXIV of the General Agreement on Tariffs and Trade (GATT) in approaching non-member countries are two of the most noteworthy. As for the sole competence of the European Commission, it is widely recognized that the process of European integration which evolved from the initial establishment of the three Communities during the 1950s[1] into a Customs Union in the 1960s and finally into a Common Market in the 1980s, prompted the European Union to adopt the CCP, which in turn became the competence of the European Commission.

Furthermore, Article XXIV of GATT or its successor, the World Trade Organization (WTO), sets out the requirement for any Customs Union to adopt the Common External Tariff (CET).[2] The European Community achieved the status of a Customs Union in 1968, and this enabled the European Community to be more powerfully represented by the European Commission. With regards to EU's extensive use of GATT Article XXIV, it is noticeable that the EU has been implementing a complex

Figure 4.1 Preferential trading arrangements of the EU: a pyramid analysis
Note: Modified and updated based on a diagram provided in Pelkmans (1997). This figure was applicable until the recent Eastern enlargement of the EU.

system of preferential trading arrangements for a long time. The preferential trading arrangements that the EU is either currently granting to non-EU countries or is involved in are numerous and complex in reality, as is shown in Figure 4.1.

Figure 4.1 exhibits – up until just before the Eastern enlargement of the EU – the hierarchy of non-EU member countries based on the degree and extent of preferences provided by the EU. The higher the countries are located in the pyramid, the stronger the preferences provided by the EU. The figure above clearly shows that the EU attached the highest priority in its external trade relations to the Central and Eastern European Countries (CEECs), which had been in the process of accession to the EU since the beginning of the 1990s. The Europe Agreements with the CEECs, and the following official negotiations with them for their membership into the EU, constituted the procedural and legal basis for the EU to treat these countries most favourably among its trading partners. These countries officially joined the EU in May 2004 and thus disappeared from the pyramid at that time.

The second-most favourable preferences are provided to the member countries of the European Free Trade Association (EFTA), which entered into the European Economic Area (EEA) agreement – a common market agreement – with the EU effective in 1993.[3] Countries in the African, Caribbean and Pacific region that were former colonies of EU member states, and Mediterranean countries, as well as remaining developing countries enjoy specific preferential market access to EU markets of different degrees.[4] However, those OECD countries that are not included in any other special agreements with the EU do not enjoy any preferential treatment, and are thus grouped as 'normal traders' for the EU, to which Most Favoured Nation (MFN) tariff rates are applied. The EU also maintains a discriminatory trading regime for products originating in selected state-trading countries, such as Cuba and North Korea.

The position of the East Asian countries in EU's preferential trading regime

Just a brief glance at Figure 4.1 confirms that no Asian countries are present in the four highest priority groups. Most of the Southeast Asian countries are beneficiaries of the EU's Generalized System of Preferences (GSP) scheme, a benefit which they share with a handful of other developing countries in Latin America and Africa. Japan and South Korea, which are member countries of the OECD, maintain normal trading relations with the EU, with MFN tariff rates imposed on their products exported to EU markets. In fact, the wide-ranging and complex system of EU's preferential trading regime results in a very small number of countries that are not enjoying any preferences in trading with the EU: of the member countries of the WTO only the United States, Canada, New Zealand, Australia, South Korea and Japan belong to this unprivileged group.[5]

Coming back to the status of Asian countries in the preferential trading regime of the EU, one distinguishing feature deserves our attention, which Figure 4.1 and recent EU strategies reveal: the EU appears to prefer inter-regional rather than inter-national relations in trading with other countries and regions. This can be explained – in addition to EU's revealed preferences provided to ACP and Mediterranean countries – more recently by the increasing number of free trade agreements (FTAs) that the EU has been negotiating with other regions: the EU has agreed to establish a FTA with the Latin American grouping MERCOSUR, and had also been considering the possibility of establishing a FTA with North America named TAFTA (Transatlantic Free Trade Area) before the idea was discarded and replaced by the Transatlantic Economic Partnership (TEP) initiative launched in 1998.

Another factor that could have accounted for East Asia showing a relatively low profile in the EU's wide-ranging and complex system of preferential trading could have been the predominance of the United States in the economic and political, as well as security relations of the Asian countries. Conversely, this served as a background for the initiative to launch an official link between the two parties, thus filling the 'missing link' between Europe and Asia in an increasingly tri-polar world economy.

Geopolitical factors underlying the EU's new approach to East Asia: a mixture of positive and negative signals

The launch of ASEM in 1996 can be regarded as the official crowning of a series of strategic approaches by the EU towards East Asia. Having been established as a summit meeting between the two continents, ASEM has positioned itself as an important inter-regional cooperation forum between the two continents. With the cooperation agenda being comprehensive and widespread, ranging from political to economic to cultural fields, ASEM has awakened attention on both sides to the importance of such cooperation, especially in the light of Asia countries' internal recognition of their too strong a dependence on the political, security-related and economic dominance of the United States in the region.

An increasing consciousness in the East Asian countries of the necessity to diversify their external relations had been effectively accommodated by the EU's newly-discovered strategic value of East Asia that had been on a continuous increase since the mid-1980s. This coincidence of mutual interest, which had been strengthening since the beginning of the 1990s, triggered a process of negotiations, thereby leading to the launch of the first ASEM Summit in Bangkok, at which 15 EU member states and ten East Asian countries (ASEAN, Vietnam + China, Japan and South Korea) met together, in 1996. ASEM, therefore, needs to be considered against the background of the overall relationship between the two continents, which contained both positive and negative aspects (Pelkmans and Shinkai, 1997), and the EU's New Asia Strategy.

Negative signals for Asia–Europe relations in the 1990s

A number of negative factors surrounded bilateral relations between Asia and Europe in the early 1990s. First, the 1986 announcement of and completion of the Single European Market by the end of 1992 generated suspicion and scepticism about the EU's trade policy stance, which faded only gradually. In fact, many major trading partners of the EU, including Asian countries such as Japan and South Korea, were concerned about EU becoming a 'fortress'[6] with higher protectionist barriers for products from non-member countries. The observed increasing direct investment of Japanese firms into Europe since the mid-1980s had been fuelled by a strong appreciation of Japanese yen and Japanese firms' pre-emptive 'tariff-jumping' strategy rather than by expectations of an improving business environment in Europe. East Asia observed cautiously the developments of the deepening process of European integration.

Secondly, during the final stage of the Uruguay Round (UR) negotiations, the revealed rigid position of the EU on the Common Agricultural Policy (CAP), with its widespread and heavy subsidy programmes, appeared to be in the way of successfully concluding deals for worldwide trade liberalization, of which East Asian countries had been main beneficiaries since the end of the Second World War. Frustrated with prolonged UR trade talks and consequently increasing opportunity costs, East Asian countries further strengthened ties with the United States, for example through the establishment of the Asia-Pacific Economic Cooperation (APEC) forum in 1989. In fact, some analysts see APEC – with its potential to be developed into a regional bloc – as a US strategy to pressurize the EU to conclude the UR negotiations with concessions on agricultural liberalization issues, which was seemingly successful (Bergsten, 1997).

Thirdly, with the EU's decision to pursue Northern (to Sweden, Austria and Finland in 1995) and Eastern (ten countries in Eastern Europe and Mediterranean region in 2004) enlargement, East Asian countries were concerned over the potential diversion of trade and investment. They had become increasingly concerned about how much of the EU's investment into Asia would be diverted to the Central and Eastern European Countries (CEECs) that had signed Europe Agreements with the EU during the first half of 1990s.

Fourthly, the EU's external relations with individual Asian countries were not without flaws. Problematic issues involved enhancing democracy (China; the Tiananmen Square incident) and human rights (ASEAN; East Timor), resolving chronic bilateral trade imbalances (Japan), and countering aggressive trade policies (South Korea; shipbuilding, steel, and so on). This set of negative signals surrounding Asia–Europe bilateral relations has functioned as a centrifugal force, leading both parties to keep their distance from each other.

Positive signals for Asia–Europe relations in the 1990s

On the other hand, there were also positive developments fostering Asia–Europe relations, which functioned, in contrast to the aforementioned negative signals, as centripetal forces, leading both parties to take favourable policy stances towards one another. First of all, with the successful conclusion of the UR negotiations and successful launch of the Single European Market, both in 1993, the EU could afford to dedicate the human resources and energy towards strengthening external relations, especially with East Asia.

Secondly, motivated by the remarkable economic performances of many East Asian countries and alerted to the proactive Asia strategy of the United States, Europe discovered an improved profile and presence in the fastest-growing Asian markets as European governments and businesses made Asia one of the top priorities in their external relations. This ultimately prompted the European Commission to elaborate on strategic concepts towards East Asia, thereby leading to the adoption of a series of strategic concept papers towards East Asia as a whole, and individual countries in the region.

Thirdly, this led the EU to start negotiating and/or concluding a series of different types of cooperation agreements with individual East Asian countries, most of which came into effect during the second half of 1990s and underlined their increasing strategic value.

Fourthly, to be fair, it can be argued that for a long time Asia for its part had also neglected Europe as a serious cooperation partner, but that attitude too was undergoing change by the mid-1990s. Asian countries were long satisfied with their strong economic and political ties with the United States and Japan, based on which they could enjoy high growth rates over the preceding two decades. In the late 1980s, they entered into an inter-regional cooperation scheme with North America through the establishment of APEC, which, above all, was expected to promote the construction of an economic community in the Asia-Pacific. With APEC, it was signalled, many Asian countries wanted to engage China, in order to stand the increasing political and economic challenges coming from this future major regional and global power. In short, it is true that Asia too was preoccupied with its own regional agenda as well as with external relations with the United States, just as the EU was preoccupied with its own integration agenda. With APEC incrementally turning out to be a vehicle to channel US business interests into the fast-growing Asian markets, Asian countries became conscious of being increasingly dependent on the United States and Japan – in both political and economic terms – and started to search for alternatives. These geopolitical factors, which prevailed in the early and mid-1990s, implied a coincidental increase in the mutual interest of Asia and Europe.

Despite these rather conflicting developments in Asia–Europe relations, nonetheless it seems that the centripetal forces of Asia–Europe relations outpaced the centrifugal forces. In particular, the new general orientation underpinning the EU strategy towards Asia had been influenced most strongly by the increasing strategic economic value of Asia in recent decades. The World Bank (World Bank, 1993), for instance, praised the Asian countries as 'miracle economies' that possessed the potential to become the centre of world economic growth in the twenty-first century. The four newly-industrialized economies (South Korea, Singapore, Taiwan and Hong Kong) which had earned the title of 'Asian Tigers' (Dragons), the liberalizing of trade and investment regimes in many Southeast Asian nations, and the major policy changes in the economy that possesses the biggest population, China, all contributed to enhancing the overall strategic value of the whole region. Following from these kinds of analyses, both the United States and the EU launched and/or revised their own strategic concepts towards Asia. The US strategy towards Big Emerging Markets (BEMs), for instance, included ambitious initiatives to pursue stronger political and economic cooperation with 17 BEMs, 12 of which were Asian countries. The EU responded with its own strategic concept towards Asia in 1994.[7]

New Asia Strategy of the European Union

In the analysis of the EU's approach towards East Asia, the New Asia Strategy (NAS) of the EU should be put at the centre of the discussion. The NAS, which was adopted in 1994 and revised in 2001, was developed in the midst of both the deepening of European integration and the prolonged UR negotiations. In some sense, the EU – with the NAS – had been preparing for the governance of the global political and economic order after these two major events. The then observed increasing strategic value of East Asia provided a timely and welcome additional impetus to intensified EU approach towards East Asia.

Table 4.1 provides an overview of EU's NAS and other individual country strategy papers and their main contents.

The original NAS strategy identified the Asian region as consisting of a group of extremely dynamic countries that have the potential to lead twenty-first-century world economic growth and development. Categorizing the Asian countries into three subgroups – Northeast Asia, Southeast Asia and South Asia – the strategy paper issued by the European Commission elaborates on ways and modalities to promote the

Table 4.1 Main contents of NAS and country strategy papers adopted by the EU during 1993–96

Date of issue	Country/region	Main contents
August 1993	Korea[1]	– Welcomes the democratization and market opening – Expects to promote bilateral economic relations that are not matching the economic powers of the two countries – Wants to establish equal partnership
July 1994	Asia[2]	– Wants to participate in the market expansion in Asia that has the potential to become the growth centre of the world economy – Specifies differentiated strategy towards three sub-groups (East, Southeast and South Asia) in the region – Wants to promote the presence of EU firms and products
March 1995	Japan[3]	– Wants to maintain and strengthen the existing economic and political dialogue channels – Making efforts to dismantle barriers to market access – Continuing the Trade Assessment Mechanism and cooperating in respecting the WTO rules
July 1995	China[4]	– Strengthening the support for China in transition – Supporting the Chinese accession to the WTO – Promoting EU firms' market and investment access to China
June 1996	ASEAN[5]	– Taking part in the dynamism of ASEAN economies – Enhancing the direct investment into ASEAN countries – Upgrading the bilateral relationship

Note: The table is translated from Park (1999).
Sources: 1 European Commission (1993).
2 European Commission (1994).
3 European Commission (1995a).
4 European Commission (1995b).
5 European Commission (1996a).

presence, profile and influence of Europe in Asia.[8] The NAS strategy focused especially on the East Asian sub-group – comprising of Southeast and Northeast Asia – as major cooperation partners for the EU. In this regard, it is noteworthy that immediately prior to and soon after the adoption of the NAS the EU adopted several strategy papers for relations with individual East Asian countries.

It is also noteworthy that in its NAS strategy paper the EU acknowledged the unique and predominant role of the United States in the field of regional security in East Asia. As such, the EU's new approach towards East Asia can be interpreted as being a balanced pursuit of strengthened political and economic cooperation with East Asia. The EU has become increasingly aware of the need for 'strengthening the EU's political and economic presence across the region, and raising this to a level commensurate with the growing global weight of an enlarged EU' as one of the core objectives in its relationship with Asia (European Commission, 2001b).

Main features of recent EU–East Asia economic relations

As noted in the above discussion, even though East Asia has not been treated preferentially by the EU, it goes without saying that the region has been an important trading partner for most EU member states. East Asia, with Japan, China and South Korea being major regional economic powers, has long been an 'engine of world economic growth', and most observers believe it will continue to be so in the twenty-first century despite the temporary setback suffered during the 1997 Asian financial crisis. A careful analysis of recent EU–East Asia trade and investment relations reveals several interesting characteristics (see Tables 4.2 and 4.3).

First, as Table 4.2 shows, Asia as a whole, including Australasia,[9] accounted for about one-quarter of EU exports to non-EU countries in 1995, and a lion's share of EU's exports to Asia were directed to East Asian countries (subdivided into Northeast and Southeast Asia). It is noteworthy that in the same year, the EU exports of manufactured products to Asia exceeded the EU exports to NAFTA member countries. In fact, it can be observed that Asia has become a more weighted trading partner for the EU since the beginning of 1990s. A moderate decrease in Asia's share as the EU's export destination, which is manifested in Table 4.2, is mainly due to Asian financial crisis and the unexpectedly strong economic performance of the United States. The remarkable economic performance of China in recent years, as well as relatively rapid recovery of South

Table 4.2 Destination of EU's exports by region (1995/2001/2005)

Region	Share in EU exports in 1995 (%)	Share in EU exports in 2001 (%)	Share in EU exports in 2005 (%)	Trade balance in 2005 (million euros)
Asia	25.9	21.1	23.1	−165,117
NEA	15.0	13.0	13.9	(−150,502)
ASEAN	6.5	4.3	4.1	(−25,308)
South Asia	2.2	1.9	2.9	(−696)
Australasia	2.1	1.9	2.2	(11,389)
Europe excluding EU	29.4	30.9	27.3	−37,600.9
Candidate countries	12.3	16.1	6.6	(16,761)
EEA + Switzerland	12.2	10.5	11.2	(−16,955)
Others	4.9	4.3	9.5	(−37,406.9)
NAFTA	20.6	28.4	27.3	103,055
US	18.0	24.7	23.5	(88,775)
Others	2.6	3.7	3.8	(14,280)
Others	24.1	19.6	22.3	−9,173.9
Total	100.0	100.0	100.0	−108,836.8

Note: Data in 1995 and 2001 are for EU15 and the 2005 data are for EU25.
Source: EUROSTAT, compacted and rearranged from European Commission (2001b), and External and intra-European Union trade – Statistical yearbook – Data 1958–2005 (30 November 2006).

Table 4.3 Destination of EU15's foreign direct investment by region (1996/1999/2005)

Region	Share in 1996 (%)	Share in 1999 (%)	Share in 2005 (%)
Asia	21.1	6.8	17.2
NEA	9.6	6.0	13.4
ASEAN	5.8	−0.6	3.2
Others	5.7	1.4	0.6
Europe excluding EU	18.7	7.5	51.2
Candidate Countries	8.9	5.1	18.3
Others	9.8	2.4	32.9
NAFTA	39.6	67.5	22.1
US	37.4	65.6	14.8
Others	2.2	1.9	7.3
Others	20.6	18.2	9.5
Total	100.0	100.0	100.0

Source: EUROSTAT, compacted and rearranged from European Commission (2001b), and EU direct investment outward flows by extra EU country of destination (5 April 2006).

Korea and other Southeast Asian countries from the crisis are expected to bring this figure back to the trend path observed since the beginning of 1990s.

Secondly, Asian countries in general, and the East Asian countries in particular, are amongst the few trading partners of the EU that could manage to show a trade surplus vis-à-vis the EU. In 2005, the EU registered a trade deficit of some 165 billion euros in trade with Asia, whereas it showed trade surpluses vis-à-vis NAFTA and some other European countries. This had, and is expected to have, some implications for the future EU trade policy towards East Asia, possibly leading to more TBR (Trade Barriers Regulation) cases.

In investment exchanges, Table 4.3 suggests that Asia is not as strongly represented as in trade relations with the EU. Asia's share of the EU's FDI in 1999 was just 6.8 per cent, but this figure does not represent the 'real' importance of the region as EU's investment partner. In fact, the sharp decrease in 1999 compared to 1996 can be interpreted as a consequence of the 1997 Asian financial crisis, as can be proved from the data showing the resurgence by 2005. The European Commission's own analysis (European Commission, 2001b) supports this view, and reports a continuously increasing share held by Asia in the EU's FDI statistics. It seems that the EU companies during the reported period have been concentrating their investment projects to the NAFTA member countries after the Asian financial crisis, considering the weakened absorption capacity of Asian countries and strengthened economic activities in the NAFTA region, thus making a full use of the flourishing new economy of the United States at that time. However, the most recent FDI performance shows a conspicuous increase of EU's FDI towards other European countries and the recovery of the investment performance to Asia.

In summary, the interest of European companies in the Asian region as their investment destination, which witnessed a strong surge in the beginning of the 1990s, has recovered and is strongly alive despite the temporary setback following the Asian financial crisis.

It is interesting to note that several surveys, including one by UNCTAD (UNCTAD, 1998), did suggest that FDI into Asia would rebound after a temporary decline, and that European investors were relatively more optimistic about the future of Asian economies than other foreign investors. This optimism has come to be realized with the strong recovery of European FDI into Asia that has been observed since 2000.

Summarizing the discussion in this section, we can draw a conclusion that despite a temporary slowdown of economic exchanges between the EU and East Asia, the latter remains an important trade and investment partner for the EU. One important consequence of this assessment is that the EU will be keenly interested in and therefore be alert to the main economic and political changes taking place in Asia.

New challenges in Asia–Europe relations

The Asian financial crisis and Asia–Europe relations

The 1997 Asian financial crisis caused a major challenge to the ASEM cooperation process. Avila (1999) suggested that the 1997 Asian financial crisis had 'demonstrated the poor institutional foundation of inter-regional organizations' in Asia, implying that existing forms of regional cooperation – such as APEC, ASEAN and ASEM – had all failed to deal with such region-wide problems as the Asian financial crisis in an effective manner. Also, Park (2003) established a linkage between this ineffectiveness and the waning interest and conceived irrelevance of inter-regional agenda like APEC and ASEM in the strategic priority scale of Asian countries. In fact, ASEM and APEC seem to have been in a stalemate situation for quite a while after the outbreak of the financial crisis in Asia. APEC's attempt to generate an additional liberalization through the Early Voluntary Sectoral Liberalization (EVSL) project failed in 1998, and ASEM's cooperation programmes were also overshadowed by their relative indifference and the sudden global security concerns due to the September 11 terrorist attacks on the United States.

In its assessment of the ASEM process during the first four years, the European Commission (2000) hinted that a certain degree of 'fatigue' existed and should be countered. The European Commission (European Commission, 2001a) goes further and points even to the necessity of reforming the process to make the machinery roll. P. Lim (2002) suggested the economic agenda had been the most successful pillar of ASEM activities, but admitted that the ASEM Trust Fund and EFEX (European Financial Expertise Network) programme – these were the support programmes proposed by the EU – failed to revive the Asian partners' interest in the ASEM process. The London, Seoul, and Copenhagen Summit Meetings of ASEM were all devoted to a substantial degree to the traditional ASEM cooperation programmes, focusing on the 'contribution to multilateral trading system', 'producing global security environments', etc. An important task for ASEM member countries, therefore, is to be creative enough to revitalize the momentum of bilateral cooperation between Asia and Europe, now that most of the crisis economies in Asia have returned to their 'normal' business cycle.

Emerging East Asian regionalism and the EU's possible response

A proliferation of regional initiatives within and surrounding East Asia is a relatively new phenomenon in the region, and poses a second challenge to future Asia–Europe relations. The challenge to Europe – be it positive or negative – has the potential to make the Asia–Europe relations different from those prevailing before the launch of ASEM. Robert Scollay (2001) and S.H. Park (2001, 2004) reported more than 20 FTA initiatives – only partly discussed or feasibility-studied, partly under serious negotiation, and even partly already effective – among and/or involving East Asian countries. Considering the traditional East Asian preferences regarding multilateralism, this is a 'new' phenomenon, as S.H. Park (2001) concluded.

If successful in their attempt to produce a region-wide integration body in the near future, the Asian countries – equipped with the long-hoped-for one-voice – will emerge as more confident cooperation partners for Europe. First, the stronger integration of East Asia might be a welcomed result from the EU perspective – regardless of being intended or not.[10] Secondly, with a better-integrated East Asia, the EU may be able to cooperate at a more elevated level than before, with the increasing possibility of establishing 'inter-regional cooperation in a real sense', as observed by Park (2003). At the same time, East Asia's own regionalism with a resulting stronger negotiating power may weaken the predominant leadership role of the United States in the region, which could mean a relative gain for the EU. Thirdly, on the other hand, a stronger East Asia may mean for the EU more difficult negotiations on contentious issues. Well-coordinated East Asian positions or even non-positions might not even allow for the inclusion of contentious issues – such as human rights, drug trafficking and immigration – onto the meeting agenda of ASEM venues, a development which has been feared by the European Commission (European Commission, 2001a).

Conclusion

Recalling the relationship between Europe and Asia since the Second World War, it can be said to have been developed in the context of multilateralism up until the 1990s. That led to the weakening position of Asia among the list of EU's preferential economic ties with external regions. However, the trend of mutual ignorance between the two continents was reversed in the 1990s due to both the growing economic importance of Asia in the world league table and the EU's strengthened interests in promoting its external relations, supported by its completion of the Single Market integration schedule, the northern and eastern enlargement, and the introduction of economic and monetary union. The relationship between the two sides has been highlighted by the formation of the dialogue meetings of ASEM, for which the New Asia Strategy of the EU, first adopted in 1994 and revised in 2001, provided an impetus.

As a result of the above analysis, it is recommended that the East Asian countries place a high priority on the ASEM process in their external strategies, recognize their ever-increasing international role through APEC and ASEM, achieve a balanced approach between regionalism and multilateralism as being in their best interests, promote strengthened intra-Asian cooperation in the future, and preserve the practice of open regionalism. It is also in the EU's interest to recognize East Asia's potential as a serious trading partner and further strengthen its external relations through ASEM and other multilateral arrangements.

The relationship between Asia and the EU had grown out of a mutual recognition of economic and political benefits, and it is constructive for both parties to nurture it. While the 1990s had certainly led to a growing awareness of the need to strengthen the ties between Asia and the EU, the Asian financial crisis did slow down the progress of increasing ties between them. Now is the time for both parties to work towards normalizing their relationship and ensuring that the result are mutually beneficial.

Asia–Europe relations in the twenty-first century will not look similar to those that prevailed before the Asian financial crisis. The East Asian experience with that financial crisis and increasing regionalism have the potential to reshape these relations, so that the ASEM process as an official cooperation forum between Asia and Europe – in order to move forward – has to take this into a serious consideration.

Notes

1. The three Communities – the European Coal and Steel Community (ECSC), the European Atomic Energy Community (EURATOM), and the European Economic Community (EEC) – were established based on Treaty of Paris and Treaty of Rome that went into force in 1953 and 1957, respectively. See Nicoll and Salmon (2001); Pelkmans (1997).
2. GATT Article XXIV, Par. 8(a)(i) states '...substantially the same duties and other regulations of commerce are applied by each of the members of the union to the trade of territories not included in the union'.

3. The common market between the EU and EFTA is called the European Economic Area (EEA). The EFTA countries, except Switzerland, ratified the EEA agreement. In this respect, the EFTA lost its relevance in the world trading system considerably.
4. These three groups of countries are provided preferential access to the EU markets based on the Lomé Convention, Euro-med Programme, and GSP scheme, respectively. For a more detailed discussion, see McDonald and Dearden (1994), especially Chapter 1.
5. In 1996 South Korea 'graduated' from the EU's GSP scheme of which it had long been a beneficiary.
6. The fear of 'Fortress Europe', which implied increasing trade and investment barriers by way of the Single European Market programme during the 1980s, is now being raised in a new context: human rights activists are fearing that, as a result of the newest enlargement to the East, the EU may become non-accessible for asylum-seekers or other potential immigrants.
7. It is often argued that EU's new approach towards Asia came too late and especially much later than that of the US mainly because the EU was too preoccupied with its internal priority issues. For example, such happenings as the German unification in late 1980s, the European Monetary System crisis in 1992 and 1993, the scheduled Northern and Eastern Enlargement, the revealed inefficacy of EU involvement in Yugoslavia conflicts tested the capacity of the EU and individual member states to the their maximum, so that little time was left to pay attention to other issues.
8. The follow-up NAS concept paper of the EU, which was adopted in 2001, includes Australasia (Australia and New Zealand) as an additional sub-region of East Asia. See European Commission (2001b).
9. The EU recently uses the term 'Australasia' to group Australia and New Zealand as part of Asia, and devotes a special chapter in its upgraded New Asia Strategy (NAS) of 2001.
10. The European Commission (2000) claims the increasing number of regionalist initiatives in East Asia as one of main achievements of ASEM.

References

Avila, J.L.V., 'Regional Cooperation in APEC and ASEM: An Institutional Perspective', a paper presented at the Conference of APEC Study Centre Consortium on *Towards APEC's Second Decade: Challenges, Opportunities and Priorities* in Auckland, New Zealand (1999).

Bergsten, F., *Open Regionalism*, IIE Working Paper 97-03 (Washington: Institute of International Economics, 1997).

European Commission, 'Relations Between the European Community and the Republic of Korea', Communication from the Commission to the Council, un-published document, Brussels (1993).

European Commission, 'Towards a New Asia Strategy', Communication from the Commission to the Council, COM (94) 314 final, Brussels (1994).

European Commission, 'A Long-term Policy for China–Europe Relations', Communication from the Commission, COM (95) 279 final, Brussels (1995a).

European Commission, 'Europe and Japan: The Next Steps', Communication from the Commission to the Council, COM (95) 73 final, Brussels (1995b).

European Commission, 'Creating a New Dynamic in EU–ASEAN Relations', Communication from the Commission to the Council, the European Parliament and the Economic and Social Committee, Final Text, Brussels (1996a).

European Commission, 'Free Trade Areas: An Appraisal', Communication from the Commission to the Council, Brussels (1996b).

European Commission, 'Perspectives and Priorities for the ASEM Process (Asia–Europe Meeting) into the New Decade', Commission Working Document, COM (2000) 241 final, Brussels (2000).

European Commission, 'Vademecum: Modalities for Future ASEM Dialogue Taking the Process Forward', Brussels (18 July 2001a).

European Commission, 'Europe and Asia: A Strategic Framework for Enhanced Partnerships', Communication from the Commission, COM (2001) 469 final, Brussels (September 2001b).

Kim, H.C., 'Introduction and Overview', in *European Integration and the Asia-Pacific Region* (Seoul: KIEP, 2003).

Lim, P., 'Whither Asia–Europe Meeting (ASEM)?', mimeo (2002).

McDonald, F., and Dearden, S., *European Economic Integration*, 2nd edn (London: Longman, 1994).

Nicoll, W., and Salmon, T.C., *Understanding the European Union* (London: Longman, 2001).

Park, S.H., 'Perspective of Long-term Economic Relations between Asia and Europe and the Strategy of Korea', *Korea Journal of EU Studies*, 4(1) (1999), 42–71 [in Korean].

Park, S.H., 'East Asian Economic Integration and Regionalism: Finding a Balance between Regionalism and Multilateralism', *Korea Review of International Studies*, 4(1) (2001), 125–45.

Park, S.H., 'East Asian Economic Integration and the Strategy of the EU', *Asia-Pacific Journal of EU Studies*, 1(1) (2003), 1–23.

Park, S.H, 'Economic Integration and Regionalism in East Asia after the Financial Crisis', a paper presented at an international conference, hosted by the Macau Institute of European Studies, 7–8 April 2004.

Pelkmans, J., *European Integration: Methods and Economic Analysis* (Amsterdam: Netherlands Open University, 1997).

Pelkmans, J., and Shinkai, H. (eds), *ASEM: How Promising a Partnership?* (Brussels: The European Institute for Asian Studies, 1997).

Scollay, Robert, 'New Regional Trading Arrangements in the Asia-Pacific Region', a paper presented at the APEC Study Center Consortium Conference on 'APEC: Heading Towards New Century and Bright Future' in Tianjin, China, 18–20 May 2001.

UNCTAD, *The Financial Crisis in Asia and Foreign Direct Investment: An Assessment*, UNCTAD/ITE/IIT/8, GE.98-51617 (Geneva: UNCTAD, 1998).

World Bank, *The East Asian Miracle: Economic Growth and Public Policy* (Oxford: Oxford University Press, 1993).

5
EU–ASEAN Relations and Policy-Learning

Yeo Lay Hwee

Relations between the Association of South-East Asian Nations (ASEAN) and the European Union (EU, formerly the European Economic Community (EEC)), which date back to 1972, constitute one of the oldest group-to-group relationships. For the ASEAN countries, the primary rationale for the relationship was economic – greater market access for ASEAN's exports and a price stabilization scheme for ASEAN's primary commodities. However, for the EEC, while the relationship was economic in form – ASEAN as an important source for raw materials – there was also a hint of political intent – ASEAN as a non-communist area of peace and economic cooperation.

After three decades of relationship, how have the two regional actors adapted their behaviour to meet the changes and expectations of each other? What were the quality and levels of this group-to-group relationship? Were there enough dialogue and information and communication flows to shape the interactions between EU and ASEAN and facilitate policy-learning? This chapter will examine the development of the EU–ASEAN relationship and discuss the implications, if any, this relationship has on the policy choices and policy development of the member states of ASEAN and the EU.

ASEAN–EU relations in a nutshell

ASEAN was founded in 1967 by Indonesia, Malaysia, Philippines, Singapore and Thailand, during a period of considerable uncertainty in Southeast Asia. At the time of its formation, ASEAN was scoffed at by many political observers, both in the region and also beyond. In a region marred by war and intra-regional conflicts, it was difficult to perceive that the leaders of these independent, sovereign states with different historical experiences would have the political will to overcome their suspicions and latent hostilities.

In the initial years, ASEAN's growth as a regional organization proceeded at a slow pace. There were very limited real integrative efforts, since sovereignty was jealously guarded. In any case, ASEAN was never intended as an instrument of integration with supranational authority. ASEAN's *raison d'être* was, and is, to turn a region in turmoil and instability into a region of peace and tranquility. It was to be an instrument for managing and containing intra-regional conflicts, and in so doing maintain and strengthen national sovereignty.

From its onset ASEAN has been an outward-oriented organization. Most of ASEAN's success really came by way of a common stance vis-à-vis third parties. This was reflected, for instance, in the role it played in the Cambodian issue in the 1980s. It has also sought to establish friendly ties with key players in the region and the world in order to secure its own interests. One channel that ASEAN used to articulate its interest was through the dialogue sessions that it established throughout the years with the major powers and other key countries in the region. Its dialogue partners include the EU, the United States, Canada, Australia, New Zealand, Japan, China, South Korea and, most recently, Russia and India. In many ways, it was such interactions with the others that helped ASEAN define its identity.

The EEC was ASEAN's first dialogue partner. Informal dialogue between ASEAN and the EEC first took place in 1972 between ASEAN ministers and the Vice-President and Commissioner of the European Commission. Initially, the dialogue was aimed exclusively to achieve greater market access for ASEAN's exports and a price stabilization scheme for ASEAN's primary commodities.

After a few annual informal meetings, it was decided in 1975 that an ASEAN–EC Joint Study Group be set up not only to look into trade matters but also to evaluate other possible areas of cooperation, such as joint ventures in the exploration of ASEAN resources, the possibility of encouraging some degree of EC participation in ASEAN manufacturing activities and of mobilizing capital for financing ASEAN projects (Luhulima, 1993).

ASEAN–EC relations were given a boost and greater political significance with the inaugural ASEAN–EC Ministerial Meeting (AEMM) in 1978. Under the direction of the AEMM, the ASEAN–EU Cooperation Agreement was formulated and signed during the second ASEAN–EC Ministerial Meeting held in Kuala Lumpur in March 1980. This Agreement was to mark the beginning of a new stage of cooperation. The main emphasis of the Agreement was on economic cooperation and development. The Agreement, a milestone in ASEAN–EC relations, extended the Most Favoured Nation (MFN) treatment to the contracting parties. More importantly, it opened up an exclusive channel for the exchange of information and requests that paved the way for EC assistance in several development projects. It opened up a second track of cooperation which specifically covered the EC and the signatories of the Cooperation Agreement.

However, despite all these positive developments in general, until the 1980s ASEAN remained at the bottom of the EC's hierarchy of relations, below even that of the African, Caribbean and Pacific (ACP) and Latin American countries. The low priority accorded was reflected both in the fact that the ACP countries received more favourable trade benefits covered by the Lomé Convention and in the irregular attendance at the AEMMs by the EC ministers. The ASEAN–EC relationship was seen very much as a donor–recipient relationship. It was an unequal relationship in which the ASEAN countries were inevitably in a weaker bargaining position (Rueland, 1996, pp. 16–17).

In contrast to this unequal economic relationship, political cooperation between ASEAN and the European Community in the 1980s was markedly more successful. Specifically, Vietnam's invasion of Cambodia (then Kampuchea) in December 1978, and the Soviet Union's invasion of Afghanistan in 1979 provided the impetus for the two regions to work closely to coordinate their positions and support each other's positions on the Cambodian and the Afghanistan issues in international fora such as the United Nations. Indeed, during the 1980 AEMM, an unprecedented joint statement was issued deploring the armed interventions of Cambodia and Afghanistan. An analysis of the votes for the UN General Assembly Resolution from 1979 to 1984 showed that ASEAN and EC did indeed vote as a bloc in support of calls for Soviet withdrawal from Afghanistan and Vietnamese withdrawal from Cambodia (Robles, 1998, p. 16). These two issues also remained dominant subjects of political discussion at successive AEMMs until their resolution in 1991.

Political relations, however, took a turn for the worse in the early 1990s because of the East Timor incident in 1991 and of differences over how to treat Burma in the midst of the Burmese ruling junta's violent suppressions of pro-democracy movements. At the same time the triumphant mood in the West following the collapse of the Berlin Wall, the break-up of the Soviet Union and the wave of democratization movements in the former communist countries of Central and Eastern Europe led western countries to start pushing other developing countries towards a greater degree of democratization. Free from the Cold War necessities of courting authoritarian but pro-western countries, Europeans introduced a policy of conditionality linking trade and aid to issues on human rights, democratization and environmental protection. The politicization of aid and economic cooperation policy heightened tension with the ASEAN nations. This new moralism of the West was criticized as 'neo-colonialism' by leaders such as Prime Minister Dr Mahathir Mohammad of Malaysia.

The past decade of continued economic growth in the ASEAN countries and the general dynamism and growing economic prowess of the East Asian region in which ASEAN is located, plus ASEAN's success as a diplomatic community, had made the latter more confident and assertive. A new sense of pride drawn from the decade of economic achievements translated to the ability to stand up to challenge the decisions or actions by the western countries. The ninth and tenth AEMMs held in 1991 and 1992 respectively were thus marked by heated exchanges over East Timor and the new conditionality of EC aid and cooperation policy.

The confidence and dynamism of ASEAN was also reflected in other, more proactive and positive measures it took in response to the new challenges in its environment. For instance, in the face of an uncertain politico-strategic situation with the rise of China, the wavering commitments of the United States to the security of the region, ASEAN first sought to bring all its dialogue relationships under the ambit of what was to be called the Post-Ministerial Conference which is held usually immediately after the annual ASEAN Foreign Ministers Meetings. It then went one step further to develop an ambitious multilateral framework for security and political dialogue – the ASEAN Regional Forum (ARF). The creation of ARF was especially significant as it reflected the willingness of ASEAN to assume new functions and responsibilities in order to shape its strategic environment.

On the economic front, faced with intensified economic competition, in the 1992 Summit in Singapore ASEAN announced the establishment of an ASEAN Free Trade Area (AFTA) by the year 2005. This deadline was subsequently brought forward to the year 2000 for certain products and by 2003, 95 per cent of manufactured goods and services were to be included in AFTA. Work also commenced on drawing up an ASEAN Investment Area (AIA) to attract more direct investments into the region.

On a bilateral basis, when ASEAN examined the past 20 years' record of its relations with the EU, ASEAN could not help but note that while promotion of economic cooperation has translated into increases in the absolute values of trade and investments, it has not altered the relative importance of each region to the other. The challenge then was to imagine new channels and identify new areas for cooperation. In the midst of EU reassessment of its own strategy towards Asia, ASEAN was quick to cash in on this and promote itself as the gateway to the wider Asia-Pacific region, and as an interlocutor for the wider dialogue between Asians and Europeans. ASEAN also recognized that future efforts to create a new dynamic would have to involve European production in Southeast Asia. Hence, the ASEAN states were relentless in driving home the message that peace and stability in the region and the launch of AFTA and AIA would provide a secure and profitable environment for Europe's direct investments.

On the background of the economic success and growing self-confidence of the ASEAN states, EU was sold on the idea of ASEAN being the linchpin of its wider Asia–Europe relations. ASEAN's attraction as a rapidly growing market of 500 million people (in anticipation of an ASEAN-10) was also in the minds of key European decision-makers when a consensus decision was taken by the EU (and, in particular, by the four big powers – United Kingdom, Germany, France and Italy) to put aside sensitive political issues and return to a pragmatic course of focusing on economics. This, of course, must be seen together in the context of EU's general shift in policy towards Asia as reflected in the July 1994 EC Communication 'Towards a New Asia Strategy' (NAS).

The pragmatic course taken was reflected in the 11th AEMM held in Karlsruhe in September 1994 which showed that ASEAN has gained the upper hand in determining the topics, style and procedure of the meeting (Rueland, 1996, p. 31). The meeting was congenial, unlike the past few meetings. East Timor was not raised and human rights issues were only mentioned briefly. Another concrete example of this pragmatic approach was the sidestepping of the issue of a new agreement that was blocked by Portugal. The ministers resolved to continue and expand their dialogue through other existing channels, and also commissioned an ASEAN–EU Eminent Persons Group to develop a comprehensive approach of ASEAN–EU relations towards the year 2000 and beyond. The European Commission's Communication 'Towards a New Asia Strategy' also pinpointed ASEAN–EU relations as the cornerstone of the new partnership that Europe would seek in Asia.

However, recommendations in both the 1996 report by the EEP on 'A Strategy for a New Partnership' and also the Communication from the Commission to the Council on 'Creating a New Dynamic in EU–ASEAN Relations' on revitalizing the ASEAN–EU ties had no chance of being translated into concrete measures. A series of events – notably the

Asian financial crisis, the launch of the Asia–Europe Meeting (ASEM), and the enlargement of ASEAN to include Cambodia, Laos and Myanmar – changed the whole dynamics and further impacted on the state of ASEAN–EU relations.

The changing dynamics and policy-learning in EU–ASEAN relations

In more than thirty years of regular contacts between the EU and ASEAN, it is interesting to see if and what, why and how the two regions have learnt from each other. With the EU as the forerunner in regional integration, the first thing one might be tempted to ask is whether ASEAN can 'learn' anything from the EU? However, one could also perhaps expand the question and ask if the two regional actors have adapted their behaviour to meet the changes and expectations of each other? What were the quality and levels of this group-to-group relationship? Were there enough dialogue and information and communication flows to shape the interactions between EU and ASEAN and facilitate policy-learning? Were there policy changes and adjustments made as a result of the learning process? Did the changes occur mainly at technical or conceptual level? Before going into an analysis of policy-learning in EU–ASEAN relations, a brief definition and discussion about what is meant by policy-learning is necessary.

Definition of policy-learning

Policy-learning covers a broad terrain with various meanings attached to it. According to Paul A. Sabatier (1993, p. 19), policy-learning is 'a relatively enduring alteration of thought or behavioral intentions that are concerned with the attainment (or revision) of the precepts of a policy belief system'. He divided policy-learning into the following three types:

- Technical learning about instruments: how the various policy instruments may be improved to achieve set goals;
- Conceptual learning: when the problem definition (the outlook on a problematique) changes, accompanied by development of new concepts and vocabulary; and
- Social learning: when there is a widely shared change in values, and ideas about a topic and about appropriate roles of policy actors, including the rules for interaction.

Peter Hall (Hall, 1990, p. 73) believed that policy-learning is informed by an understanding of policy failure providing an impetus to place new ideas on the policy and political agendas. Learning occurs when policy makers adjust their cognitive understanding of policy development and modify policy in the light of knowledge gained from past policy experience.

According to Hall (1993, p. 284), there are three orders of policy-learning. 'First Order' learning involves 'satisficing' and making minor adjustments in the precise settings of policy instruments – this is very much similar to the technical learning as propounded by Paul Sabatier. 'Second Order' learning is characterized by re-tooling, limited experimentation and the introduction of new policy techniques. Changes at these two levels are characteristic of normal politics. 'Third Order' change involves a radical shift in 'the hierarchy of goals and sets of instruments employed to guide policy'. This 'Third Order' learning is a mix of what Sabatier would call conceptual and social learning. It involves significant departures in policy on the basis of a completely different conceptualization of policy problems.

Another much simpler and much used definition given by David Dolowitz and David Marsh (1996) refers policy-learning to 'a process of policy transfer, emulation and lesson-drawing in which knowledge about policies, administrative arrangements, institutions in one time and/or place is used in the development of policies, administrative arrangements and institutions in another time and/or place.'

Policy-learning between states or governments is not unusual. In different periods of time, governments have looked at each other's experiences in areas where common problems were identified or innovations turned out to be successful. With increasing interdependence and improvements in communications, policy-learning – whether it is lesson-drawing or emulation or transfer – is becoming more common. However, our knowledge on what learning is actually concerned with and how actors engage in a learning process is still quite limited as there is not much literature yet on these. While it is often assumed that policy-learning is undertaken to 'improve policy', this may not be necessarily true as it could be 'enforced' or perhaps undertaken for other political objectives.

When studying policy-learning, therefore, distinctions should be drawn between technical learning (about instruments); conceptual learning (about goals and strategies) and social learning (about societal values, responsibilities, appropriate ways of interacting and policy approaches).

While cross-border learning between governments/states are happening with increasing frequency, much less has been discussed or studied at the inter-regional level. In considering EU–ASEAN relations, the focus here is to look at how their interactions may result in policy-learning on regional integration. Does ASEAN as a regional entity look consciously at the EU regional model and policies adopted by the EU in promoting European integration to draw some lessons to be used for their own policy designs? Has the long interaction between ASEAN and EU result in evolution of common norms, common policies governing the relations between the two regional entities?

The potential for policy-learning

In the years of interaction, particularly through development assistance in areas such as environment, energy, trade facilitation, individual ASEAN states receiving aid in specific sectors such as forestry, energy might make some policy adjustments with increased knowledge and capacity building made possible by the EU partners. Policy-learning here is therefore only in the First Order or confined to technical learning. One would assume that armed with better knowledge and capacity, policy makers would be privy to a wider set of policy instruments, leading to different policy choices.

However, in terms of broader inter-regional interactions, whether policy-learning has occurred at a regional level by the two regional entities representing the region is really up for debate. Has ASEAN learned from the EU experience of regional integration, and is there anything that the EU has learned from the so-called 'ASEAN Way' of regional cooperation? These are highly contentious and certainly worth debating.

Regional integration and community-building

The EU is considered to be the forerunner of regional integration, beginning with the 1952 European Coal and Steel Community (ECSC) which became the European Economic Community (EEC) with the signing of the Treaty of Rome in 1958. Therefore, in a policy-learning context, one is tempted to think that, as a late-comer, ASEAN would be the one watching and learning from the EU experience so as to avoid costly mistakes and leverage on workable and successful experiments by the EU. Of course, this is far from reality. From the very beginning the *raison d'être* for forming ASEAN was very different from the EU. ASEAN was not about regional integration but arose out of the need to contain regional tensions in order to focus on domestic development as a counterweight to internal communist insurgencies and communal problems.

This *raison d'être* of ASEAN was explicitly stated in its founding declaration, which expressed the determination of its member states 'to ensure their stability and security from external interference ... in order to preserve their national identities' (the ASEAN Declaration). This explains why from the very beginning ASEAN has taken the form of 'state-to-state cooperation where diplomacy is the main instrument' (Wanandi, 2001, p. 25). Regional economic integration was never mentioned as an ASEAN objective in the founding declaration.

ASEAN's growth as a regional organization proceeded at a very slow pace and there were very few real integrative efforts in the first two decades. Economic cooperation among the ASEAN states was also minimal. However, as the global and regional picture began to change with the relentless forces of globalization, the collapse of communism, and the opening of China's market, ASEAN also has to re-orientate its focus. The socioeconomic landscape of ASEAN has changed considerably by the late 1980s. Societies and economies have been opening up. In the face of these political changes, economic challenges and growing interdependence, ASEAN began to look more actively into closer economic cooperation and the ASEAN Free Trade Agreement (AFTA) was signed in 1992. To further cement regional economic cooperation to meet the challenges from other regions and emerging economies, the idea of creating an ASEAN Investment Area (AIA) was also adopted. AFTA and AIA marked a perceptible shift in policy beliefs from a staunchly nationalistic approach to economic development to a wider approach taking into account regional cooperation leading to some sort of integration.

For a long time ASEAN has resisted any attempts to compare itself with the EU, and has dismissed the EU integration model as not relevant for ASEAN. ASEAN is a loosely-knit organization with a penchant for informality, flexibility and pragmatism. It has pride itself for developing a *modus operandi*, the 'ASEAN Way'. The much-touted 'ASEAN Way' is one that entails behavioural norms that prescribe 'respect for sovereignty and non-interference in internal affairs, peaceful resolution of conflicts, and non-use of force' (Nischalke, 2000, p. 90); as well as procedural norms that privilege informalism and non-confrontational behaviour as encapsulated in the concepts of *musyawarah* (consultation) and *mufakat* (consensus) (Nischalke, 2002, p. 93).

However, the inability of ASEAN to use its 'ASEAN Way' to address and deal with the fallout from the Asian financial crisis and other regional problems such as the haze that enveloped the region in 1997 has led to a serious re-think of the direction and the *modus operandi* of the organization. Core policy beliefs with regards to the norms and procedures of regional cooperation are now being challenged. The risks of becoming irrelevant forced ASEAN to do some serious soul-searching and face up to the need to change its way of doing things. There was, hence, a surge in talks within the policy community and particularly those in the epistemic community about institutionalization and developing new regional mechanisms to face up to the new realities. Suddenly the EU experience becomes an area of interest at least in the immediate aftermath of the Asian financial crisis.

While the long-standing EU–ASEAN relations did not contribute directly to a policy shift in approaches to regional cooperation by the ASEAN countries, EU avails itself if not as a model, at least as a subject for study and for lessons-drawing. It was interesting therefore to see that since the crisis, the discourse coming from ASEAN has been moving towards the need to build institutions and there are more serious attempts and studies to understand how the EU works. Of course, no one made the big leap in embracing the EU model entirely, but there are calls to adapt some of the EU norms and institutions to the ASEAN realities. One example is the call to strengthen the ASEAN Secretariat. While not calling for the ASEAN Secretariat to have supranational authority akin to that of the European Commission, there is a push for 'devolving sufficient authority to regional mechanisms and institutions to enable them to review and coordinate between the different countries' (Tay and Estanislao, 2001, p. 19).

More concretely, the EU has offered to help to strengthen the institutional capacity of the ASEAN Secretariat through its ASEAN Programme for Regional Integration Support (APRIS). In its Regional Indicative Programme for ASEAN, the Commission explained that APRIS was conceived after the Asian financial crisis, which underscored the need for closer economic integration between ASEAN countries.

> APRIS is a facility through which the ASEAN Secretariat obtains flexible and responsive technical assistance from the EU, where know-how and experience is shared on aspects of regional cooperation relevant to ASEAN's integration, with the primary focus on strategic planning. Support for the ASEAN Secretariat through APRIS takes the form of technical assistance, for the delivery of policy papers, work programmes and other studies, institutional capacity building and training.[1]

One can easily dispute the suggestion that the policy shifts within ASEAN are as a result of the EU. Indeed, it is not a direct result of the

EU–ASEAN interactions, but rather because of a combination of factors as set forth earlier – the rise of China, the Asian financial crisis, and so on. But it cannot be denied that the interactions with EU and the assistance rendered have influenced the discourse. More important is the role played by the epistemic communities in the two regions, or perhaps more accurately the experts and scholars involved in Track II diplomacy, particularly those within the ASEAN–ISIS network of think-tanks.

The role of the epistemic community or policy network or community, particularly transnational networks, in the diffusion and dissemination of ideas and policy paradigms is important in any discussions about policy-learning. The section below will examine the role of ASEAN–ISIS in shifting the change in discourse on regional cooperation and discuss its ability or inability to engender real policy-learning among the state policy actors.

The role of ASEAN–ISIS in policy-learning

How can researchers in an epistemic community or policy networks influence policy change? In Southeast Asia, unofficial diplomacy has made significant contributions in the area of regional cooperation. According to Herman Kraft in his paper on 'Unofficial Diplomacy in Southeast Asia: The Role of ASEAN-ISIS', Track II activities have grown in tandem with Track I channels and have become directly involved in policy advocacy and policy formulation by providing policy frameworks for officials too busy to put together proposals (Kraft, 2000, p. 4).

The ASEAN-Institutes of Strategic and International Studies (ASEAN-ISIS) is a network of think-tanks in ASEAN involved in policy research. Founded in 1984, it has been credited for policy recommendations leading to the establishment of the ASEAN Regional Forum in 1994 and, more recently, the idea of an ASEAN Economic Community and ASEAN Security Community.

The ASEAN-ISIS comes close to being a policy network in which communities with a limited number of people, with frequent contact, persistent membership and consensus on basic values, work together to advance ASEAN's development. Whether the ASEAN-ISIS representatives fit the bill of an epistemic community is open for debate. However, what is clear is that ASEAN-ISIS works in conjunction with ASEAN and, since 1993, its representatives have consulted annually with the senior officials of ASEAN member states. It has submitted policy recommendations in the form of memoranda to the ASEAN governments on various issues (Kraft, 2000, p. 5). The latest was the ASEAN-ISIS memo on the ASEAN Charter to the Eminent Persons Group (EPG) for the ASEAN Charter.

In the area of regional integration and community building, ASEAN-ISIS has been actively involved in dialogue with European partners and has been in the forefront of pushing for greater regional integration after the Asian financial crisis. The annual ASEAN-ISIS–EU think-tanks dialogue, which began in 1999, was one such channel. They are in some sense a central force in promoting collective policy-learning. Policy ideas are spread and some start to take root. Though the network has recently also come under critical scrutiny for being too close to governments and too elitist, closeness to government is a comparative advantage because it gives ASEAN-ISIS some influence on government policy. Of course, it can also become a disadvantage as it results in self-censorship and may limit the ability of ASEAN-ISIS to provide critical thinking when it is most needed.

Multilateralism and cooperative security dialogue

Evolving clearly from the concept of a European community as embodied in the EU, multilateralism in security has become clearly part of the European identity. This is in contrast to ASEAN where security dialogue until the early 1990s was still very much in the bilateral mode, with US as the main security provider in a sort of hub and spokes framework. The launch of the ASEAN Regional Forum (ARF) in 1994 was a major shift towards a more multilateral approach towards comprehensive and cooperative security.

The ARF emerged from ASEAN in the 1990s. The end of the Cold War, the rise of China and a proliferation of security matters of a non-military nature left the Asia-Pacific searching for a new organizing principle for security. Again the search for a new framework was informed by the discourse within ASEAN-ISIS, which in turn was coloured by the interactions and partnerships of ASEAN-ISIS with its counterparts in Australia, Canada, Japan, US and the European Community.

> Based on the ASEAN-ISIS experience, the Council for Security Cooperation in the Asia-Pacific (CSCAP) was formed in June 1993. The underlying goal enunciated by the ASEAN-ISIS founders of CSCAP was to create an alternative conception of security in the Asia-Pacific based on cooperation rather than military balances. (Simon, 2002, pp. 12–13)

Again it is not possible to prove a direct policy linkage between the EU and ASEAN with regards to the change in approach adopted towards security dialogue. But some shades of similarities that ARF shared with the Conference on Security and Cooperation in Europe (CSCE) forced one to consider whether or not Europe's head-start in developing new frameworks and institutions for security dialogue made an inevitable mark on the new evolving framework in Asia pioneered by ASEAN. The role of Track II institutions and their impact on the learning curve and the discourse at the official track level is again something to be considered.

The issue of applicability of the European model to the Asia-Pacific will always be a point of contention within ASEAN and the ARF. But the founding principles of ARF are in fact close to the CSCE philosophy that Joachim Kruse argued for in his monograph 'The OSCE and Cooperative Security in Europe: Lessons for Asia', so that the ARF might be seen as an attempt to test how applicable is the CSCE philosophy in the Asia-Pacific (Krause, 2003, p. 127).

Inter-regionalism as a feature of international relations

The EU (and its predecessor EC) has been in the forefront of pushing for inter-regional or group-to-group dialogue. Such dialogues entered a remarkable period of growth in the early 1980s. These inter-regional or group-to-group dialogues are seen as an additional element or level to manage global interdependence. They fill the gaps between bilateralism and universalism. Also, it brings about more 'consistency' in Europe's international profile at a time when the EC/EU has not really developed a Common Foreign and Security Policy (CFSP). Besides the EU–ASEAN other examples of such dialogue are those with the ACP Group, Andean Pact, Gulf Cooperation Council (GCC), Arab League and more recently the Euro-Mediterranean partnership, and EU-Mercosur partnership.

ASEAN in the 1990s also developed a penchant for such inter-regional dialogue, and it has been the driving force behind several inter-regional or group-to-group initiatives such as the Asia–Europe Meeting (ASEM) process, the Forum for East Asia and Latin America Cooperation (FEALAC), and the Asia–Middle East (AMED) dialogue.

However, it could suggest that the EU's and ASEAN's 'love' of inter-regional dialogues are driven by different factors. The EU's inter-regionalism is driven mainly by an institutionalist consideration that underscores the importance of institutional cooperation as a way to manage complex interdependence, and perhaps also an element of social constructivism that stresses the formation of regional perceptions and identities triggered by inter-regional interactions. In addition, the EU's pursuit of inter-regionalism, as argued by Vinod Aggarwal and Edward Fogarty, is driven by what they see as a 'desire to promote its political-institutional influence around the world' (Aggarwal and Fogarty, 2003, p. 387).

On the other hand, realism and neo-realism still very much colour the international relations approach of ASEAN member states. Hence the focus of inter-regional dialogues is perhaps more on the balancing aspect, though it has also been argued that in the case of the Asia–Europe Meeting (ASEM), an element of constructivism may have also been envisaged.

What ASEAN has learned from the EU in this aspect is taking the form and adapting it in some way to suit its own interests. Inter-regional dialogues promoted by ASEAN tend to be informal, less institutionalized and more flexible. The configuration of Asia differs in the different inter-regional dialogues jump-started by ASEAN, making ASEAN the only constant 'regional' player in these dialogues.

The ASEAN charter – strengthening ASEAN and giving ASEAN a legal personality

On 12 December 2005, during the eleventh ASEAN Summit in Kuala Lumpur ASEAN leaders decided that it is time for the Association to have a formal charter as the basis for cooperation. The decision was a recognition of the need to promote necessary changes in order to adapt to the changing environment and its challenges. The leaders understand the need for ASEAN to deepen its integration, strengthen its institutions and processes to cope with the various transnational challenges. More specifically, as pointed out by the former ASEAN Secretary-General, Rodolfo Severino, the reason for having a charter is as follows:

> A charter would help establish the association as a juridical personality and a legal entity. It would make clear the association's objectives. The charter would enshrine the values and principles to which the association's members adhere and which, in a real sense, define its very nature. The charter would envision the arrangements for the further integration of the regional economy and define the institutions, mechanisms and processes for dealing with transnational problems. It would establish the organs of the association and delineate their respective functions, responsibilities, rights and limitation, the relationships among the organs, and their decision-making processes. Among these organs would be an objective and credible dispute-settlement mechanism. The charter would mark out the relationship between the association and the member-states. It would specify the

ways for the charter to take effect and when. It would lay down the rules for amendments to be made.²

An Eminent Persons Group (EPG) for the ASEAN Charter was convened in 2006. The EPG was tasked to study ASEAN and made 'bold and visionary' recommendations on what should go into the Charter. The EPG met a number of times in 2006 and carried out consultations with leaders, officials, parliamentarians, academics and civil society to get ideas for the EPG report.

Most significantly, the EPG members also made a visit to the European Union to study the EU's integration experience and problems and also dialogue with parliamentarians and officials from the EU to understand how the EU works through its various institutions and procedures. The visit afforded the EPG members a better understanding of the issues that need to be contemplated as ASEAN deepens to become a rule-based organization.

The decision to have a Charter to take ASEAN towards a more structured intergovernmental organization in the context of legally binding rules and agreements was remarkable considering the fact that for more than 30 years, ASEAN has resisted formal institutionalization with an emphasis on binding rules. Instead it has clung on to the so-called 'ASEAN Way', which is informal, with its emphasis on consultation, consensus-building and non-binding agreements relying on voluntary implementation. Once the decision was taken to transform ASEAN into a more rules-based organization, it is perhaps not surprising that officials should look to the EU for 'inspiration' and some of the changes recommended reflected learning and adaptation from the EU integration experience.

ASEAN's institutions and decision-making processes will remain decidedly intergovernmental and hence although the ASEAN Secretariat will be strengthened and the power and role of the ASEAN Secretary-General will also be enhanced, there is no decision at this juncture to create any supranational authority. However, the reality of interdependence and the need to have a much more coordinated regional approach and policies to confront the various challenges have been recognized by the leaders. Hence, for the first time, ASEAN has moved away from the jealously guarded principle of non-intervention. The EPG has recommended that ASEAN 'calibrate the traditionally policy of non-intervention in areas where the common interest dictates closer cooperation'. The unanimous decision-making process is also tweaked to allow more flexibility of applying the 'ASEAN minus X and ASEAN 2 plus X' formula on certain issues.

Other organizational changes proposed also appeared to bear some broad similarities to the EU. For example, the ASEAN Summit will now be replaced by the ASEAN Council (the supreme policy-making organ of ASEAN comprising the leaders of the ASEAN members). The various ASEAN Ministerial Meetings will be consolidated and grouped into Councils of the ASEAN Community – comprising the Council of ASEAN Economic Community, Council of ASEAN Security Community and Council of ASEAN Socio-cultural Community.

Because it has remained essentially intergovernmental, the ASEAN Secretary-General and Secretariat will not be in the same league as the European Commission. But the Secretary-General of ASEAN will have his/her role and power enhanced – in addition to discharging all the functions and responsibilities entrusted by the ASEAN Council and the Councils of the ASEAN Community, he/she can now initiate plans and programmes of activities for ASEAN regional cooperation, harmonize, facilitate and monitor progress in the implementation of all approved ASEAN activities and submit reports on non-compliance, and represent ASEAN as an observer in other international, regional and sub-regional forums.

Another important adaptation is the recommendation to have Permanent Representatives accredited to ASEAN. The Permanent Representatives from the member states, appointed by their respective governments with the rank of Ambassadors will attend meetings at the ASEAN Committees.

Again, as in the other examples, while the impetus for drafting an ASEAN Charter to strengthen ASEAN and confer ASEAN with a legal personality is a result of many factors not related to the EU, the EU as a forerunner in regional integration, and a highly successful regional organization avails itself as a subject for study and lessons-drawing.

All the above examples from regional integration to inter-regionalism to multilateralism are not perfect examples of deep policy-learning and hence illustrate the limits and constraints to policy-learning in the context of ASEAN–EU relations.

The limits and constraints to policy-learning

While crisis can act as an impetus for policy change, this alone is not sufficient. The interpretation and analysis of the causes of the crisis must be exploited skillfully by those policy actors serious about genuine change.

The EU may be a willing master in imparting its lessons on regional integration, but ASEAN is not entirely ready or prepared as a student. The diversities within ASEAN meant that while some have a greater capacity for learning, others may adopt lessons only for symbolic purposes or as a strategic device to secure political support rather than as a result of improved understanding. The lack of discussions and deliberations in the policy-making process in some of the less democratic ASEAN countries has also constrained the ability to produce adequate knowledge about the desired changes.

There is certainly some emulation which involves the borrowing of ideas and adapting policy approaches, tools or structures to local conditions (Stone, 2000, p. 6). However, the level of actual policy-learning in the area of regional integration has remained stuck at best on what Hall sees as first order learning. There is no convergence on values with the EU on things such as pooled sovereignty and supranational authority. ASEAN is not on a par with the EU on its goals of regional integration. ASEAN's interest is on tightening its economic cooperation to allow it to compete more effectively as a region vis-à-vis other economies such as China and India. Hence, the focus of its learning has been on economic policy instruments and techniques.

There are real limits and constraints on policy-learning between EU and ASEAN, particularly in the area of regional integration, because the starting conditions and the end goals of the two regional entities are very different. Though the decision of ASEAN to form an ASEAN Free Trade Area has brought ASEAN closer to the regional integration path as exemplified by the EU in its early stages, there are key differences. The enlargement of ASEAN to include Cambodia, Laos and Myanmar further constrained the ability for ASEAN to deepen the integration process. Hence parallel to the rhetoric and push towards 'community-building' is the parallel 'coalition of the willing' approach to move ASEAN forward.

Interestingly enough, EU's relations with ASEAN – though supposedly a group-to-group dialogue – have also begun to show considerable flexibility from a rigid inter-regional approach. The most significant shift was captured in the Commission's most recent Communication on 'A New Partnership with South East Asia' (2003). Through its long-standing EC–ASEAN cooperation programmes, the Commission has tried to engender certain change and tried to promote cooperation at the regional level. It, however, has admitted that 'some of these programmes in retrospect have been overly ambitious and were not paced with ASEAN's own agenda. The initiatives have sometimes been in advance of the realities of ASEAN integration and lacked sufficient ownership on behalf of

ASEAN.' Region-to-region cooperation has proven to be more complex than bilateral cooperation.

Thus, drawing on lessons learned from earlier programmes, the new approach towards cooperation with ASEAN as spelt out in the Communication on 'A New Partnership with South East Asia' was to first establish 'true mutual interest' at least with one ASEAN counterpart, and then adopting an approach which can be bilateral, regional or a mix of both. This in some way borders on similar 'coalition of the willing' approach to that developing within ASEAN.

This is also interesting in light of the fact that ASEAN has caught on with the promotion of 'inter-regional' dialogue in the broadest sense in its search for new partnerships with other regions such as Latin America and the Middle East. However, after establishing the broad framework, the practical way forward is through a sort of 'coalition of the willing' approach. Therefore in these areas, we see some sort of mutual learning – ASEAN's adaptation of EU's regionalism and inter-regionalism, and EU's policy shifts towards ASEAN in accepting a 'coalition of the willing' approach in advancing the partnership.

Conclusion

Policy shifts or changes are common place in politics and can be brought about by many factors. Here in this chapter we are concerned about policy-learning, an acquisition of new knowledge about problems and solutions, as a source of change. Studies of policy-learning are very much concerned with the effects of organizational learning. Looking at the long-standing inter-regional dialogue between EU and ASEAN, and following the changing discourse on regional integration, particularly the paths taken by ASEAN towards regional cooperation, one is inclined to ask how much influence the EU has on ASEAN in this area.

The initial conclusion drawn from the above discussion on policy-learning and the changing dynamics of ASEAN–EU relations showed that there are real limits and constraints on what ASEAN can learn from the EU in the area of regional integration. ASEAN as a regional organization is still in flux after the Asian financial crisis and the enlargement that took place at the time the crisis was in full swing was a costly mistake for ASEAN. Nonetheless, the past few years has seen an ASEAN that is more open to a dialogue on institutionalization of regional cooperative mechanisms and more willing to draw lessons and study more carefully what the EU model can offer for possible adaptation.

Notes

1. This is found in the Regional Indicative Programme 2005–06 for ASEAN, prepared by DG Relex of the European Commission (available on its website).
2. *Framing the ASEAN Charter: An ISEAS Perspective*, Compiled by Rodolfo C. Severino (Singapore: ISEAS, 2006), pp. 7–8.

References

Aggarwal, Vinod K., and Fogarty, Edward, 'Explaining Trends in EU Interregionalism' (2003). Available at http://ist-socrates.berkeley.edu/~basc/pdf/articles/Explaining%20Trends%20in%20EU%20Interregionalism.pdf.

Communication from the Commission, 'A New Partnership with South East Asia', COM 399/4 (2003). Available at http://europa.eu.int/comm/external_relations/library/publications/09_sea_en. pdf.

Dolowitz, David, and Marsh, David, 'Who Learns from Whom?: A Review of the Policy Transfer Literature', *Political Studies*, 44(2)(1996), 343–57.

Hall, Peter A., 'Policy Paradigms, Experts and the State: The Case of Macroeconomic Policy Making in Britain', in S. Brooks and A-G. Gagnon (eds), *Social Scientists, Policy and the State* (New York: Praeger, 1990), pp. 53–78.

Hall, Peter A., 'Policy Paradigms, Social Learning and the State: The Case of Economic Policy Making in Britain', *Comparative Politics*, 25 (1993), 275–97.

Kan, Hester, 'Opening the Black Box: Developing a Framework to Analyze Processes of cross-national learning'. Available at www.bath.ac.uk/eri/events/EVENT05-ESPANET/ESPAnet%20school/Bath%20YRW%20Kan.pdf.

Kemp, Rene, and Weehuizen, Rifka, 'Policy Learning: What Does it Mean and How Should we Analyze It?'. Available at http://www.step.no/publin/reports/d15policy/learning.pdf.

Kraft, Herman Joseph, 'Unofficial Diplomacy in Southeast Asia: The Role of ASEAN-ISIS', *CANCAPS Papier* No. 22 (published by the Consortium of Asia-Pacific Security, York University, 2000).

Krause, Joachim, 'The OSCE and Cooperative Security in Europe: Lessons for Asia', IDSS Monograph No. 6 (Singapore: Institute for Defence and Strategic Studies, 2003).

Luhulima, C.P.F., 'ASEAN–European Community Relations: Some Dimensions of Inter-regional Cooperation', in Lai To Lee and Arnold Wehmhoerner (eds), *ASEAN and the European Community in the 1990s* (Singapore: Singapore Institute of International Affairs, 1993), pp. 79–101.

Nischalke, Tobias I., 'Insights from ASEAN's Foreign Policy Cooperation: The "ASEAN Way", a Real Spirit or a Phantom?', *Contemporary Southeast Asia*, 22(1) (April 2000), 89–112.

Nischalke, Tobais I., 'Does ASEAN Measure Up? Post-Cold War Diplomacy and the Idea of Regional Community', *The Pacific Review*, 15(1) (2002), 89–117.

Regional Indicative Programme 2005-06-ASEAN. Available at http://europa.eu.int/comm/external_relations/asean/csp/rip_05-06_en.pdf.

Report of the Eminent Persons Group (EPG) on the ASEAN Charter. www.aseansec.org/19247.pdf.

Robles, Alfredo C. Jr., 'ASEAN and the European Union: Conceptions of Interregional Relations and Regionalization in Southeast Asia', paper presented at the Joint Conference of the International Studies Association, Vienna, 16–19 September 1998.

Rueland, Juergen, *The Asia–Europe Meeting (ASEM): Towards a New Euro-Asian Relationship*, Rostocker Informationen zu Politik und Verwaltung Heft 5, Universitat Rostock, Germany (1996).

Sabatier, Paul A., 'Policy Change over a Decade or More', in Paul A. Sabatier and Hank Jenkins-Smith (eds), *Policy Change and Learning: An Advocacy Coalition Approach* (Boulder: Westview Press, 1993), pp. 13–39.

Simon, Sheldon W., 'The ASEAN Regional Forum Views the Council for Security Cooperation in the Asia Pacific: How Track II Assists Track I', *National Bureau of Asian Research Analysis*, 13(4), (July 2002), 5–23.

Stone, Diane, 'Learning Lessons, Policy Transfer and the International Diffusion of Policy Ideas' (2000). Available at www.eldis.org/fulltext/poltrans.pdf.

Tay, Simon S.C., and Estanislao, Jesus P., 'The Relevance of ASEAN: Crisis and Change', in Simon S.C. Tay, Jesus P. Estanislao, and Hadi Soesastro (eds), *Reinventing ASEAN* (Singapore: Institute of Southeast Asian Studies, 2001), pp. 3–24.

Wanandi, Jusuf, 'ASEAN's Past and the Challenges Ahead: Aspects of Politics and Security', in Simon S.C. Tay, Jesus P. Estanislao and Hadi Soesastro (eds), *Reinventing ASEAN* (Singapore: Institute of Southeast Asian Studies, 2001), pp. 25–41.

Website: www.aseansec.org.

Yeo, Lay Hwee, 'The Role of ASEAN in EU–East Asian Relations', *ASIEN*, 72 (July 1999), 19–28.

6
Asian Migrants in Europe: the Need for a Global Perspective

Leo Douw

Over the past ten years Asian migration to the European Union (EU) has gradually gained in importance as an area of policy making.[1] The Amsterdam Treaty (1997, enacted in 1999) and the Tampere Council (1999) are the most important hallmarks of this trend: they reflect the widely felt need among policy makers at the top of the EU, in particular within the European Commission, to liberalize external migration and thus fulfil the EU's fundamental commitment to the principles of liberal democracy (Angenendt and Hernandez, 2004, p. 3; Batistella, 2002). Nevertheless, progress is slow, and EU policies have retained their defensive character: they serve to control and restrain external migration flows rather than facilitate them (Angenendt and Hernandez, 2004, pp. 6–8; Angenendt and Kruse, 2004, pp. 100–1).

This chapter argues that the construction of a global perspective on Asian migrants in Europe is needed to improve the quality of governance on non-European immigration and support the liberalization of international and inter-regional migration policies. For too long, migration has been conceived of as being individually motivated and as a temporary and socially marginal phenomenon. In addition, the separation of migration studies and the study of minority communities should be overcome. This mode of thinking pertains to the Cold War period, when all over the world nation-building was focused on putting the domestic resources of national states to their optimal uses and international flows of capital, commodities and labour were of limited importance. Despite all the problems which beset it, however, migration is usually in the interest of both the sending and the receiving countries, and is also actively promoted or at least permitted at both ends of the migration chain. In this respect it resembles trade and investment: state involvement in facilitating and promoting international flows of goods and capital are considered as normal, so the question is: why is this so problematic in the case of flows of people? The basic answer to this question is that the movement of human beings involves more than just the optimal allocation of labour power in which the receiving countries are interested, and thus requires more regulation than liberal ideals allow for: labour, just like land and money, cannot be commodified as easily as material goods (Polanyi, 1957). Global migration also entails the worldwide redistribution of work and income (Batistella, 2002). Migration between Asian countries and the EU is part of the much broader and irreversible process of urbanization that is going on in Asia, and thus has a compulsive motive behind it: migrants often stay abroad for the rest of their lives and even if they return to their own countries usually do not return to the rural settings from where most of them originated.

Only during the 1990s did researchers and politicians gradually begin to open their minds towards migration as a global phenomenon that was as much part of the international economy as international trade and investment. This was the atmosphere in which the policy intentions of the Amsterdam Treaty and the Tampere Council were formulated. After the terrorist attacks on the World Trade Center on September 11 2001, the need to expand cooperation on migrant policies was felt even more, but, at the same time, the fear of terrorism hardened the previously existing limitations: the EU member states remained anxious to guard their own borders, and the EU focussed exclusively on policing its outer boundaries and control unregulated migration (Angenendt and Kruse, 2004, p. 123). The classic division between international migration as the movement of people across borders and the integration of migrant communities in their host societies became politicized and thereby even more visible. This hinders the solution of the problems entailed by external migration flows, such as human trafficking and smuggling, the implementation of refugee and asylum policies, and the integration of migrant communities with their host societies.

As a start, it is necessary to better know which global forces keep international migration moving. Therefore, below we will sum up those aspects of migration that should become more articulate in the consciousness of European citizens. Thereafter, how the development of migration policies has proceeded thus far and what remains to be done will be examined. It should be noted that most of the examples in this chapter will be taken from migration flows between China and the EU, but those will be supplemented by other flows between Asia and the EU and will be taken to represent more general patterns in the occurrence of those flows.

The role of national states

The main argument for taking a more structural approach to migrant policies on the demand side is the persistent need for migrant workers because the EU member states have been experiencing a decline in their birth rates and a concomitant increased ageing of the population for a long time. The postwar baby-boomers need migrant inflows in order to secure their pensions (Angenendt and Hernandez, 2004, p. 11; Angenendt and Orren, n.d., pp. 24–5). Migrant inflows from Asia are useful also because demand will not be limited to low-skilled labour, but will also include high-skilled labour in the future, and Asian countries, including China, are increasingly able to supply that need. Asian migrants are increasingly diversified, and nowadays include students, academics, businessmen, and diplomats, who all are more flexible from the past in their employment possibilities. Also, second-generation Asian people are bigger physically and much better educated and socialized in Western European societies than their parents could ever be, and thus provide some of the future needs. Demand is also generated by the migrants' economic spheres, especially when they are as self-centred and self-contained as the Chinese ones: they draw in new migrants because they are the cheapest to be had, and because of access to the existing human trafficking and migration networks. Those networks are partly invigorated because they have increasingly come to deal in Asian products, as for example in the case of the Chinese state-owned enterprises, to which northern Chinese migrants often cater for their trade.

Even though for several decades to come demand will probably be concentrated on the European side, in the longer term, competition for migrants may increase between East Asia and Europe because of China's one-child policies, amongst other factors (Skeldon, 2005). Looking at Asian migration more broadly, there are several areas where economic growth happens and on which Asian migration focuses – including the Middle East, Thailand, Taiwan, South Korea and Japan. In the future those countries may develop into being competitors for labour migration even more strongly and quickly than China.

National governments in Europe, of course, have been impeding the development of proactive EU migration policies rather than stimulating them. National governments in Asia, however, are often actively engaged in facilitating international migration: China and the Philippines both have been labour-sending countries since the 1970s, the Philippines most conspicuously so. Both China and the Philippines obviously had an economic interest: remittances are good for the balance of payments, and may to a certain extent be expected to support economic development.

In addition, other motives may also play a role. The Philippines government has been consciously organizing emigration on a vast scale since the mid-1970s (van den Muijzenberg, 2003). Getting rid of surplus labour should be mentioned here, also in the higher-skilled social classes. In the Philippines highly-educated women are often trained for migration; while China usually provides no previous training, its national government feels responsible, and there is an elaborate system of regulations and institutions responsible for labour migration, topped by the Ministry of Labour, and government supervision at both the national and the local level (Xiang, 2003, pp. 32–3).

Direct political influence is more difficult to trace as a background force to migration policies, especially because most Asian migrant communities in Europe are too small to be counted on. In addition, any Chinese government has too much of a troubled past in mobilizing Chinese overseas, particularly in Southeast Asia, for its purposes not to be very cautious in this respect. Nevertheless, one may suppose that migrant flows are being used in the ongoing political games. Deng Xiaoping is rumoured to have said, during quarrels with the Japanese government during the 1980s, that he would release 25,000 migrants if his requests could not be honoured. In the problematic relations between China and Israel deals on weapons are being traded against deals on migrants (Shichor, 1998). Therefore, even 'high politics' cannot be said to be immune from migrant issues, and here, of course, security issues are immediately around the corner.

Even if national governments cooperate over migration, local governments may circumvent their regulations and policies, which fact adds to the problems to be solved. In China, for example, local officialdom may have a strong interest in sending out migrants, not only because it often has to deal with the problems of labour surpluses, which may engender social unrest, but also because it vies for remittances, donations, and investments. It is very questionable whether effective economic development results from migrants' contributions (Scharping, 1999; Pieke et al., 2004, p. 26), but the existence of these motivations make it understandable that efforts to promote and also regularize migration by the Chinese national government are often counteracted and circumvented, if not obstructed by local officialdom (Xiang, 2003, pp. 24, 36; Chin, 2003, p. 57). This must be counted as one reason why it will be difficult for national governments and regional organizations such as the EU and the Association of South-East Asian Nations (ASEAN) to collaborate over migration. Most importantly, however, the compulsion deriving from those situations make it clear that migration is not in any sense a temporary or marginal phenomenon too many people are involved in it or have an interest in it for us to expect that it will subside by itself. Mentalities are also important: success is expected from migrants, for whose expatriation usually huge amounts of money have either been paid by family and friends or borrowed from human traffickers. The migrant myth, which promises mountains of gold only if the transfer to the destination country can be achieved, keeps the trajectories going, and is often the cause for those who fail to have success as migrants to be looked down upon and themselves turn towards criminal activities (Li, 1999a).

Migrants' trajectories and the global urbanization process

Examining *the sending* side of migrant trajectories, it is useful to be conscious that both in China and the Philippines, as in other Asian countries, migrations to Europe and elsewhere are actually an extension of domestic migrations, which in their turn are usually part of local urbanization processes. In China, there are notoriously 100–120 million migrants continuously adrift – mostly peasants who try and find work in the quickly developing coastal zones. In the Philippines migration abroad extended from circular domestic migration flows that had been very old (van den Muijzenberg, 2003, pp. 129–32). These patterns have come into being since the end of World War II, if not earlier.

There is not only horizontal mobility occurring, but also vertical mobility, in the sense that migrants often do not return to their villages but continue working in urban and industrial occupations – in either the sending or the host countries. Return to the home villages, in the case of the overwhelming majority of rural migrants, seems rare; it either happens when they become rich and/or retire, or it does not happen at all. Nowadays, for the migrants themselves it has become even more difficult to see the difference between domestic and foreign migration, thanks to the communications revolution: a flight from Sichuan province to Beijing or Amsterdam makes a difference of only about ten hours, and the reception may not be so much less inhospitable or difficult in the last destination than in the first one. Also, migrants have much better opportunities to keep in touch with their home bases by cheap flights, the internet, and mobile telephones.

It is significant, in this context, that migrations to Europe are only a trickle in comparison to internal Asian migrations. From 1969 to 1989 12 million Chinese workers migrated to the Middle East (Dupont, 2001, p. 159). During that period, the number of Chinese descendants in Europe amounted to several 100,000s (Angenendt and Orren, n.d., p. 5; Pieke and Benton, 1998, *passim*). Furthermore, mentioned earlier, are the 'permanent' 100 million migrants within China since the late 1980s. In the early 2000s, even though the number of Filipinos in Europe amounted to 800,000–900,000 workers, the bulk of the overseas Filipino workers were absorbed by the Asian labour market (van den Muijzenberg, 2003, pp. 132–7). Asylum-seekers from Asia in Europe have increased over the years, but the number of refugees within the borders of Asian borders is staggering. Maybe Thailand is the best example, even if it may not be representative: in the period 1975–97 there were 160,000 Vietnamese boat people (compared to 70,000 in France, the largest recipient in Europe), around 200,000 Cambodians, 360,000 Laotians, 500,000–1.75 million refugees and illegal workers from Myanmar, and probably around 500,000–1 million displaced people from along the border with Myanmar (Dupont, 2001, p. 143).

Finally, it seems useful to look upon migration flows as partly tentative: itinerant populations are continuously on the move – for example, in Suriname (in Latin America) during the 1990s every month some 1,000 Chinese landed, but only 300 remained, depending on their success in finding employment there; many went on to other destinations tentatively, notoriously so to the United States.[2]

Migration configurations

The concept of migration configurations may help us better understand the structural character of migration processes and the problems it raises for policy making. A migration configuration consists of 'the connections between the total sum of social institutions and practices in areas of origin, transit, and destination that produce and sustain a particular flow of (or, more commonly, a set of closely connected flows) of migrants' (Pieke *et al.*, 2004, pp. 19, 60–3).

This definition serves to remind us first, to look at both ends of the migration chain/flow and the trajectory that connects those two locations; secondly, to look not at individual migrants, but at the combined whole of social institutions that cause and sustain a particular flow of migrants; and, thirdly, to pay due attention to the differences between any configuration of migration flows.

Frank Pieke and his colleagues have researched two different Fujianese communities, whose migrations may serve as an illustration of the configuration concept (Pieke et al., 2004). The first is Fuqing, a harbour located on the coast of northern Fujian province in China. Fuqing had been a migrant sending place since the beginning of the twentieth century. Liem Siu-lioung of the Salim conglomerate in Indonesia derives from there and he has recently made Fuqing culture part of his companies' corporate culture and used the link to access investment opportunities in China. At the more modest scale of migrant workers, migration picked up quickly after 1978 when China adopted a more permissive attitude towards emigration, and previously existing networks in Southeast Asia could be build on to facilitate migrations, particularly towards Eastern and Southern Europe. Sanming, the other place picked by Pieke et al., has a completely different configuration. It is situated in the mountainous parts of inland northern Fujian and had experienced no migration abroad before 1978. It did have substantial domestic immigration, however: in the 1960s and 1970s Sanming was part of the Third Front (*Sanxian*) policies, meant to transfer industries inland from the coastal areas, because the former were considered all too vulnerable to foreign attacks. Consequently, a migrant population was built up from other parts of China, but when migration abroad emerged as an alternative to local employment after the late 1970s, no previously existing networks could be used to get abroad, and local officials linked up with Zhejiangese people who had long-standing relations with Europe. Consequently, they traversed very different trajectories from the Fuqing migrants when travelling to their destination countries, and also had their own patterns of building up an existence once there.

Mixed patterns require more subtle approaches when making and implementing policies than when more uniformity and coordination exists. Regional backgrounds have always been very different for Chinese migrants to Europe. One may distinguish four broad waves of migration from China to Europe over the course of the twentieth century, which have produced quite distinct migrant communities (Pieke and Benton, 1998, pp. 6–9).

First, there were the small traders from Wenzhou and Qingtian in central China. Their routes towards Europe remain somewhat contested. They probably came overland, via Moscow, as well as overseas and spread throughout European countries; their flow subsided after 1949, but resumed from the mid-1970s. Secondly, there were the Cantonese seamen, who came to the major ports of North West Europe, and mostly, but not all, had disappeared by the 1940s. After the Second World War chain migration emerged from the New Territories area of Hong Kong to the United Kingdom (UK), with large numbers in the catering trade, which then spread on to the Continent. Thirdly, decolonization and other political transformations in Southeast Asia led to further waves of migration of Chinese descendants towards Europe. From the later 1970s some 75,000 boat refugees came from Vietnam to France and elsewhere in Europe. France, of course, had a community from its colonies already; 10,000 came from Indonesia to the Netherlands, and then on to several other countries in Europe, first upon Indonesian independence in the late 1940s, then after the pogroms in the 1950s and 1960s. Other former colonies, such as Malaysia and Singapore, also delivered Chinese migrants; those migrations typically ended in the booming catering trades in the UK, the Netherlands, Belgium, Spain, and other countries throughout the 1960s and 1970s.

Finally, contemporary patterns emerged, under the heading of 'New Migration' after the 1970s (Thunø, 2001; Xiang, 2003, pp. 27–34), which added migrants of more variegated social and regional backgrounds to the existing communities: those mentioned from north Fujian belong to this category, who came from the late 1980s, often through human smuggling by *shetou* (snakeheads); they usually landed in Germany and the USA, but were often left in other European countries as well, by circumstances such as lack of money and trickery by *shetou*. In Eastern Europe many well-educated city-dwellers came from northern China, closely linked to Chinese state enterprises and Chinese networks and, unlike many of the other groups mentioned above, of self-contained communities with few or no links to the home country, aside from the common sending of remittances and donations. These new migrants competed with western capitalist enterprises in Eastern Europe and were later motivated by the expansion of the EU in 2004. New migrants landed in Southern Europe as well, especially in the leather and textile sectors. In 2004, in Spain, the first conspicuous anti-Chinese riot occurred, addressing the competition for local industries coming from Chinese factories and sweatshops. Lastly, the waves of asylum-seekers increased, which began from the Tiananmen Incident in 1989 and was added to by a sudden wave of adolescent refugees in the early 2000s.

The boundless variety of migration configurations reveals the multivariate dynamics of migration trajectories and should be better known among policy-makers in order to enable them to formulate a more proactive set of migration policies. There is one level at which migration configurations play a pertinent role, namely in checking out the stories told by individual asylum-seekers. Very often, non-governmental organizations (NGOs) such as Amnesty International and Asia Watch appear not to have sufficient know-how available to check out those stories. As an expert on China one may be confronted with questions like, in 1989, had there been demonstrations in Fuzhou, and is a claim of being pursued by the Chinese government of a private entrepreneur (*getihu*) during that time valid? Or otherwise, one finds very complicated stories, stretching over years or even decades, which can never be fully verified, or even understood, by anyone who is not very thoroughly acquainted with China's history.[3]

The ignorance about migrants in the receiving countries

Aside from their relatively small numbers, migrants from Asia also suffer from social and cultural invisibility: for example, the Chinese communities in the Netherlands and the rest of Europe generally only come to the public eye after grave accidents or in times of crisis. There was a crisis in the restaurant sector at the end of the 1980s in the Netherlands, which suddenly brought Chinese social workers on television and invoked a parliamentary investigation into the situation of the Chinese in the Netherlands (Pieke, 1988). During the summer of 2002 there was a sudden occurrence of Chinese demonstrations against mafia practices in Rotterdam. Among the 'accidents' may be counted the 2004 case of the drowning of the cockle-pickers in Morecambe Bay in northern England, where the victims died because they could not read English-language signs warning about the irregular tides. The world was shocked four years earlier, in 2000, by the death by suffocation of 58 Chinese migrants from Fujian province in a container, which was transporting them from Rotterdam to Dover. The driver, who was Dutch, was judged guilty and punished rather soon, and others in the trafficking network have been prosecuted, but the main suspect has been released recently because of a lack of evidence. It is generally known, however, that the Chinese community is afraid to cooperate with the police for fear of revenge; one may also presume that passivity is maintained because restaurant owners have no interest in an improvement of the organization of those transports, which would supposedly make them more expensive. But all of these public occurrences remained isolated events, ignored nearly as much as the unpredictable celebrations of the Chinese New Year.

To begin with it is very difficult to establish at the precise number of Asian migrants. Different sources produce different numbers. Methods of registration differ by member country and make comparison very difficult: counting may be by nationality or by ethnicity; illegal migrants may or may not be included in estimates; naturalization, which is remarkably high for Indians as an example but also occurs among Chinese, may obscure parts of the migrant populations.[4] Some scholars go as far as to refuse to mention any estimate of the number of migrants in their target population.[5]

One of the reasons for the public ignorance of Asian communities in Europe may be their economic self-sufficiency, especially when that is centred upon private entrepreneurship. The very widespread Chinese catering trade is a fine example, which, despite the many changes that have occurred in the composition of the Chinese migrant communities, still forms the core of Chinese economic activity in Europe. The sector is suspected of being able to survive in part, however, by exploiting illegal migrants (Vogels, Geense and Martens, 1999, pp. 122–4, 176–7). This contributes to the interest of Chinese migrant communities to convey a public image of being closed and undivided, to run their own businesses and not to mix up with the local population. In addition, among the first-generation migrants there is no discussion or affinity with western religious creeds; actually, there is little interest in religion at all, not even in Chinese religion, which is practiced individually and involves personal and usually eclectic choices (Geense and Pels, 1998, pp. 57, 115–19, 148–9). Finally, the location of Chinese communities may be centred on Chinatowns, which may increase their distinction and visibility, but also their isolation.

The internal divisions among Asian migrant populations are even less understood, with academic studies about those much less developed than among other minorities. Despite the fact that the Chinese in Europe can rightly be described as 'the first Europeans', because they refuse to distinguish sharply amongst individual European countries (Christiansen, 1998), their degree of organization in Europe is conspicuously lower than elsewhere. The number of voluntary associations in Europe has grown faster than in the rest of the world over the period from the 1950s to the 1990s, but remains small, with less than 2 per cent of the worldwide total.

The rapid growth of these associations from the 1970s onwards might be considered as a signal of strength, because they apparently reflect a high degree of organization. Nevertheless there is sufficient reason to believe that associations, at least in the Chinese case, also reflect the existing internal divisions within the Chinese communities and therefore actually impede their public performance. They may be organized according to particularistic principles deriving from their origins, as is consistent with the migration configuration concept: surname, shared

Table 6.1 Chinese voluntary associations in Europe (1950s–1990s)

	World	Europe
1950	4,847	22
1991	9,093	174

Source: Li (1999b), p. 222.

provenance, shared dialect, profession or religion, and shared political principles (or ideologies) may all be used as attributes to base organizations on. In doing so, moreover, organizations may cover residents throughout the whole of Europe or only those in one or a few countries. In addition, the importance of personal or family-like networks may cut across organizations, or divide them further; Gordon Redding's description of Chinese networks as having weak organization but strong personal linkages seems quite applicable still to European networks as well (Redding, 1990; Eshuis, 2001). Finally, class contradictions usually cause a relative lack of interest among common Chinese for voluntary associations despite whatever positive function the latter may have (Li, 1999b, pp. 217–19).

There is still a long way to go yet in order to overcome public ignorance of the European Chinese communities, and to overcome the resistance within those communities to exposing their real problems: self-sufficiency, social isolation, and a public imagery of closeness and homogeneity also entail a lack of outside control, which, as noted above, is a root cause of harsh exploitation and also stimulates human trafficking and smuggling.

The importance of security issues

In view of their lack of social visibility, it is small wonder that Asian migrants play little role in European politics, but that may be expected to change in the future. Thus far, negotiations on issues about migration have worked as a stimulant for regional cooperation, even though they also kept national governments divided in many cases and thus have a potential to influence negotiations on international security. Migrants are very much part of the security setting for other reasons as well. Refugees emerge from violent conflicts, and may add to political tensions. In addition, there is no clear dividing line between legal and illegal business, let alone between the activities of terrorists, smugglers and political dissidents. The formation of diasporic communities, however idealistically portrayed, may alienate migrants from their social environment and intensify ethnic conflict. Ethnic conflicts may be sparked off in the international arena: the Turkish migrants' presence in Germany can no longer become ignored when discussing Turkey's entry into the EU. The lack of political leverage of Asian migrants may be backed up and increased by the rise of the newly successful economies in Asia, such as India and China; there are certainly claims on Chinese descendants that may be used for political purposes in the future, to which the second generation of Chinese descendants may respond. India too has recently become active in engendering diasporic communities, which may help its economy to develop, but also may increase the visibility of its migrants abroad.

To many these developments seem frightening, but in view of the problems involved, as sketched above, it can be seen quickly that solutions need more time and are essentially long-term propositions. First, a completely new international security system has emerged from the globalization process since the 1980s and a new security setting took definite shape only in the 1990s, when the Cold War ended with the fall of the Soviet Union and the first Gulf War marked the rise of US hegemony. Adaptation to this new situation and the building of new institutions takes time and energy, but was undertaken with considerable dynamism and has resulted in regional and global forums such as the ASEAN Regional Forum (ARF), the Asia Pacific Economic Cooperation (APEC), and the Asia–Europe Meeting (ASEM). In particular, the latter body, usually depicted as a process rather than an institution, may grow into being a platform for policy formation on interregional migration (Lazcko, 2003, p. 7; Angenendt and Hernandez, 2004, pp. 3–4).

European citizenship and the social sciences

The social sciences have not yet adapted to those institutional changes; rather, they have entered a period of transformation. Mainstream political scientists, commonly labelled as neo-liberals and neo-realists since the 1980s, look upon national states as 'hard' units, which can be pinned down on their fixed material interests, but it seems questionable whether this approach suffices for the problems of our times. The neo-realist scepticism about the goodwill of national states to pursue anything but their perceived interests, but also the neo-liberal confidence in the productive capacity of cooperative institution building for the achievement of free trade, democracy and greater international security both have their limits. A more subtle approach is needed, in which soft power plays a bigger role, and is acknowledged as an important force to achieve improvements in international relations. Peaceful institution building has been tried and is commonly appraised as the distinguishing trait of European diplomacy: the support of rural democracy in China, the environment, human resource management, and labour rights may be mentioned as fields where cooperation can at least be seriously tried out and experimented with (Shin and Segal, 1997; Singh, 2001). International migration is clearly another such field.

There is also a new transnational, or cosmopolitan social class emerging, which may be supposed to constitute a new public domain and civil society in the longer term, of transnational NGOs, businesspeople, professionals and artists, to whom academics may attach themselves and who may increasingly contribute their ideas and action to the existing diplomatic channels and methods, with which they seem to be merging and interacting in a much more intensive manner from the past. Europe numbers some 250 NGOs that are engaged in the representation of migrants' interests (Geddes and Guiraudon, 2004, pp. 340–4). There is a fine example of a Korean NGO, which worked to the benefit of migrants in South Korea, enhancing their political visibility and representation (Lim, 2003; Moore and Tubilewicz, 2001); Amnesty International takes on similar roles for refugees. Also, academic and student exchanges may play a much bigger part in supporting new approaches in the future.

Those developments create new possibilities for idealism and the construction of new national identities and institutions, and may supplement or counteract the focus on national interest as defined in the past. There is a completely new sociology emerging up on the subject of borderlands and international migration (van Schendel and Abraham, 2005), which is due to supplant the traditional focus in migration studies on '(national) minorities': concepts such as migration configurations, which do take into account the migration chains from beginning to end and their multi-sited social embedding, are quickly becoming commonplace, and start from movement, fluidity and change rather than from the fixity of the nation state (Marcus, 1995). Andrew Geddes designed a more flexible approach to borders and border crossing by distinguishing between territorial, organizational and conceptual borders: the latter two need not overlap with the first one or with one another, and thus facilitate the positioning of migrants in different social settings, whose borders transcend the conventional national ones (Geddes, 2005a, 2005b). New approaches have been opened up very recently also by studies which explore the linkages between migration and minorities, and between security concerns and migrants' rights protection (Sasse and Thielemann, 2005, pp. 665–6; Sasse, 2005; Cholewinski, 2005; Hughes, 2005; Guglielmo and Waters, 2005; Toggenburg, 2005). In short, in terms of the International Relations schools of thought, a more 'constructivist', or sociological, approach should be developed in order to increase international security, rather than rely on the neo-liberal and neo-realist creeds.[6]

Policy trajectories

International cooperation is imperative for the enhancement of knowledge on border-crossing migration flows and the improvement of policy making in this sphere. The lack of instruments to regulate and facilitate migration flows in the EU is dangerous, because it stimulates illegal migration. General policies are not migrant-friendly and have for a long time supported the notion of a 'Fortress Europe', which only works to limit legal and reduce illegal migration. Only over the past five years has a more proactive and liberal flow of policy documents been produced, but the proposed policies are mainly the work of the European Commission and are not usually compulsory for the member states. There is certainly no free immigration, but there exists a strictly limited and circumscribed set of categories under which migrations may be legalized: asylum, family reunification, special (short-term) contracts, special recruitment schemes (for highly skilled labour), foreign students, and citizenship programmes for ethnic communities abroad (Angenendt and Orren, n.d., pp. 12–16). For this reason there are too many illegal, semi-legal, forced and not-accepted asylum-seeking migrants. The rather liberal attitudes, which were relatively widespread during the 1990s and were reflected by the popularity of the idea of the multicultural society, were halted after September 11 2001. After that date, the integration of migrant communities in their host societies became the focal point for the formulation of migrant policies, especially at the national level (Sasse, 2005, p. 674; Cholewinski, 2005, p. 697). This made the public debate on migration a highly politicized one, at the exact time when immigration and asylum-seeking began to decrease in volume, due to increased border controls and also for economic reasons (Angenendt and Hernandez, 2004, pp. 6–8; Angenendt and Kruse, 2004). Consequently, the unhappy bifurcation treated above between concerns about migration and those about minorities were invigorated. This is a problem for the policy makers at the top of the EU, particularly in the European Commission, who need broad popular support in order to get their liberalization programme accepted, as reflected in the Amsterdam Treaty and the Tampere Council.

Immigration is increasingly coordinated at the EU level, but national sovereignty is still predominant, for aside from the anti-immigration atmosphere since the early 2000s, differences in the attitudes among the EU member states also impede the enactment of more liberal policies towards external migration. National interests and historical traditions differ: Germany has very different traditions from France, and both differ in many respects from the UK and smaller countries, such as the Netherlands. In this connection it is useful to realize that internal migration in the EU has been liberalized only recently and that Asian countries have a tendency to lag behind the EU in regulating migration (Batistella, 2002; see also below).

Within the EU, during the period 1974–85, discussions began on opening the internal borders for persons. In 1985, the so-called Schengen One agreement arranged for the step-by-step reduction of border controls (involving only France, Germany, Luxembourg, Belgium, and the Netherlands). In 1987, the ad hoc Working Group on Immigration elaborated arrangements on asylum, visa, communication, false documents and external borders. Then followed Schengen Two and the Dublin Convention in 1990. The former arranged for visa regulations, asylum, police and justice cooperation, and the Schengen Information System (SIS); the latter proposed to allow asylum-seekers to only make one application for asylum; this was not a final agreement, because many complaints had been raised against this system. In 1992, the Maastricht Treaty made the EC responsible for visa regulations, but achieved no cooperation on the harmonization of asylum and migration policies.

Following this, in 1997, the Amsterdam Treaty was concluded; this determined to harmonize asylum and migration by the year 2004, something which has not yet happened. The Amsterdam Treaty was enacted in 1999, the same year as the EU meeting in Tampere which agreed on very liberal policies and produced 20 documents on asylum and migration, but imposed no obligation on the member countries to cooperate. This demonstrates the fact that in the area of asylum and migration policy national sovereignty is still predominant (Angenendt and Orren, n.d., pp. 20–3).

In the inter-regional context, it is important, of course, that the ASEM talks kicked off in 1996 and migration policies were an obvious topic for its agenda. ASEM may become a platform for multilateral negotiations, but it also seems clear that the EU and its member states should take the lead. Asian governments thus far have depended mainly on intra-Asian bilateral negotiations – for example, between Thailand and all its adjoining countries (see above), Malaysia and Singapore with Indonesia, and China with Indonesia and Japan. In addition, they cannot be expected to be more liberal in their approaches to migration than the European countries: for example, when the EU toned down its measures on temporary labour, which impeded permanent settlement, the Asian countries immediately followed suit (Batistella, 2002, p. 405).

Concluding remarks

The construction of a global perspective on migration is a complex task, but it is imperative in order to gain sufficient support for a proactive and rational set of policies, directed at both ends of the migration chain and the migration trajectory in between. In order to achieve such a perspective one has to look at many things simultaneously: the role of states in facilitating and stimulating migration; the existence of ever-changing migration configurations and the consequent need for a multifaceted approach of migration; the creation of institutions for the regulation of migration, both at the supranational and the below-state levels (including NGOs); and, finally, the problems of international diplomacy and security: migrants are very much part of the international security setting.

Nevertheless, working towards those ends is a valuable process, because it is the only way for the EU to realize its fundamental commitment to liberal-democratic values. Moreover, if pursued with vigour and enthusiasm, and if accepted by the EU's Asian counterparts, cooperation in many adjoining fields may be improved and global peace promoted.

Notes

1. A good recent overview of the reasons why external migration will have continued relevance for EU policy making is provided by Sasse and Thielemann (2005), pp. 655–62.
2. Oral information provided by a knowledgeable informant.
3. The examples are taken from applications by Chinese asylum-seekers, who had asked for advice from an international NGO, which in turn consulted the author.
4. Compare for an example the numbers provided by a report of the OECD, 2001, *Trends in International Migration* (quoted in Angenendt and Orren, n.d., p. 5), with the numbers in Pieke and Benton (1998), *passim*.

5. See for example Pieke *et al.* (2004).
6. For an argument why political scientists in the field of EU studies should engage in migrant studies, see Geddes (2006).

References

Angenendt, Steffen, and Hernandez, Carolina G., 'Migration and Asylum as Political Challenges for European–Asian Cooperation', in Carolina G. Hernandez and Steffen Angenendt (eds), *Foreign Workers, Refugees, and Irregular Immigrants: Political Challenges and Perspectives for Asia–Europe Cooperation* (Manila, Tokyo: Council for Asia–Europe Cooperation, 2004), pp. 3–29.

Angenendt, Steffen, and Kruse, Imke, 'Forced Migration and Refugee Protection in the European Union', in Carolina G. Hernandez and Steffen Angenendt (eds), *Foreign Workers, Refugees, and Irregular Immigrants: Political Challenges and perspectives for Asia–Europe Cooperation* (Manila, Tokyo: Council for Asia–Europe Cooperation, 2004), pp. 100–39.

Angenendt, Steffen, and Orren, Henry Edward, *Asian Migration to Europe and European Migration and Refugee Policies*, paper (German Council on Foreign Relations, no data).

Batistella, Graziano, 'International Migration in Asia vis-à-vis Europe: An Introduction', *Asian and Pacific Migration Journal*, 11(4) (2002), 405–15.

Chin, James K., 'Reducing Irregular Migration from China', *International Migration*, 41(3) (2003), 49–70.

Cholewinski, Ryszard, 'Migrants as Minorities: Integration and Inclusion in the Enlarged European Union', *Journal of Common Market Studies*, 43(4) (2005), 695–716.

Christiansen, Flemming, 'Chinese Identity in Europe', in Frank, Pieke and Gregor Benton (eds), *The Chinese in Europe* (London: Macmillan, 1998), pp. 42–87.

Dupont, Alan, *East Asia Imperiled: Transnational Challenges to Security* (Cambridge: Cambridge University Press, 2001).

Eshuis, Roswitha, 'Chinese Initiatieven, De rol van organisatie-initiatieven voor politieke participatie van Chinezen' ('Chinese Initiatives: The Role of Organization-Initiatives for Political Participation by Chinese') (Amsterdam: University of Amsterdam, MA Thesis, 2001).

Geddes, Andrew, and Guiraudon, Virginie, 'Britain, France, and EU Anti-Discrimination Policy: The Emergence of an EU Policy Paradigm', *West European Politics*, 27(2) (2004), 334–53.

Geddes, Andrew, 'Europe's Border Relationships and International Migration Relations', *Journal of Common Market Studies*, 43(4) (2005a), 787–806.

Geddes, Andrew, 'Chronicle of a Crisis Foretold: The Politics of Irregular Migration, Human Trafficking and People Smuggling in the UK', *British Journal of Politics and International Relations*, 7 (2005b), 324–39.

Geddes, Andrew, 'Migration and the study of Politics', *British Journal of Politics and International Relations*, 8 (2006), 611–20.

Geense, Paul, and Pels, Trees, *Opvoeding in Chinese Gezinnen in Nederland (Education in Chinese Families in the Netherlands)* (Assen: Van Gorcum, 1998).

Guglielmo, Rachel, and Waters, Timothy William, 'Migrating Towards Minority Status: Shifting European Policy Towards Roma', *Journal of Common Market Studies*, 43(4) (2005), 763–86.

Hughes, James, ' "Exit" in Deeply Divided Societies: Regimes of Discrimination in Estonia and Latvia and the Potential for Russophone Migration', *Journal of Common Market Studies*, 43(4) (2005), 739–62.

Laczko, Frank, 'Introduction; Understanding International Migration between China and Europe', *International Migration*, 41(3) (2003), 5–19.

Li, Minghuan, ' "To Get Rich Quickly in Europe" – Reflections on Migration Motivation in Wenzhou', Frank N. Pieke and Hein Mallee (eds), *Internal and International Migration: Chinese Perspectives* (London: Curzon, 1999a), pp. 181–99.

Li, Minghuan, '*We Need Two Worlds*': *Chinese Immigrant Associations in a Western Society* (Amsterdam: Amsterdam University Press, 1999b).

Lim, Timothy C., 'Racing from the Bottom in South Korea? The Nexus between Civil Society and Transnational Migrants', *Asian Survey*, (43)3 (2003), 423–42.

Marcus, George E., 'Ethnography in/of the World System: the Emergence of Multi-sited Ethnography', *Annual Review of Anthropology*, 24 (1995), 95–117.

Moore, Marketa, and Tubilewicz, Czeslaw, 'Chinese Migrants in the Czech Republic, Perfect Strangers', *Asian Survey*, (41)4 (2001), 611–28.

Pieke, Frank, *De positie van de Chinezen in Nederland (The Position of the Chinese in the Netherlands)* (Leiden: Documentatiecentrum voor het Huidige China, 1988).

Pieke, Frank, and Benton, Gregor (eds), *The Chinese in Europe* (London: Macmillan, 1998).

Pieke, Frank N., Nyiri, Pal, Thunø, Mette, and Ceccagno, Antonella, *Transnational Chinese: Fujianese Migrants in Europe* (Stanford (Cal): Stanford University Press, 2004).

Polanyi, Karl, 'The Self-Regulating Market and the Fictitious Commodities: Labor, Land, and Money', in Karl Polanyi, *The Great Transformation: The Political and Economic Origins of Our Time* (Boston: Beacon Press, 1957[1944]), pp. 68–76.

Redding, Gordon, *The Spirit of Chinese Capitalism* (Berlin, New York: Walter de Gruyter, 1990).

Sasse, Gwendolyn, 'Securitization or Securing Rights? Exploring the Conceptual Foundations of Policies towards Minorities and Migrants in Europe', *Journal of Common Market Studies*, 43(4) (2005), 673–93.

Sasse, Gwendolyn, and Thielemann, Eiko, 'A Research Agenda for the Study of Migrants and Minorities in Europe', *Journal of Common Market Studies*, 43(4) (2005), pp. 655–71.

Scharping, Thomas, 'Selectivity, Migration Reasons and Backward Linkages of Rural-Urban Migrants: a Sample Survey of Foshan and Shenzhen in Comparative Perspective', in Frank N. Pieke and Hein Mallee (eds), *Internal and International Migration: Chinese Perspectives* (London: Curzon, 1999), pp. 73–103.

Schendel, Willem van, and Abraham, Itty (eds), *Illicit Flows: How States, Borders and Language Produce Illicitness* (Bloomington: Indiana University Press, 2005).

Shichor, Yitzak, 'Israel's Military Transfers to China and Taiwan', *Survival*, 40(1) (1998), 68–91.

Shin, Dong-Ik, and Segal, Gerald, 'Getting Serious about Asia–Europe security Cooperation', *Survival*, 39(1) (1997), 138–55.

Singh, Daljit, 'Europe's Role in Asian Security', in Wim Stokhof and Paul van der Velde (eds), *Asian–European Perspectives* (International Institute for Asian Studies, 2001), pp. 94–107.

Skeldon, Ron, 'The End of Exceptionalism', keynote speech, Copenhagen: Fifth Conference of the International Society for the Study of Chinese Overseas, 10–14 May 2005.

Thunø, Mette, 'Reaching Out and Incorporating Chinese Overseas: the Transnational Scope of the PRC by the End of the Twentieth Century', *The China Quarterly*, 168 (2001), 939–58.

Toggenburg, Gabriel N., 'Who is Managing Ethnic and Cultural Diversity in the European Condominion? The Moments of Entry, Integration and Preservation', *Journal of Common Market Studies*, 43(4) (2005), 717–38.

van den Muijzenberg, Otto, 'Birds of Passage May Nest in Foreign Lands: Filipino Migrants and Sojourners in Europe', in, Chrissi Inglessi, Antigone Lyberaki, Hans Vermeulen and Gert Jan van Wijngaarden (eds), *Immigration and Integration in Northern versus Southern Europe* (Athens: Netherlands Institute in Athens, 2003), pp. 127–67.

Vogels, Ria, Geense, Paul, and Martens, Edwin, *De Maatschappelijke Positie van Chinezen in Nederland (The Social Position of the Chinese in the Netherlands)* (Assen: Van Gorcum & Comp., 1999).

Xiang, Biao, *Emigration from China: a Sending Country Perspective* (Singapore: Asia Research Institute, National University of Singapore. Published by Blackwell, 2003).

Part II
Patterns of Bilateralism

7
A European Strategy Towards China? The Limits of Integration in Foreign Policy Making

Richard Balme

Introduction

In 2005, the European Union (EU) and China celebrated 30 years of official relations. With a real boom in trade relations, propelled further by China's accession to the World Trade Organization (WTO) in 2001, and the development of close political dialogue, Europe–China relations have been transformed profoundly in recent decades. This can easily be understood given the dual process of European integration on the one hand, and the transition in its political economy on the Chinese side, yielding intensive changes at both the domestic and the international levels. The EU and China are now recognized as key players in contemporary international politics, while their relations are – and will obviously remain – critical to the globalization process. However usual the reality of diplomatic summits, trade or tourism may appear today, a number of obstacles did stand in the way of these developments, particularly the legacy of the colonial past and of the Cold War in Asia, the hegemony of the US in international relations, and the persisting difficulties of European countries to act collectively in the international arena. The development of these relations therefore required a long process of delineating policy making and institution building. It can also be noticed that the distance in space and differences in size and pace of development added to the complexity of these relations. Briefly stated, the European 'soft power' interacts with the regional and increasingly global 'hard power' of China, whose process of state building can be considered still in the making when compared to Europe. In this case, 'players' in international relations have few things in common beyond diplomatic protocol and therefore they develop complex, asymmetric and multi-levelled relations.

This chapter analyses the development of European policy towards China and how it was able to emerge and consolidate among EU member states and institutions with the progress of European integration. China is considered as a case study for exploring the degree of integration of European foreign policy making across different areas as well as between member states and EU institutions. The influence of trade, security, human rights and cooperation issues in the dynamics of Sino-European relations is reviewed and the contribution of EU–China relations to multilateralism and global governance is assessed.

The development of a European Union policy towards China

Relations between the EU and China have developed rapidly in recent years, and as such have attracted significant amounts of media coverage. The recent controversies over the arms embargo and Chinese textile exports to the EU were only the latest turbulences in a well-established set of political, economic and cooperative relations. In 2004, the EU became China's largest trading partner, while China is now the EU's second biggest trade partner after the United States (US). This of course matters much in shaping European policy towards China. But it is also the result of a long process of diplomatic activity.

The development of these relations went through several different phases (detailed in Gosset, 2005). The first period was from 1975 to 1989. Formal diplomatic relations between the then European Community (EC) and China were established in May 1975, with the visit of European Commissioner Sir Christopher Soames to Beijing. Interestingly, 1975 pre-dated the end of the Cultural Revolution in China. The establishment of EU–China relations corresponds to China putting distance between itself and the Soviet Union and moving closer to the West, especially to the US, after 1971 and to the beginning of political cooperation within the EC. With China's 'Four Modernizations' policy in place, trade (1978) and cooperation (1984) agreements could be signed, interparliamentary (1980) and interministerial (1984) meetings introduced, and the first visit of the President of the Commission to Beijing organized (in 1979 Roy Jenkins met with Deng Xiaoping). The opening of the EC Delegation office in Beijing in 1988 occurred during the presidency of Jacques Delors, in a period that saw the completion of the single market and intense institutional developments in Europe, while China's economic modernization was raising hopes of some political liberalization.

Things changed drastically with the Tiananmen tragedy, opening a new period from 1989 to 1997. The brutality of the 4 June massacre deeply shocked European publics and governments, coming as it did only a few months before the fall of the Berlin Wall and the end of communism in central Europe. The event made it plain that Chinese authorities would not allow their country to be part of the 'third wave' of democratization, and that the economic reforms in the country would not be mirrored by rapid political liberalization. During the events, the European Parliament urged the Chinese government to enter into dialogue with students. On 7 June the then EC-12 decided to suspend economic and cultural relations with China, and on 27 June the Council decided to suspend arms exports to China, to reduce cooperation projects, and to favour the extension of visas for Chinese students.[1]

Nevertheless, by late 1990 economic relations and high-level contacts had resumed. This was in large part due to the context of the first Iraq war and to the efforts to persuade China to impose sanctions within the United Nations Security Council (Moller, 2002). More generally, a strategy aimed at isolating China quickly proved mainly symbolic, ineffective in changing the Chinese government's attitude, and potentially dangerous. During the same period, the Maastricht Treaty enforcing the Single Market in 1993 raised the profile of the EU in the GATT and then WTO negotiations, and defined a legal frame for the common foreign and security policy (CFSP). 1995 is also the year of the second opening-up of the Chinese economy, in order to build the appropriate legal and judicial environment to access the WTO.

Both political and economic considerations (recession in Europe) therefore quickly pushed the EU to progressively normalize its relations with China. A new framework for bilateral political dialogue was set up in June 1994 to encourage Chinese participation in global affairs, including regular meetings between the EU Troika and China at ministerial level, as well as high-level political consultations between the Commission and Chinese authorities. The landmark of this new policy was the Commission's first communication on China, 'A Long Term Policy for Relations between China and Europe', released in October 1995. Both China and the EU took their places in the first Asia–Europe Meeting (ASEM) in Bangkok in March 1996.

On the human rights front, the EU supported resolutions critical of China in the UN's Human Rights Commission (UNHRC) in Geneva in the early 1990s. 1995 was the only year where Americans and Europeans actually agreed to have a draft debated, although China finally escaped condemnation. In the same year the EU-15 expressed their concern about the lack of due process for the long-standing dissident Wei Jinsheng. But Chinese authorities also took the initiative in a bilateral dialogue on human rights, and later on they made it clear that they expected Europeans to abstain from seeking condemnation of China within the UNHRC. In 1997 the last attempt initiated by the Netherlands and Denmark failed again, and the EU–China Human Rights Dialogue, which had been suspended in 1996, was resumed. This situation has been stable since then.

The third period under consideration ranges from 1998 to 2005. This period can legitimately be considered as the most dynamic in recent Europe–China relations. With the handovers of Hong Kong in 1997 and Macau in 1999, the colonial relationship between Europe and China finally came to a close. The Asian crisis also changed the whole political economy structure of the region, while the EU adopted a single currency and went through a crucial process of enlargement. The whole global situation has also been deeply affected by the post-September 11 context, the second war in Iraq and the issues of weapons of mass destruction and non-proliferation. For different reasons, the EU and China share interests in trade, cooperation, and the promotion of 'multilateralism' or 'multipolarity' in international relations. Both China and Europe upgraded their international status in developing relations, and the boom in economic, cultural and political relations, sometimes referred to as a honeymoon during these years, has to be understood in this perspective. In March 1998 the Commission released a new policy paper on 'Building a Comprehensive partnership with China' and in April the first EU–China Summit took place in London. In May 2000 the EU and China concluded their bilateral negotiations on China's accession to the WTO, and the EU played an active role in facilitating China's membership (Griese, 2005).

Preceding the sixth EU–China Summit, the Chinese government released its first policy paper towards the EU in October 2003. Two agreements were signed during the Summit, establishing a new dialogue on industrial policy, and cementing China's participation in Galileo, the EU's system of radio satellite navigation. Two other dialogues were initiated – on intellectual property rights and on tourism. A joint declaration on non-proliferation and arms control was issued in Brussels in December 2004. EU–China relations turned so positively that the Chinese authorities expected the arms embargo to be lifted in 2004, and used the time frame of the approaching celebration of the thirtieth anniversary to continue pressing on the issue. After delaying the decision (see below), Commissioner for External Relations Benita

Ferrero-Waldner indicated during her celebration visit in Beijing in May 2005 the expectation of the EU to launch negotiations to establish a new framework agreement, to create a high-level coordination mechanism, and to work towards readmission agreements and visa facilitation. The Chinese government was invited once again to help create the conditions for lifting of the arms embargo, and encouraged to ratify the International Convention on Civil and Political Rights (ICCPR).[2] Despite these late incidents, relations had undoubtedly expanded and intensified well beyond the existing institutional framework, highlighting the need for a new agreement.

The last period runs from 2005 to the present. After periods of normalization and 'honeymoon', it is sometimes referred to by diplomats as a time of 'maturity'. What is true is that mutual expectations came back to greater realism. To Chinese authorities, European powers proved in the end unable or unwilling to lift the arms embargo, and still hesitant to recognize China as a fully-fledged market economy. At the same time, the rejection of the European constitutional treaty postponed further the perspective of a greater influence for Europe in international affairs. For Europeans, the Chinese government has made few concessions to western public opinion on human rights and, unsurprisingly, faces domestic difficulties when implementing its WTO commitments in terms of intellectual property rights (IPR), market access, or sector-based trade agreements. Both parties increasingly have to manage the domestic implications of globalization and, from this perspective, interact increasingly along political rationales. Without changing the nature of these relations, tensions have become more apparent with the implementation of agreements adopted in the previous phase.

Two new Commission policy papers in October 2006, 'EU–China: Closer Partners, Growing Responsibilities', and 'Competition and Partnership', followed by the Conclusions from the Council adopted on 11 December 2006, displayed a more direct and demanding style in relation to China. Nevertheless they also run a risk of disjointing the position of the Commission from that of the member states. The next sections explore in more detail the ups and downs of the integration of European foreign policies toward China through a number of specific issues.

The politics of European trade with China

One of the major consequences of the domestic policy changes in China, coupled with the development of relations with the EU, has been the impressively rapid growth in EU–China trade. Between 1999 and 2004, total trade more than doubled (multiplied by 2.4), with exports growing from 19.6 to 47.9 billion euros, and imports from 52.4 to 126.6 billion euros. The EU-25 deficit in trade with China grew from 32.8 in 1999 to 78.3 billion euros in 2004. This dramatic growth has been observed since the beginning of the 1980s, with China progressively raising its position in EU trade. By 2004 the EU had became the first trading partner of China, and China the second trading partner of the EU after the US. Perhaps more significantly, the growth in EU–China trade exceeds by far the growth of exchanges between the EU and other parts of the world.

Trade is dominated by manufactured goods. Two-thirds of EU-25 exports to China are registered as machinery and vehicles, and a further 20 per cent as other manufactured articles. Until 2004, the main EU-25 export products to China were motor cars and aircraft, while the main imports were computers and parts (including monitors and printers), mobile phones and digital cameras. The distribution of trade among EU member states is more difficult to depict (due to intra-European trade), but major trends can be mapped. The main exporter to China is Germany, with 20.9 billion euros in 2004, followed by France (5.3 billion), Italy (4.4), the United Kingdom (UK) (3.4). With Belgium and the Netherlands, these countries account for more than 80 per cent of EU-25 exports to China – 44 per cent by Germany alone. Imports from China are somewhat less concentrated but again, Germany comes first with 28.5 billion euros (23 per cent), followed by the UK (20.5 billion euros), the Netherlands (18.7 billion euros), Italy (11.8) and France (11.6). All member states record a deficit in trade with China, except Finland with a small surplus of 0.58 billion euros, due to the success of its mobile phone industry. The largest deficits are registered by the UK (17 billion euros), the Netherlands (16 billion euros),[3] Germany (7.5 billion), Italy (7.3) and France (6.2).

Significantly, Hong Kong's once-dominant role in Europe's China trade has been declining dramatically. Hong Kong accounted for more than half of EU exports to China (including Hong Kong) until 1997; this share fell to 30.9 per cent in 2003. Hong Kong represented 65 per cent of total Chinese imports to Europe in 1980, 18.3 per cent in 1997, and 8.9 per cent in 2003. More recently, the regional growth of China's foreign trade, initially concentrated in the Pearl River Delta, has also been shifting to other regions, in particular to the Yangtze River Delta. The same applies to foreign direct investment (FDI) in China, some 10 per cent of which comes from EU-25. The role of both Hong Kong and South China in EU–China relations undoubtedly and rapidly became more relatively balanced since 1997 (Freeman, 2005).

Several controversies are related to these trade relations. Member states unquestionably supported China's accession to the WTO in December 2001, both as evidence of China's constructive engagement in international institutions (as pursued by the EU's policy), and as a tool to develop access to China's domestic market, an issue of very keen interest to national governments seeking trade promotion. Chinese authorities made significant concessions to both the US and the EU as part of the preceding negotiations (Dejean de la Batie, 2002), and since that time they have been claiming that they should be granted Market Economy Status (MES) by the EU within the WTO. This somewhat technical issue relates to the method used to define reference prices in designing trade defence instruments. The MES would allow for considering the domestic market, rather than a third country, as a reference in deciding about anti-dumping procedures. The issue concerns a very marginal volume of trade and is essentially symbolic. It would basically acknowledge the fulfillment of China's obligation within the WTO and the end of its transition period. But it also remains to date (April 2007) as an irritant, precisely as Europeans more actively contest the persisting difficulties in access to the Chinese market, which have become increasingly apparent with time (European Commission, 2006).

Another issue lies with the trade deficit, which has been coupled with the question of the exchange rate of the Chinese currency, the RMB. The US increasingly accuses Chinese authorities of using both *de facto* restrictions to market access to limit imports and the underrating of the RMB to sustain exports. The EU is far less vocal on the currency issue, and acknowledges the limited flexibility adopted by the Chinese government. It also recognizes that the trade deficit with China, nominally less important in volume than for the USA, substitutes for rather than adds to the total trade deficit with Asia. The EU is also less exposed, from a political perspective, to the tremendous accumulation of foreign currency reserves by China, mainly in US dollars, linked to the deficit.

If the deficit is not a politically sensitive issue for Europeans, other controversies are more critical. IPR, for instance, are regularly addressed by the European side, with growing insistence. An official Dialogue on IPR has been in place since 2003. Major difficulties lie more with the lack of implementation of existing rules than with the creation of new ones. Cooperation programmes are developed in this respect, but with limited effects. As exemplified by the case of textiles after the lifting of quotas in January 2005, the implementation of agreements reached under the WTO negotiations also generate sudden economic flux and brutal social changes, leading to tensions in bilateral relations. After pressure exerted by national governments and lobbying from textile industries, the European Commission on 6 April 2005 published guidelines indicating under which circumstances it would consider safeguard action against imports from China.[4] After some reaction from the Chinese Ministry of Commerce, these tensions were eased without formal WTO procedure in the following months, after the European Commission adopted a regulation to clear blocked Chinese textile imports in September 2005. Nevertheless, such difficulties are likely to intensify and to expand to other sectors with the development of trade liberalization.[5] The launching of the Dialogue on trade in 2004, and the opening of negotiations for a new Partnership and Cooperation Agreement in 2006, must be understood in this perspective.

Trade politics are crucial in EU–China relations, for a set of converging reasons: the persisting high level of growth and market potential development in China, coupled with a nearly opposite situation in Europe; the absence of any direct strategic interaction on security issues between Europe and China since 1997, placing economic relations at the top of the bilateral agenda; and the leading role of the European Commission in what is one of the most integrated areas of EU institutions' competencies. On the other hand, the discrepancy between trade agreements, handled by the EU, and trade promotion, where member states openly compete in their relations with Chinese authorities,[6] is worth noticing, as it significantly restricts the integration of European foreign policies towards China.

Political dialogue and human rights

Based on a series of policy papers, the EU China's policy relies on a strategy of 'constructive engagement' with China in world affairs.[7] In the words of the EU website:

> The commitment of the EU to the strengthening of its political dialogue with China is notably based upon recognition that China, as a UN Security Council member, a growing economic and political power, and an increasingly assertive member of the international community, can exert a significant influence on a wide series of issues of global concern.

A broad EU–China political dialogue was formally established in 1994, through an exchange of letters, 'in recognition of China's status as an emerging power on the international scene'. This dialogue has grown into a regular series of meetings at several levels.[8] The scope of the dialogue has broadened gradually over time to cover issues ranging from non-proliferation to the security situation in Asia, from global warming to the fight against illegal migration and trafficking in human beings. The 2003 policy paper defined concrete and practical action points for the implementation of EU policy towards China for the ensuing two–three years: in particular, an enhancement of political dialogue through a better focusing of the existing mechanisms and the systematic inclusion of global and regional governance and security issues; dialogue on illegal immigration would be more results-oriented, and negotiations to sign a readmission agreement were to be launched; ways of improving the efficiency and impact of the human rights dialogue were also specified. At the EU–China Summit in the Hague on 8 December 2004, a joint declaration on non-proliferation, agreements on peaceful nuclear research, customs cooperation and the prolongation of the Science and Technology Agreement were signed. Four cooperation agreements were also concluded. Both parties stressed the importance of further deepening their relationship, turning it into a 'strategic partnership'.

Two issues have been in the forefront of the agenda of this dialogue – the human rights situation in China and the arms embargo.

Human rights

Human rights have been a major theme of EU–China relations since the Tiananmen Square crackdown in 1989. The beginning of the Human Rights Dialogue responded primarily to the EU's necessity to restore and develop links with China, and to the ineffectiveness of its own regime of sanctions to alter Chinese domestic policy. It was also thought of as an alternative to the US approach, at the time trying to link trade policy to human rights.[9] German Chancellor Helmut Kohl in 1995 and French President Jacques Chirac in 1997 asserted the need to take differences in human rights approaches into account. The EU–China dialogue on human rights (initially distinct from the Political Dialogue) was initiated in January 1996, but was interrupted by China after Denmark (plus nine other EU member states) tabled a critical resolution at the 1997 UNHRC session. Later in 1997, China decided to resume the dialogue. Since then, the dialogue has been held twice a year. For the EU, the human rights dialogue constitutes a platform to engage China on sensitive issues, and to allow for the channeling of EU concerns directly to the Chinese authorities. The EU seeks to promote a 'positive' and 'results-oriented' approach through dialogue and cooperation, and intends to see it connected to decision-making in China so that it brings tangible improvements. The Commission supports the process through its cooperation programmes. Since 1997, several projects (on village governance, legal cooperation, promotion of women's rights, networking on Human Rights Covenants etc.) have been carried out.

In terms of direct consequences the 'net impact' of the Dialogue is impossible to assess precisely (Dejean de la Batie, 2002). Indeed, Chinese authorities claim a different conception of human rights, enlarged to social and economic well-being, and tend to minimize the importance or political and civil rights, at least in the assessment of the current situation. The understanding of 'improvements' therefore substantially varies. Other dialogues are also conducted between China and Japan, Canada, Australia, Norway, Switzerland, and, within the EU, Germany, the UK and Hungary. A similar dialogue was established with the United States in the 1990s, but this has been suspended since 2002. Chinese authorities never establish any formal link between bilateral dialogues (less so even sanctions) and human rights developments. Therefore changes in the human rights situation in China need to be attributed to the conjunction of bilateral dialogues, intermittent international public pressure, and above all to domestic political considerations.

From a procedural perspective, some improvements have been achieved. China signed in 1997 and ratified in 2001 the UN Covenant on Economic, Social and Cultural Rights, although with a reserve on unions' rights. In 1998 China signed the UN Covenant on Civil and Political Rights, it has not yet ratified it, and has not indicated any time frame for doing so. China signed a memorandum of understanding with the UN High Commissioner for Human Rights, initiating some forms of cooperation. And Chinese authorities agree to receive lists of individual cases and to provide answers, although on an informal basis.

Nevertheless, most of this progress has been made since the EU–China dialogue was initiated and few demonstrable improvements have occurred in more recent years. However, the rare liberations of dissidents by Chinese authorities related to the international context, if any, are generally linked to the development of Sino-US relations, or interpreted as such. International non-governmental organizations (NGOs), influential on western public opinion, point a dark picture of human rights in China, according to which Chinese authorities continue to detain political prisoners, to restrict religious freedoms, and to exert brutal repression in Tibet and Xinjiang. Interventions by the EU in favour of North Korean refugees fleeing into China have been of no effect. China still denies the Red Cross access to visit its political prisoners. The death penalty is used widely and Chinese authorities remain reluctant to communicate data about it. The expected positive impact of the 2007 reform, introducing review of death penalty cases by the People's Supreme Court, still needs to fully produce its effects.

Such a picture is definitely embarrassing for EU institutions and the governments of member states. The European Parliament occasionally issues positions on human rights in China, and visits by Chinese officials to Europe are usually punctuated by activists' demonstrations, which are an irritant to the Chinese leadership. NGOs are also critical in their assessment of the Dialogue itself (Human Rights in China, 2004), denouncing the lack of transparency, the exclusion of NGOs, the absence of benchmarking to assess results, and the way it affects human rights issues at the UN (see below). European leaders are sometimes more vocal on human rights when they visit Beijing, in accordance with their constituencies (German Foreign Minister Joshka Fischer, for instance). But in the absence of a major crisis, European public opinion is less sensitive to the human rights situation in China than to the trade issue.

The major limitation of the EU Human Rights Dialogue lies with its link to the UNHRC. The existence of the dialogue does not preclude as such the EU from expressing publicly its concerns about human rights violations in China. In 2001 and 2002, in its opening statements to the annual UNHRC sessions, the EU Presidency expressed serious concern about the human rights situation in China. Demarches are also made, including at the highest level, to express European concerns whenever necessary. As exemplified by previous practices and by Sino-US relations, the Dialogue nevertheless remains unofficially linked to the absence of resolution against China at the UNHRC. Every year at the annual session China proposes a 'motion of non action', in order to exclude resolution projects concerning China from the agenda. EU member states agree to oppose this motion of non-action, arguing that all cases brought to the Commission should be discussed, but not to initiate cases against China. In 2001 they clarified their strategy and indicated that they would later support a resolution passing through the motion of non-action, which has not occurred to date. Through these diplomatic contortions, China obtained some respectability in the UN institutions. Such a situation, however, does not contribute, beyond formalism, to the promotion of multilateralism at the global level, one objective which is nevertheless vocally claimed to be shared by both parties. Whether the Human Rights Council newly established in 2006 will produce more tangible results remains to be seen.

The arms embargo

It was in this context that the lifting of the arms embargo, instituted in 1989, became a major issue. It is easy to understand how access to the WTO, the development of political and human rights dialogue, and the absence of resolutions against China at the UNHRC justified such a request on the Chinese side. Following Deng Xiaoping's southern China tour in 1992, the reform and opening policy has been considered as confirmed by the Chinese leadership and has been progressively implemented and expanded in its own style and pace. Consequently, Chinese foreign policy is currently conceived as instrumental in securing a domestic policy of development of productive capacity, economic growth and social prosperity. International reputation (the Olympics in 2008 and the World Expo in 2010) and respectability are part of this project, and being listed with Myanmar or Sudan among countries on which the EU is applying sanctions is definitely perceived as an offense.

On the part of the Europeans, the arms embargo is equally perceived as outdated. The initial formulation by the European Council in Madrid (27 June 1989) was loose enough to be interpreted differently by individual member states. It was further specified in 1994 to exclude lethal weapons and ammunitions, but remained silent on the issues of dual technologies and components. In 1998, the EU adopted a much more specific 'Code of Conduct', more in conformity with international covenants, although not legally binding. The Code of Conduct, applicable to all third countries, is more binding that the embargo against China itself, and makes it outdated.

France and Italy delivered some weapons in reference to contracts signed before 1989 (Crotales and Aspide missiles, and Super-Frelon and Dauphin helicopters). Italy and the UK delivered 'non-lethal' equipment, such as radars and aircraft materials (Dejean de la Batie, 2002). Between 1989 and 2004, China bought a total of 13 weapon systems from the EU, ten of which came from France. EU arms exports to China actually multiplied sixfold between 2001 and 2003 (after the adoption of the Code of Conduct), from 63 to 428 million euros (Godement, 2005). Although these data are far from complete, they reveal that arms sales from the EU to China have been continuing. The same applies to the USA, despite a more restrictive regulation excluding 'non-lethal weapons'. The embargo situation may remain relative, but is nevertheless real, when one considers the surge of Chinese arms imports from Russia, Ukraine, Uzbekistan and Israel.

The strategic implications of the debate are not easy to disentangle. Opponents to the lifting of the embargo (particularly the US) invoke the possibility of boosting the arms race across the Taiwan Strait. Chinese and EU authorities deny any intention of selling and buying more weapons for the time being, and underline the need to levy an 'obsolete' measure that is discriminatory in respect of China. Strategic implications are probably more medium- or long-term in nature, and rely on the diversification of arms suppliers to China, in both technological and political terms (Godement, 2005; Shambaugh, 2002, 2004, 2005; Shao, 2005).

Chinese authorities pressurized the Commission and member states on the issue in 2003 and 2004. France promoted the initiative among the EU; France and Germany, and later in 2004 the UK publicized their support for the lifting of the embargo. After Paul Rueda's report was issued in November 2004, member states engaged in negotiations for a tightening of the 'Code of Conduct' that would justify the lifting of the embargo in front of European public opinion and the US. Further positive signals were issued by European leaders in early 2005 and, after several delays, Chinese authorities expected the lifting to be announced for the celebration of the thirtieth anniversary of EU–China relations. However, the momentum was disrupted by US opposition to the measure, and by the anti-secession law passed by the Chinese National People's Congress authorizing the use of force to stop Taiwan from seceding. Both US President George Bush, visiting Europe in February 2005, and Secretary of State Condoleezza Rice, in Asia in March 2005, firmly opposed the lifting of the embargo, in order not to jeopardize the US efforts to stabilize the region. The US Congress in particular was extremely vocal and threatened to restrict arms trade with Europe, a serious economic and security threat when the interconnections of US and European, especially British, defence industries are considered. A top EU envoy to Washington, Annalisa Giannella, failed to persuade the Congress of the rationale behind the planned measure, and the atmosphere surrounding the adoption of the anti-secession law ended in delaying the measure, as admitted by an informal meeting of EU foreign ministers in Luxembourg.

This diplomatic episode is quite revealing. First, as is shown by the time clash between the embargo issue and the anti-secession law, absolutely no connection was made by Chinese authorities between the two issues, and, as expected, 'domestic' politics (the issue of Taiwan) remained for important than EU–China relations, even when it comes to arms sales. Secondly, it is worth noticing that the EU and member states, with the exception of the UK in a more intermediate position, conceive of their relations with China with little consideration for security issues in Asia, where they are not directly involved. Japan, for instance, repeatedly expressed its concern and opposition to the lifting of the embargo, so far with little effect on European diplomacy. This obviously differs from the US attitude based on their symbolic and effective implication in the region. It also runs the risk of forming coalition blocks in East Asia, at odds with objectives of combined regionalism and multilateralism. And, last but not least, although the motive of US pressure is not officially invoked by the Europeans, nonetheless, the EU, Chinese and third countries (Russia and Japan) interpret it predominantly as the main reason for the new delay in lifting the embargo, and as one obvious limitation to the EU's foreign policy independence.

From the above developments it is clear that the scheme of bargaining human rights improvements against access to advanced technologies for military industries is at best outdated, and has produced no tangible results when applied to China. The EU arms embargo has indeed been ineffective from this point of view, and European chancelleries have for some considerable time ceased to link political and human rights dialogues to possible sanctions on trade or security issues. To a significant extent, European diplomacy on this point is facing a gap with the perception conveyed by western medias and human rights activists. The EU also revealed both a deficit of consensus among its member states and a lack of independence in failing to implement its own decision. Both the EU enlargement and the rejection of the European constitution by France and the Netherlands widened the gap between the expectations and the realities of European integration. The EU currently appears to experience divisions among its major power-houses, as well as between the Commission and its member states. In such a context, bilateral relations, at least with large member states, tended to gain in influence in the most recent period. Probably more relevant than the arms embargo, in terms of both past and future evolution, is the convergence of China and the EU on the non-proliferation of WMD, their mutual support of their roles regarding North Korea and Iran, and their commitment to international covenants. But who, except the US, would have the capacity to control for compliance with non-proliferation (Chan, 2005)?

Cooperation programmes and sectoral dialogues

The EU cooperation programme with China aims to provide support for China's transition process, the sustainability of its economic and social reforms, and its further integration into the international community and the world economy. While poverty alleviation is still an important issue in China – and a cross-cutting objective of a number of EU programmes – the EU co-operation strategy intends to transcend the more traditional approach to development assistance and to constitute a response to China's needs. Although little research or evaluation is available on these programmes at this stage, they are in fact quite revealing of the changing face of these relations.

The indicative financing for co-operation with China under the 2002–06 Country Strategy Paper (CSP) amounted to €250 million. Some 50 per cent of these credits went to social and economic reforms, 30 per cent to sustainable development and 20 per cent to the 'promotion of good governance'. The objectives of the CSP are put into action through National Indicative Programmes (NIPs). Other, thematic programmes aimed at promoting specific aspects of development are also being used. Examples are the European Initiative on Democracy and Human Rights (EIDHR), and the non-governmental organization (NGO) co-financing programme. These cooperation programmes include training programmes (a Sino-European Business School in Shanghai, development of European studies, training on AIDS prevention, public administration, and a project of a Sino-European Law School in Beijing); judicial cooperation; village governance; intellectual property rights; economic, social and cultural rights in Yunnan; the WTO accession process; enterprise reform; environmental cooperation projects, and so forth. The limitations of these programmes lie in their financial volume, and in the declining importance of foreign aid in fast-developing China. Although the EU and its member states are collectively the world's largest donor of aid, their contribution in China has for some time been well behind Japan. More decisively, although poverty in China remains a major issue, the country's dependence on international aid is comparatively weak since in many ways it is overwhelmed by the volume of incoming FDI.

In parallel, a series of so-called sectoral dialogues covering more than 20 areas have now been established, ranging from environment protection to science and technology and from industrial policy to education and culture. Recent Chinese competition legislation was drafted with reference to the EU model. Like the EU, China is also committed to eradicating market fragmentation in order to reap the full benefits of a large internal market. Regarding regional policies and other income redistribution mechanisms, achieving 'balanced development' is now an explicit goal of China's economic policy. For its part, the EU has a wealth of experience in regional and rural development policies which squarely address the issues related to disparities in regional growth. Chinese and EU specialists have started exchanging experiences on these issues with the intention of intensifying cooperation in the years to come. China and the EU are also both major players in international trade and very close interaction, at all levels, on trade issues is in place. In many areas, both sides are simultaneously confronted with new challenges, such as rapid advances in science and technology, or problems with health protection. In some areas Europe could usefully benefit from Chinese know-how and experience. Civil nuclear research is an example of such an area mentioned by the European Commission, where Europe will soon have to close down its ageing experimental nuclear reactors, whereas China is currently building state-of-the-art facilities. As a consequence of the conclusion of a new Euratom agreement, China agreed to share the technology behind its new facilities with European researchers.

Exchanges take place under different denominations depending on the specific context of the sector. They are referred to as 'dialogues', 'regular exchanges', or simply as 'cooperation', and they take place at various hierarchical levels, from working level to ministerial level. A variety of participants may be involved, including officials, politicians, business organizations, and private companies. Proceedings are organized in a flexible way and take the form of working groups, conferences, annual formal meetings or simply informal exchanges. Specialists from well over a dozen Directorates General in the European Commission are involved in regular exchanges with their respective counterparts in China.

Sectoral dialogues are crucial in many respects. They have expanded EU–China relations well beyond the traditional diplomatic milieus and well beyond the exposed issues of trade, arms sales and human rights. They also pave the way for business and other operators by upgrading the institutional environment for exchanges. They form the basis for interactions between a wide variety of decision-makers, for exchanges of best practices, benchmarking, the mutual adaptation of policy values and policy instruments. In sum, they favour mutual policy learning and, within the measure of realism, they contribute to improve the quality of governance in China. According to the Commission, they act as a 'stabilizing element' within the relationship that helps to counterbalance other more sensitive issues such as human rights, migration, or trade negotiations.

Conclusion: Europe, China and multilateralism

There are several different ways to look at EU–China relations. From a 'realistic' state-centric perspective, they feature an interesting clash between the soft power of a post-national political structure, and the hard power of China, where state and nation building are still at stake. Strategic interactions between the two entities are limited (there is no territorial contiguity, and neither strategically interferes in the regional affairs of the other). Stability in Central Asia, the behaviour of Russia, and peace in the Middle East are shared but remote interests. The only long-term strategic interest shared by Europe and China is probably the US, as both are in position of potentially challenging its hegemony over the next decades. So far, in this understanding of EU–China relations, soft power clearly and unsurprisingly does not magically override the hard realities of regional security, progressive state building and economic development. But these relations are not a zero-sum game either, and mutual benefits and influences can be identified both in terms of ideas (multi-polarity) and resources (trade) on both European and Chinese sides.

One alternative way to consider these relations is inspired more by the prism of transnationalism and neo-functionalism. Economic and cultural globalization would simply perforate national sovereignties, diffuse common social and political patterns, and sustain the development of supranational institutions. The economic and social transition of China, coupled with its access to WTO and its engagement in major international organizations, at first sight supports this view. But the specificity of the Chinese trajectory sheds doubts on the idea of a simple causality of the process of globalization. In the Chinese case state capacities are indeed developed and reinforced through the policy of opening. If international institutions and regional organizations matter, they are largely a supplement to rather than a substitute for bilateral relations. Since 2005, due to the stalemate in European integration, bilateral relations have become prevalent.

Finally, a more institutionalist approach may consider both state resilience and path-dependency in transnational integration. What we witness in the EU–China case are probably elements of inter-regional (in this sense, global) modes of governance on key transnational issues such as migration, environment, non-proliferation, health and, for better or worse, human rights. Such governance structures are networks developed at the articulation of states' bureaucracies and international organizations. They appear quite familiar to European studies scholars, as they are often depicted as characteristic of EU policy making. They can be effective in policy making, as they provide a high level of expertise in mobilizing stakeholders and decision-makers. But they also tend to largely exclude citizens and civic groups from decision-making processes. These multilateral networks supplement international organizations to provide governance structures dealing with globalization, so far without clear articulation to democratic representation.

Notes

1. Declaration of European Council, Madrid, 27 June 1989, 'The European Council, recalling the declaration of the Twelve of 6 June, strongly condemns the brutal repression taking place in China. It expresses its dismay at the pursuit of executions in spite of all the appeals of the international community. It solemnly requests the Chinese authorities to stop the executions and to put an end to the repressive actions against those who legitimately claim their democratic rights. The European Council requests the Chinese authorities to respect human rights and to take into account the hopes for freedom and democracy deeply felt by the population. It underlines that this is an essential element for the pursuit of the policy of reforms and openness that has been supported by the European Community and its Member States. ... In the present circumstances, the European Council thinks it necessary to adopt the following measures: raising the issue of human rights in China in the appropriate international foray; asking for the admittance of independent observers to attend the trials and to visit the prisons; interruption by the Member States of the Community of military cooperation and an embargo on trade in arms with China; suspension of bilateral ministerial and high-level contacts; postponement by the Community and its Member States of new cooperation projects; reduction of programmes of cultural, scientific and technical cooperation to only those activities that might maintain a meaning in the present circumstances; prolongation by the Member States of visas to the Chinese students who wish it. Taking into account the climate of uncertainty created in the economic field by the present policy of the Chinese authorities, the European Council advocates the postponement of the examination of new requests for credit insurance and the postponement of the examination of new credits of the World Bank.'
2. Press Release indicated: 'Commenting on 30 years of EU–China diplomatic relations, Commissioner Ferrero-Waldner said, "Both the EU and China have changed beyond recognition in 30 years and so has our relationship. Our existing Trade and Economic Cooperation Agreement simply don't live up to the dynamism of today's partnership. It's time to reflect the vibrancy of our relations with an ambitious new agreement that will help us move to a fully-fledged strategic partnership"' (EU website accessed 14 May 2005).
3. The figure for the UK is misleading as a large part of UK exports to China transits through Hong Kong. Similarly, data for the Netherlands incorporate the 'Rotterdam effect', where Chinese exports to Europe via Rotterdam are counted as if the Netherlands were their final destination.
4. 'The guidelines relate to the textiles-specific safeguard clause written into China's Protocol of Accession to the WTO in 2001 which was incorporated into EU law in 2003. They establish procedures and criteria for the use of safeguard proceedings. The guidelines, like the safeguard clause itself, respond to the potential market disruption that could be caused by a sudden and sustained surge in Chinese textile exports to the EU. As well as threatening EU textile producers, such a surge could displace textile imports from highly vulnerable developing countries with an historic dependence on trade with the EU market. This problem is of particular concern for textile producers

in Europe's Mediterranean partners. The guidelines establish alert zones for each category of Chinese textiles imports allowing for increases in China's current market share. To reach these alert zones Chinese exports will need to show a rapid and sustained rise over a defined period. If these thresholds are reached, the Commission, acting on its own initiative or at the request of a Member State, will undertake an investigation. Informal consultations with the Chinese will allow China to act to provide sufficient remedy. If no remedy is achieved, formal WTO consultations with the Chinese authorities would require them to act to limit textiles exports in the affected categories. If this is still insufficient, safeguards can be invoked. Safeguards would take the form of quantitative import restrictions applicable for a year, but extendable on reapplication. These measures can only be used until 2008. The guidelines also allow for emergency procedures in the case of a rise in imports of such magnitude that serious material injury to EU industry is imminent. In this case formal consultation with the Chinese could be launched without a preceding investigation' (EU Website accessed 14 May 2005).
5. The EU also initiated an anti-dumping proceeding concerning imports of certain footwear originating in China and Vietnam in July 2005.
6. Competition for large industrial projects in China usually mobilizes European firms from different countries, and their American, Japanese or Korean counterparts.
7. The DG Relex website summarizes these objectives in the following way: 'to engage China further, both bilaterally and on the world stage, through an upgraded political dialogue; to support China's transition to an open society based upon the rule of law and respect for human rights; to encourage the integration of China in the world economy through bringing it fully into the world trading system, and supporting the process of economic and social reform that is continuing in China to raise the EU's profile in China'.
8. The Framework of the EU–China Political Dialogue is currently the following: – Annual summits, at the level of the Heads of State or Government, between China and the EU, their location alternating between China and the EU. – Meetings when needed between the EU Troika Foreign Ministers and their Chinese counterpart, in addition to annual meetings in the margins of the United Nations General Assembly. – Annual meetings of EU Troika political directors with their Chinese counterpart, the location of the meeting alternating between China (Beijing) and the EU. – Annual meetings (in Beijing) between EU Troika Asia Pacific directors and their Chinese counterpart on Asian and Pacific issues, the location of the meeting alternating between China and the EU. – Meetings at least once a year between EU Troika and Chinese experts on international security, arms control, non-proliferation and export control issues. – A meeting every six months between the Minister of Foreign Affairs of China and the Ambassadors from the European Union posted in Beijing. – A meeting every six months between the Minister of Foreign Affairs of the country holding the EU Presidency and the Ambassador of China posted in the Presidency's capital.
9. In 1993, US President Bill Clinton threatened not to renew the status of Most Favored Nation (MFN) to China, without obtaining substantial improvements on human rights' situation. The Congress often pressures the US administration on human rights in trade policy. With the access of China to the WTO,

however, China has benefited from 'normal trade relations' with the US on a permanent basis since January 2002.

References

Bridges, Brian, and Santos Neves, Miguel (eds), *Europe, China and the Two SARS* (New York: St Martins Press, 2000).

Chan, Gerald, 'China's Compliance Diplomacy in Arms Control and Non-Proliferation', Department of Government and International Studies, Hong Kong Baptist University, GIS Working Paper No. 8 (May 2005), 1–31.

China Quarterly, 'China and Europe since 1978. A European Perspective', Special issue, No. 169 (March 2002).

Dejean de la Batie, Herve, 'La Politique Chinoise de l'Union Européenne', *IFRI Centre Asie*, Policy Papers No. 1 (2002).

European Commission, *China, Country Strategy Paper*, Commission Working Document (2002). Brussels: European Commission.

European Commission, *National Indicative Programme 2005–2006, China*, Commission Working Document (2004). Brussels: European Commission.

European Commission, *Competition and Partnership: a Policy Paper on EU–China Trade and Investment*, Commission Working Document, 24 October 2006. Brussels: European Commission.

Freeman, Duncan, 'Europe and Hong Kong: Challenges in an Evolving Relationship', *European Policy Centre*, Brussels, Issue Paper No. 25 (February 2005).

Godement, François, 'La Relation Chine–Europe et ses implications strategiques', *Centre Asie IFRI*, March 2005.

Gosset, David, 'China and Europe: Toward a Meaningful Relationship', *Perspectives*, 3(7) (2005).

Griese, Olaf, 'L'Union Europeenne et la Chine: une normalization par le commerce?', in D. Helly and F. Petiteville, *L'Union Europeenne Acteur International* (Paris: L'Harmattan, 2005).

Human Rights in China, *Behind Closed Doors: Bilateral Dialogues on Human Right*, Hong Kong (2004).

Moller, Kay, 'Diplomatic Relations and Mutual Strategic Perceptions: China and the European Union', *China Quarterly*, 169 (March 2002), 10–32.

Shambaugh, David, 'European and American Approaches to China: Different Beds, Same Dreams?', Sigur Center for Asian Studies, the George Washington University, Asia Papers No. 15 (March 2002).

Shambaugh, David, 'China and Europe: The Emerging Axis', *Current History* (September 2004), 243–8.

Shambaugh, David, 'Lifting the EU Arms Embargo on China: An American Perspective', Discussion Paper prepared for the CSIS/SWP Conference, *China Rise: Diverging US–EU Approaches and Perceptions*, Berlin, 28–9 April 2005.

Shao, Cheng Tang, 'The EU's Policy towards China and the Arms Embargo', *Asia–Europe Journal*, 3(3) (October 2005), 313–21.

8
China's Strategic Thinking: The Role of the European Union
Ting Wai

Introduction: realism and idealism in Chinese foreign policies after the end of the Cold War

Ever since the end of the Cold War, China has been wishing for a more peaceful security environment, so that it could concentrate its energies on the modernization of the nation. In the early 1990s, Chinese strategic analysts gave a somewhat rosy picture of the future international community, which was determined by the phenomenon of *yichao duoqiang*, a phrase which means that the future international political order would be determined by the existence of one superpower with a number of great powers. The capabilities of these great powers, which are not global powers but only regional powers, cannot match that of the sole superpower, the United States (US). However, the superpower is not able to monopolize world issues, and it needs the assistance of those regional powers to maintain order in the various regions of the world. Moreover, Chinese analysts were quite optimistic about the future of warfare, as they predicted that no world wars would occur in future, while limited (*jubu*) wars, which are limited to a region or civil wars, would still be numerous.

However, from the late 1990s, Chinese leaders and scholars began to complain about the border security environment of China. After the end of the Cold War, there were only two major outstanding items relating to external relations in the foreign policy agenda of the Chinese government – namely the Taiwan issue, which is in any case considered not as a foreign policy issue but rather as a domestic issue of China, and the sovereignty of the archipelagos in the South China Sea. Beijing wants to concentrate its energies on these two major issues, which are regarded as the 'primary contradiction' in the Chinese Marxist terminology. All the other issues should be regarded as of secondary importance. Geopolitically speaking, China wishes to maintain stability in all of its border regions, so that it can concentrate only on the southeastern part of China. However, things did not turn out as the Chinese leaders hoped, and China is now burdened with many challenges along its long borders.

In the northeastern part of China, the Beijing government started to experience troubles in its relationship with the North Korean regime after the advent to power of Kim Jong II. Since 1994 the latter, through a number of brinkmanship activities, has deliberately provoked a number of crises. The US–North Korean Agreed Framework, signed in October 1994, provided only a temporary solution to the North Korean nuclear issue. Faced by the hawkish attitude of the Bush administration, from 2002 the nuclear issue was re-ignited with the reopening of the heavy-water reactors closed down in 1994 and the alleged project to enrich uranium with the assistance of Pakistan. Though North Korea is labelled by the US as a member of the 'axis of evil' with Iraq and Iran, the communist regime has not succumbed to the pressure of the US. Rather the opposite; it has adopted a very high-profile approach facing the strong rhetoric of the neo-conservatives in the Bush administration and has continued its own plan of nuclear development, in the hope of getting the maximum benefits possible in any future diplomatic 'exchanges' (Ting, 2003, pp. 99–120).

It is always stipulated in the West that China could still play a pivotal role in the Korean Peninsula crisis, as it continues to exert some influence on the North Korean regime, which is a long-term ally of China. However, though China still aspires to play the role as a 'middleman' between North Korea and the West, and it is still able to do so at present, what North Korea wants to achieve is to deal directly with the US and Japan through launching the crises. As a consequence, the intermediary role played by China is no longer fundamental to the future solution of the crisis. China is still instrumental in bringing the countries concerned together in convening the six-party talks, but it has no particular leverage in bringing the opponent parties to a consensus. What China could do is thus very limited. In addition, if North Korea is equipped with nuclear weapons, as some American strategic analysts assert, then it may already have six to eight atomic bombs, which is really a nightmare also for China (Kristof, 2005, p. 8; Shaplen and Laney, 2005, p. 8). The North Korean bombs would certainly trigger South Korea and even Japan into fabricating nuclear weapons, especially the latter, which has already accumulated tons of plutonium and is able to produce nuclear bombs within a very short time. This is what strategists call the 'recessed deterrence'. Possession of nuclear arms by these regional powers that are democratic and remain loyal allies of the US is regarded as detrimental to Chinese interest.

On the southwestern border of China, Beijing could not enjoy tranquility either. China always has a long-term 'friend', Pakistan, that serves as a kind of buffer against the ambitious and rising regional power, India. However, after the explosions of nuclear weapons by these two countries in May 1998, China started to lament about the worsening of security environment in this region. The high official responsible for arms control within the Chinese Ministry of Foreign Affairs, Sha Zukang,[1] complained in 1999 that the Chinese security environment had worsened, not improved, since the end of the Cold War, as it was now surrounded by nuclear states. Though Indian officials pointed at China as potential enemy number one, China's wish to maintain stability along the border regions causes it to adopt a more reconciliatory attitude vis-à-vis India. Interestingly, relations between India and China, and also between India and Pakistan, have improved since 1998. The Chinese geopolitical calculus towards South Asia and Central Asia was to cultivate a peaceful South Asia and to build up a better relationship with the Muslim states in Central Asia, which are crucial for China's future energy supplies. Unfortunately, as a result of the September 11 incident, the Bush administration succeeded in penetrating into Central Asia by establishing bases there for US military actions against the Taliban in Afghanistan. The US even succeeded both in convincing Pakistani President Musharaff to align with it in combating terrorism and in establishing an even better relationship with India, which always maintains that the relationship between the richest and largest democratic states should be excellent. So Central Asia, which originally was considered as a kind of 'power vacuum', has become a sphere of influence of the US.

China is dragged by the North Koreans in the northeast and is under 'check and balance' by US forces in the southwest. But even the northwestern part of China is not particularly peaceful, as the Uighur separatist movement is still active in the vast Xinjiang province, where the separatists want to establish a new state, Eastern Turkistan, of which the exile government headquarters is found in the US. Though China has already conducted joint military exercises with some states in Central Asia in fighting against terrorism in this region, and has secured the endorsement of the US that the Eastern Turkistan Movement is a terrorist association, China indeed feels that it is under the pressure imposed by 'containment' and 'engagement' of the US from different directions, so that it could not feel free to concentrate its efforts against Taiwan and the neighbouring states with which it has sovereignty conflicts.

Facing this unfavourable external environment, China's room for manoeuvre is under serious constraints. In order to ameliorate the situation so as to create the best atmosphere for its development, China seeks to appease its neighbours, by providing them with benefits arising from China's phenomenal rates of economic growth, and by assuring them that China will never become a hegemony that poses a threat to the others. In order to break through the geopolitical constraints imposed by this unfavourable external environment, China has sought to advance its relationship with the countries of ASEAN (the Association of South-East Asian Nations) by constructing a free trade area by the year 2010. At the same time, China has also attempted to develop its relationship with Europe, in order to achieve a 'breakthrough' when faced with the challenges of the US–Japan alliance. These ideas reflect the realist approach in Chinese foreign policies in counterbalancing the forces that are sceptical about China's rise, and to ensure that despite the not-so-favourable external environment, China could still continue to enhance its economic and military capabilities.

The above analysis, which is realist in nature, reflects only one aspect of Chinese foreign policies. What is interesting is that there also exists a normative aspect, which shows Chinese thinking in promoting a more just and righteous international political order. The best synopsis of such thinking was given by President Hu Jintao during his visit to Moscow in May 2003, where he proposed five points for the establishment of a just and reasonable international political and economic order. These include:

1. promoting the democratization of international relations;
2. maintaining and respecting the plurality of the world;
3. establishing a new security view basing on mutual trust, mutual benefits, equality and collaboration;
4. promoting the balanced development of world economy;
5. respecting and promoting the functions of the United Nations and its Security Council. (Meng, 2004, p. 112)

These five points can be considered as the basic framework of Chinese ideas on the new international political order, especially in this era when the international order is dominated by the unilateralism proposed by the neo-conservatives in the US government. In terms of strategy, China is willing to be integrated into the international system, and to play the role of a responsible power aiming to reform the international political and economic order. China has been stressing the importance of the revision and transformation of international institutions and regimes. In making these normative ideas more concrete, Chinese scholars specializing in researching the rise of powers propose six crucial points for China to consider in the construction of the new international order:

1. The foundations for China in order to participate actively in the construction of new international order are the increase in power and promotion of interests of China. Only through the increase in power could China work better and become an influential figure in shaping the future of the international community.
2. China should stress the ideational factor in the construction of the international political order. If international order is the result of 'distribution of ideas', then China should contribute more to the ideas of such an order. Apart from the five basic points proposed by Hu, it is stipulated that the competition and conflicts among nation-states should be resolved by mutual cooperation and collaboration.
3. China insists on the significant effects of international institutions in the future international political order. The construction of 'righteous' international norms should be the right channel in the future creation of international institutions and regimes.
4. China emphasizes the significance and functions of the United Nations. The ideals of this foundation of the system of international norms for the United Nations are valid and righteous, but the United Nations has always been suffering from some limitations, such as the dominant role of great powers in determining the functions and agenda of the United Nations. So the United Nations should think of how to promote the participation of smaller nations, to help implementing the democratization of international relations, and to be more effective in solving the global problems.
5. Starting from the mid-1990s, China accepts the idea of regionalization, and wishes to participate in the formation of an East Asian regional order. This is considered as the foundation for China for the future development of a new international political and economic order. The active participation of China in the ASEAN-plus-one process so as to facilitate mutual benefits and to share the experience of economic development is considered as an asset that is helping to

raise the profile of China in the future construction of regional order and international order.
6. China should act as a responsible great power and be willing to share the responsibility to shape the future of international political order. China should build up a positive image in maintaining the so-called 'international morality' in international relations. China hopefully can transform itself from an influential regional power to a global power, albeit not in the near future, and to promote peace and stability in the international community. (Meng, 2004, pp. 115–19)

On the one hand, the *realpolitik* in the thinking of Chinese diplomacy facing the unfavourable external environment determines that China has to appease the neighbours, while at the same time seeking friendly relationships in other continents, especially with the very influential and potential global actor, Europe. It is even said that a Europe–China axis is currently being formed to confront the US–Japan alliance (Johnson, 2005). On the other hand, the idealism in Chinese foreign policy determines that Beijing seeks to establish a new international political and economic order that reflect China's ideas and visions. According to Chinese scholars who are specialists in European Union (EU) studies, the EU has different views from the US regarding the future of the international order, but these are close to Chinese thinking. The decision-making process of the EU 'emphasizes on common interests, sharing of power, and abiding by the restrictive common rules of the games', and the EU favours 'multilateralism' in solving the problems of international affairs (Feng, 2002, pp. 58–60). Therefore from both the realist and idealist points of view in understanding Chinese foreign policy, Europe, and more precisely the EU, is considered as a major actor/partner in the formulation of a new order in the thinking of Chinese leaders. However, it should also be noted that though China appears to be favourable to the international role and responsibility of the EU, Chinese leaders and analysts are still sceptical about the eventual goal of Europeans in 'westernizing' and 'transforming' China. This ideological burden is a heritage of the 1989 Tiananmen incident, after which the western powers, especially the US, were accused of sabotaging and transforming the Chinese communist regime by the alleged 'peaceful evolution'. Though due to the rapid growth of the market economy and the corresponding massive transformation of the Chinese society, the ideological factor plays less of a role in China's relations with the outside world today, this is nevertheless a factor that still needs to be taken into consideration, as can be seen from the numerous writings of Chinese scholars.

China–EU relations: economic and financial aspects

China has been undergoing tremendous economic growth since the beginning of the open door and reform policy in late 1978. The average annual growth since that time has reached 9.4 per cent. The total trade volume was worth US$1,422 billion in 2005, equating to an average annual growth of 16 per cent since the beginning of the open and reform policy in 1979, while the foreign currency reserves exceeded US$1,066 billion as at the end of 2006.[2] The number of people living below subsistence level reached 26 million, in comparison to 250 million in 1978.[3]

In 2004 China became the world's third largest trader and in 2002 became the largest recipient of foreign direct investment (FDI) in the world. Since 2004, Europe has become China's first trading partner, while in 2003 the EU ranked only third. For the EU, China has become the second largest trading partner, just behind the USA, since 2002. In 2005, China's trade with the EU amounted to US$227.5 billion, in comparison to US$212.3 billion with the USA, and US$184.6 billion with Japan (International Monetary Fund, 2006, pp. 133–5). For the EU, this means an increase of 28.2 per cent, for the USA, 25.0 per cent, and for Japan, 9.9 per cent from the previous year. The increase from 2003 to 2004 was more remarkable. For the EU, the increase is 41.4 per cent in relation to 2003, while for the USA, the increase is 34.3 per cent, and for Japan it is 25.6 per cent (Johnson, 2005, p. 2). From 2002 to 2003, the increase in EU–China trade was 44.4 per cent, US–China trade 29.9 per cent, and Japan–China trade, 30.9 per cent. Trade figures between China and the EU, US and Japan are shown in Tables 8.1–8.3.

From Table 8.3, it is clear that the volume of China's total trade with the EU has tripled between 2000 and 2005. China's exports have surged significantly, with an increase of 253 per cent from 2000 to 2005, while China's imports also increased by 140 per cent during the same period. The increases in EU–China trade are consistently faster than the increases in US–China and Japan–China trade. In the first three months of 2005 alone, the value of total trade between the EU and China amounts to US$65.2 billion, which marks an increase of 25.2 per cent over the same period in 2004. As a comparison, US–China trade in the same period reached US$61.3 billion, an increase of 24 per cent; Japan–China trade reached US$57.5 billion, an increase of 10.9 per cent (*Hong Kong Economic Journal*, 14 May 2005, p. 6). The continuous increase in EU–China trade is considered by the Chinese authorities as epitomizing the better relationship between the EU and China.

Regarding the EU's FDI into China, up to the end of 2005, the number of projects invested by the members of the EU had reached 21,427, and the actual value of investments amounted to US$47.3 billion. In the year 2005 alone the EU invested in 2,846 projects, with the actual value of investments amounting to US$5.2 billion (Qiu, 2004; *China Commercial Yearbook*, since 2004). Yet the total number of EU projects still only constituted 3.87 per cent of the total FDI that China has absorbed since 1979, while the US represents 8.86 per cent, and Japan, 6.35 per cent

Table 8.1 China's trade statistics – exports (in US$ billion)

	China's exports to		
Year	EU	US	Japan
2005	143.9	163.3	84.1
2004	107.3	125.1	73.5
2003	72.2	92.6	59.4
2002	48.2	70.1	48.5
2001	41.0	54.4	45.1
2000	38.2	52.2	41.7
1999	30.3	42.0	32.4
1998	28.2	38.0	29.7
1997	23.9	32.7	31.8

Source: *Direction of Trade Statistics Yearbook*, International Monetary Fund (2004, 2005, 2006).

Table 8.2 China's trade statistics – imports (in US$ billion)

	China's imports from		
Year	EU	US	Japan
2005	73.6	49.0	100.5
2004	70.1	44.8	94.4
2003	53.1	33.9	74.2
2002	38.6	27.3	53.5
2001	35.8	26.2	42.8
2000	29.8	21.7	40.1
1999	25.5	19.5	33.8
1998	20.7	17.0	28.3
1997	19.2	16.3	29.0

Source: *Direction of Trade Statistics Yearbook*, International Monetary Fund (2004, 2005, 2006).

(Qiu, 2004; *China Commercial Yearbook*, since 2004). There is still a long way to go for the EU to catch up with the performance of the US and Japan. The comparison among the Western triad's investments in China can be seen from Table 8.4, which is compiled based on the statistics given by Chinese authorities.

It is interesting to note that in terms of the number of projects, the EU still lags behind the US and Japan; moreover, the increase in FDI can only be noted since the late 1990s. However, the total value of investment is usually large and is comparable to that of the US and Japan, which means that the value of the average EU project is larger than the others (Song, 2001, pp. 24–7). The investment per project appears to be more significant, which can be explained by the fact that the Europeans are willing to invest high value-added projects in China, and seem to be more willing to transfer the relatively advanced technology badly needed in China, such as investing in the automobile, telecommunications and medical industries. This is the basic reason why the Chinese are more receptive to European investments, which contain higher value and more technology. From a realist point of view, this is beneficial to developing the Chinese economic capabilities. From an idealist point of view, more and more enterprises, including particularly small and medium-sized enterprises, attracted to China would certainly become a linkage for fostering closer cooperation and mutual understanding between China and the European continent.

In strengthening the economic and political cooperation to reach the status of 'comprehensive strategic partnership' as proclaimed by

Table 8.3 China's total trade with the Western Triad (in US$ billion)

Year	EU	US	Japan
2005	227.5	212.3	184.6
2004	177.4	169.9	167.9
2003	125.3	126.5	133.6
2002	86.8	97.4	102.0
2001	76.8	80.6	87.9
2000	68.0	73.9	81.8
1999	55.8	61.5	66.2
1998	48.9	55.0	58.0
1997	43.1	49.0	60.8

Source: *Direction of Trade Statistics Yearbook*, International Monetary Fund (2004, 2005, 2006).

Table 8.4 Investments of the EU, US and Japan in China

			Accumulated						
Year	No. of projects			Pledged value of investment*			Actual value of investment*		
	EU	US	Japan	EU	US	Japan	EU	US	Japan
2005	21,427	49,006	35,124				47.3	51.1	53.9
2004	18,581	45,265	31,855	74.3	98.6	66.7	42.1	48.0	46.9
2003	16,158	41,340	28,401	66.0	86.4	57.4	37.9	44.1	41.4
2002	14,084	37,268	25,147	60.0	76.3	49.5	33.9	40.2	36.3
2001	12,598	33,905	22,402	55.6	68.1	44.2	30.2	34.9	32.1
2000	11,384	31,181	20,352	50.4	60.3	38.7	26.1	30.2	27.8
1999	10,207	28,628	18,738	40.6	52.4	35.0	21.9	25.8	24.9
1998	9,330	26,581	17,602	36.4	46.3	32.5	17.4	21.4	21.9
1997		24,366	16,404		40.1	29.8		17.5	18.5
1996		22,100	14,991		35.7	26.4		13.7	14.2
1995		over 19,600	13,257		28.8	21.8		10.2	10.7

			by year						
Year	No. of projects			Pledged value of investment*			Actual value of investment*		
	EU	US	Japan	EU	US	Japan	EU	US	Japan
2003	2,074	4,060	3,254	5.9	10.2	8.0	3.9	4.2	5.1
2002	1,486	3,363	2,745	4.5	8.2	5.3	3.7	5.4	4.2
2001	1,214	2,594	2,019	5.2	7.5	5.4	4.2	4.9	4.3
2000	1,130	2,553	1,614	8.9	7.9	3.7	4.5	4.4	2.9
1999	877	2,047	1,136	4.2	6.1	2.5	4.5	4.4	3.0
1998	994	2,215	1,198	5.9	6.2	2.7	4.3	3.9	3.4
1997	834	2,166	1,402	4.2	4.9	3.4	4.2	3.2	4.3
1996	1,167	2,517	1,742	6.8	6.9	5.1	2.7	3.4	3.7
1995	1,582	3,372	2,935	7.4	8.1	7.6	2.1	2.5	3.1
1994									
1993	1,543	6,750	3,488	3.0	6.8	3.0	0.6	2.1	1.3

Note: *Billions of US dollars.
Source: Yearbook of China's Foreign Economic Relations and Trade (Beijing: China Foreign Economic Relations and Trade, consecutive years), and China Commercial Yearbook since 2004.

the Chinese Premier, Wen Jiabao,[4] the EU and China have instituted several projects recently. The first major project is the Galileo global satellite navigation cooperation agreement, to which China has pledged to contribute 2 billion euros. This Sino-European system is definitely designed to produce an alternative to the GSP system produced by the US which, to date, is the only system used all over the world. A global satellite navigation system technology training centre has been established in Beijing. The Americans are afraid that this system can be used against American satellites. In fact, China has already launched its own satellite navigation system called Compass. Altogether four satellites of Compass have already been launched, and by 2008 they should satisfy the demand of China and the surrounding areas. By the year 2011, the system would become a global navigation system that will significantly enhance the capability of the People's Liberation Army (PLA) to carry out precision attacks. It is believed that the Chinese navigation system has incorporated technology and engineering data from European sources (Ge, 2007, p. A28).

In February 2004, during the EU–China Summit, a memorandum was signed on 'tourist destination status' that facilitates the travel of Chinese tourists in Europe. Most of the countries within the EU are granted 'Authorized Destination Status' so that they could receive Chinese tourists. In addition, the EU and China did agree during the sixth Summit to establish a dialogue on environmental protection. This is a major concern of the Europeans who are keen to help China to address the challenges regarding sustainable development.

Another controversial issue in EU–China economic relations is the massive increase in Chinese exports of textile products into the European market, after the abolition of the global quota scheme on 1 January 2005, a concrete result of the Uruguay Round of multilateral trade negotiations more than a decade ago. Just a few months after the quotas were abolished, both the EU and the US envisaged methods to limit the inflow of Chinese clothing. The US decided to disallow the import of three categories of textile products since May 2005, causing widespread dissatisfaction amongst Chinese manufacturers.[5] For the EU, the Trade Commissioner Peter Mandelson started an inquiry into nine categories of textiles in April 2005, after Chinese imports in these categories in the first three months of 2005 had increased variously from 51 per cent to 534 per cent over the same period in 2004.[6]

US and EU measures attempting to restrict Chinese exports of textile products aroused severe rebukes from the Chinese government. Both the US and the EU have long been promoting the idea of free trade, but when their own interests are affected, they return to protectionist measures and disregard the norms and regulations of the World Trade Organization (WTO). In fact, in December 2004, the Chinese Ministry of Commerce did launch eight measures to limit the over-growth of Chinese textile exports, including imposing export duties, directing the enterprises to export to order, and promoting self-discipline within the industry (*Ta Kung Pao*, 27 April 2005, p. A19). China warned the EU that an inquiry to the exports of Chinese textile products that would lead to special restrictions is contradictory to the rules of WTO and detrimental to the bilateral trading relationship. Chinese Minister of Commerce Bo Xilai even said that in international commerce, double standards should not be adopted. It is hypocritical to talk about free trade when one's products have a competitive edge in the world market, while restricting those few products from the developing countries that have a competitive edge in comparison to the same products of the developed world.[7] The clothing and textile industries in both Europe and USA have long been defended by protectionist measures, and have not really tried to improve their competitiveness in the last decade by equipping themselves with state-of-the-art technology or by lowering labour costs, while China does excel in improving the productivity of its textile industry.[8] Despite all these sound counter-arguments pronounced by the Chinese government, evidently a large-scale trade war would not result, given the stable political relations and mutually beneficial economic relations between the EU and China.

The confrontation between the EU and China over the massive imports of Chinese textiles products to Europe in 2005 resulted in the spectacular increase of export tariffs by the Chinese authorities for 74 types of products, starting from 1 June 2005 (*Ta Kung Pao*, 21 May 2005, p. A4). Export tariffs for some textile products were increased by as much as five times (Chen, 2005, p. B4). However, following the indifferent attitude of the EU in the face of this conciliatory move of China, Bo Xilai suddenly announced the abolishment of export tariffs for 81 products on 30 May 2005, in order to show his discontent towards the 'unfair' attitude of the EU (*Ta Kung Pao*, 31 May 2005, p. A1). This triggered a rapid response from the EU, and the resulting negotiation arrived at a 'win–win' situation that catered for the needs of both parties. For ten products, both sides agreed to allow an annual increase of 8 to 12.5 per cent, with the basis of calculation being from April 2004 to March 2005 for nine products, and March 2004 to February 2005 for another product (*Ta Kung Pao*, 16 June 2005, p. A14). This is clearly beneficial to China as it takes into consideration the rapid increase in imports in the first three months of 2005 and takes this as the basis for future increases. The compromise also satisfies the EU as it limits the increases of Chinese products until 2008. China claims this agreement as a model for the reconciliation of interests as the EU does not take unilateral actions, but always tries to solve the problems in a compromising attitude. Since the agreement was valid only from 12 July 2005, before that date 80 million textile items had accumulated in the European customs offices. The EU and China had to negotiate again and in September 2005 they agreed on using the quota of 2006 for some products while for other products they would transfer the quota from other products (*Ta Kung Pao*, 6 September 2005, p. A2). Though China had to make a sacrifice and allow the control of textile products by quota, it praised the goodwill of the EU in allowing China to export more.

Although a trade war may seem unlikely, Chinese experts still express their serious concerns about the 'protectionist tendencies' of the EU. In 2006, Chinese-fabricated shoes suffered from a 16 per cent 'anti-dumping tax' imposed by the EU for two years (*Ta Kung Pao*, 1 November 2005, p. A29). In its document on EU–China relations issued in October 2006, the European Commission insisted that 'Europe should continue to offer open and fair access to China's exports and to adjust to the competitive challenge... China for its part should reciprocate by strengthening its commitment to open markets and fair competition' (European Commission, 2006, p. 7). But it also stressed that 'trade defence measures will remain an instrument to ensure fair conditions of trade' (European Commission, 2006, p. 8). That is to say, the EU's openness to Chinese products is subject to whether the Chinese market is 'open enough' for European products. This caused severe criticisms from Chinese analysts, who explicitly pointed out that this condition is only a pretext for trade protectionism (Lu, 2006, p. A29). For the Europeans, fair trade is always more important than free trade.

To date China is not satisfied with the EU's reluctance to grant 'market economy status' to China, even though that status has been granted to Russia and Ukraine, whose market economies are far less perfect than that of China. The double standard adopted is seen as a kind of discrimination against China. Even though this 'market economy status' will eventually be granted to China, Chinese analysts are keen to point out that in future while conventional protectionist measures such as tariffs, quota, anti-dumping and so on would cease to be effective, new kinds of barriers such as 'technology barriers' will certainly be imposed. These barriers include environment standards, hygienic standards, security standards, and so on, which would become very effective in restricting imports from China. There even exists a 'New Commercial Policy Instrument' in the trade policy of the EU that can be used by the EU in order to get rid of negative influences to the European market caused by the trading measures of another country (Dai, 2005, pp. 79, 82). In its 2003 EU Policy

Paper, China urged the EU to grant 'market economy status' to China, to reduce and eventually abolish the discriminatory measures, such as antidumping, and to compensate for China's losses in commercial interests due to the enlargement of the EU.[9] However, from the EU side, it is hoped that the conclusion of a new 'Partnership and Cooperation Agreement (PCA)' with China would help in addressing the trade and investment issues through a more balanced approach (European Commission, 2006, p. 14).

So from the realist perspective, the EU and China may have some minor problems regarding trade, but these will remain secondary in comparison to their common wish to develop multilateralism in the international political order against the unilateralism of the US. However, it is no exaggeration to say that ideology still plays a role in the Chinese conception of bilateral relations, as the Chinese are still perplexed by the western attempts to transform China. This is why when the EU does put pressure on China concerning human rights issues and political reform, China seems to react – but never wholeheartedly.

Embracing or resisting westernization: social and cultural implications

Though Chinese analysts have praised the evolution of EU–China relations, especially in recent years, not only regarding the substantial benefits rendered to China, but also on the positive effects of such cooperation on the equilibrium within the international order, they also express concern over the 'hidden agenda' of the Europeans. Returning to all the documents of the European Commission on strengthening relations with China, the five aims for EU–China relations are always reiterated in each document:

1. Engaging China further, through an upgraded political dialogue, in the international community;
2. Supporting China's transition to an open society based upon the rule of law and the respect for human rights;
3. Integrating China further in the world economy by bringing it more fully into the world trading system and by supporting the process of economic and social reform underway in the country, including in the context of sustainable development;
4. Making better use of existing European resources;
5. Raising the EU's profile in China. (European Commission, 1998)

The last two items are of lesser importance, while the first three aims reflect the basic policy of the EU. However, Chinese scholars point out that these three aims also reflect the attitude of the Europeans in attempting to transform China according to the value system of the Europeans. This is basically the posture of a 'teacher' (Dai, 2005, p. 77). Another scholar indicates that the Europeans still possess the mentality of a 'saviour' facing the 'backward' Asian nations:

> It is difficult to eliminate the unequal cultural factor in Asia-Europe relations. Europe still insists that western culture, value system and social institutions should be the future direction for change of the non-western nations and regions. Europe always gives the image as 'saviour' facing the Asians, and the donations, economic assistance and humanitarian aid usually carry political conditions... (Yu, 2002, pp. 36–9, 44)

The EU and China have been engaged in a regular series of dialogues on human rights since 1997. It is envisaged by the European Commission that this can help through 'improving the human rights situation on the ground by encouraging China to respect and promote human rights and fundamental freedoms and to cooperate with international human rights mechanisms' (European Commission, 2001, p. 10). The form of dialogue is considered as a progress by Chinese analysts, as now the EU tends to treat China as a real partner on equal basis. This is contrary to the past, since from 1990 to 1996 the EU always tried to condemn China during the annual meeting of the United Nations Human Rights Committee (UNHRC) at Geneva. The human rights dialogue is seen by China as a recognition and access to respectability, whereas the EU intends to use the process of dialogue to narrow down their divergences and convince China to resolve their conflicts on human rights issues. From the EU perspective, it is clear that political and economic interests prevail over the issue of human rights or democratization within China, especially since it will take a long time to ensure improvements in the latter. Using dialogue and cooperation, therefore, is considered as a viable and more discreet solution to which the Chinese appear to be more receptive and which could possibly produce some substantive results (Su, 2002, p. 64).

Nonetheless, Chinese analysts are especially obsessed by the European 'attempts' to 'socialize' China so that it would abide by international norms and to 'teach' China about the issues of human rights, rule of law, and law enforcement. In an earlier work on EU–China relations, it is stressed that

> The European Commission and member governments should expand training opportunities for judges and lawyers, which will not only equip them to use these new economic laws effectively, but also expose them to western legal tradition and practice. This could, in the long run, create a more tolerant human rights environment in China. (Grant, 1995, p. 3)

Training programmes have thus been created to train Chinese legal professionals, including lawyers, judges and police officers according to the western tradition, and to promote better law enforcement. Through actions in China,

> The EC is therefore committed to developing practices and general principles useful for interpreting existing laws and regulations within expected bounds, offering a sense of fairness and of justice. In this respect, the EC should focus particularly on supporting the ability to interpret laws on the part of the judiciary. Legislative reforms supporting the judiciary are key, as is the regularization of procedures and review of administrative law and practice. (European Commission, 2002, pp. 28–9)

> The EC's action should also focus on efforts to strengthen understanding of law and legal processes by citizens and various levels of officials, particularly locally and provincially, to make sue that law is applied consistently around the country. (European Commission, 2002, p. 29)

In the document 'EU Strategy Towards China', issued in May 2001, it is emphasized as an action point that the EU should 'continue implementation and preparation of EU human rights-related assistance programmes addressing the rule and legal reform, economic, social, cultural, civil and political rights and democracy' (European Commission, 2001, pp. 11–12). Though China did not refuse these training programmes, since they could at least help Chinese jurists to learn more about the western legal systems, Chinese leaders are quite skeptical about the European ideas to transform China or 'westernize' China.

One authoritative account of EU–China relations, indeed, emphasized that 'the international functions of the EU have a dual character. Actively promoting multilateralism and external adventurous intervention coexist. It should not be considered as a 'moral model' in international relations' (Huo, 2005, p. 4). Political integration within the EU lags behind economic integration and its international influence also lags behind EU's comprehensive economic power. That is to say, the external actions of the EU are still very much determined by the great powers within the EU, especially the United Kingdom, France and Germany. It is stipulated that the 'humanitarian intervention' carried out by France and Britain following the USA in Kosovo, and the intervention in the presidential election in Ukraine still reflect the influence of the great powers and their attempt to transform the 'non-western' states. The same article stresses that though in the China policy of the EU, 'the strategic and economic considerations are still more important than ideology, it has never abolished the attempts to 'westernize' China or 'divide' China' (Huo, 2005, p. 4). The EU is only using 'supporting China's transition to an open society based upon the rule of law and the respect for democracy' as a pretext. The ultimate goal is to push China to receive western ideology. While the EU since 1997 has used human rights dialogue to engage China, rather than using confrontation, 'the original idea of the EU to make use of human rights issue to influence and transform China has not been changed' (Huo, 2005, p. 4).

Although the rule of law and human rights are supreme values that must be defended by the EU and promoted to China, one should not forget that China is still under the so-called one-party dictatorship and that the 'state apparatus' like police and judges are all instruments of the governing Chinese Communist Party to exercise its rule. There is no judicial independence in China as the verdict of the court has to abide by what the party committee and party secretary of the court have decided. Without major political reforms, the uses of these EU programmes on law enforcement and human rights are doubtful in the short run, but, optimistically speaking, they might be useful in the long run, as more liberal-minded jurists would then become more receptive to western ideas and thus become more favourable towards political and legal reform.

The usefulness of the EU's concern over China joining the two covenants on human rights is similarly questionable. China did sign the 'International Covenant for Social, Economic and Cultural Rights' (ICSCCR) in October 1997, and the 'International Covenant for Civil and Political Rights' (ICCPR) in October 1998, creating a worldwide hope that China would eventually abide by the two international agreements in regard the protection of human rights within the nation. However, although the first document was ratified by the National People's Congress (NPC) in March 2001, the second one, which is obviously more important, has not yet been ratified. The EU apparently is not satisfied with the human rights conditions in China. The *Laogai* (re-education through forced labour) still exists and is deemed to be offending human rights. Freedom of expression, religion and association are not guaranteed, and, as highlighted by the EU, 'a significant gap still exists between the current human rights situation in China and internationally accepted standards' (European Commission, 2003, p. 12). China signed the ICCPR in order to show that it is committed to 'join the world' and abide by international norms in human rights. But China's much-delayed ratification denotes that it is not yet ready to fully accept all the norms that are of 'international accepted standards'. What the EU could do is rather limited, though it is emphasized that 'it is clear that dialogue is an acceptable option only if progress is achieved on the ground' (European Commission, 2001, p. 11). The EU has been using the dialogue as a method, a low-profile approach taking into consideration the dignity and pride of the Chinese nation, to encourage China to improve human rights conditions (Zhu and Zhang, 2002, pp. 87–90; European Commission, 2006, p. 13). This seems to be not very successful, and the EU needs to think of an even more subtle way to apply pressure to China in this regard.

Political and strategic perspectives

China has been undergoing a series of changes in its perceptions of the outside world and their implications for its domestic development. Just after the end of the Cold War, China still suffered from political and economic sanctions imposed by the West due to the 1989 incident. It desperately wanted to have a breakthrough in the sanctions and found that European states were not as staunch as the US in maintaining those measures against the interests of China, despite some setbacks, such as the French sale of 60 Mirage fighters to Taiwan in 1992. During the crises across the Taiwan Strait in summer 1995 and March 1996, China tested its missiles directed against Taiwan. It was the period when China showed rather strong nationalist and irredentist sentiments, epitomized in a book called *China Can Say No!* However, the Chinese economy continued to grow and from the late 1990s onwards serious debates on the so-called 'rise' of China started. Though China was still not very rich, China's eventual rise to a status of power was no longer questionable. When China became a 'power', it tended to acquire a better appreciation of the positions of other powers regarding some strategic issues, for instance, it seemed to appreciate better why the US forbids other countries to export weapons of mass destruction (WMD) and why it is so keen on the non-proliferation of WMD and missile technology. As a result, China appears to be more prudent in exporting the relevant technologies and the strategic materials starting from the new century, and accordingly passed a series of laws in 2002 and 2003 on export control and non-proliferation.

The (potential) acquisition of 'great power status' also enforces Chinese analysts to think about how to act and live peacefully with its neighbours. Starting from the late 1990s, China has been conscious of the question whether China does have any soft power (culture, values, institutions and ideologies), when it is clear that China's hard power (economic and military capabilities) is increasing at a tremendous rate. Indeed, Chinese scholars are perplexed by the lack of soft power in comparison to other powers, as China could not well develop since the Opium War due to the humiliations imposed by imperialists and numerous wars. It was only in the last two decades of the twentieth century that China had a peaceful development. A country possessing hard power but not soft power appears awful in the eyes of the neighbouring countries. So starting from late 1990s, China has been anxious about 'cultivating' its soft power. The above-mentioned ideational component of foreign policy may be regarded as an aspect of soft power. Beijing would like to promote its ideas of peaceful coexistence, mutual non-intervention, respect of sovereignty, cooperation and consensus of countries in litigation, and settling international disputes by diplomatic means etc., hoping that more nation-states would abide by these norms. China aims to create international norms and international institutions that can reflect these 'Chinese ideas', such as the creation of the 'Shanghai Cooperation Organization', with the participation of four Central Asian states plus Russia.

Facing the unilateralism of the Bush administration, which also supports the rearmament of Japan and is willing to have Japan share more global responsibilities, China finds it necessary to counterbalance the strengthened US–Japan alliance, and it turns to Europe. It is because Europe's ideas about maintaining a peaceful international order are somewhat similar to Chinese thinking, as a prominent Chinese specialist argues:

> In the international political arena, the EU is trying to gradually become a leading force that is radically different from the US which is seeking a status of world hegemony. Not only does the EU want to become the leading force in Europe, it also seeks to reinforce its own style in the world. Their international 'power need' adopts a 'mild model' which is different from the American power politics and

unilateralism. It urges the states to contact, dialogue and cooperate with the others in order to enlarge the consensus and resolve the conflicts, and not to resort to confrontation. In settling the international affairs, the EU puts emphasis on multilateralism, stressing on common interests, distribution of rights and abiding by the restrictive common rules of the games... Europe offers a different model from the US... it pays attention to market economy, but does not allow the market society to develop, in other words, it does not practice the American model of market economy plus market society. (Qiu, 2004)

This quotation is in tune with Chinese scholarly thinking simply because it corresponds to China's views regarding the actions of great powers in the international arena. These common views become the adhesive that brings the two 'poles' together in counterbalancing the unipolar tendency of the US.

Indeed, it is difficult to imagine a world 'dominated' entirely by the US, despite the fact that American presidents are keen on leading the world. A unipolar world is impossible as it implies that all major powers are under the leadership of the United States. However, the scenario as epitomized by Samuel Huntington, of a uni-multipolar world, is likely to come to pass. The superpower is definitely more superior to other powers in terms of military capabilities, but in terms of regional political and economic influence, other regional powers, including especially the EU and China, play a very crucial role. Apart from unilateralism, President George W. Bush also relies on multilateralism at the same time, as reflected by the six-party talks in the resolution of the crisis on the Korean peninsula.

The idea of two poles coming together to counterbalance the most powerful pole has been proposed recently by scholars in China as well as in the West. However, a Chinese scholar, Ye Zicheng, does not think that the idea of 'poles' and multipolarity in the international arena would necessarily lead to peace and stability. A multipolar world can also be a source of conflicts and wars. He maintains that the idea of 'poles' is simply a legacy of the European politics and is a concept of great power politics. Moreover, it is difficult to characterize the world order today, as it is not bipolar as during the Cold War, nor multipolar as in nineteenth-century Europe. Today the relationship between all the great powers and the US has a dual character: there exist conflicts and 'contradictions', but there exists an aspect of cooperation. It is thus difficult to say that these great powers and the US are counterbalancing each other. What is worse, the idea of 'poles' implies a certain degree of 'exclusiveness' or even 'confrontation' (Ye, 2004, pp. 1–29). So, Ye proposes the strategy of 'great power cooperation'. This can reduce the potential 'conflict' between China and the US resulting from China collaborating with the others. In fact, China must also cooperate with the USA in many aspects, even though it is opposed to unilateralism and a unipolar world. The idea of 'great power cooperation' could also reduce the potential conflicts arising from some other countries which aspire to become a pole.

In reality, despite the controversies after the advent to power of President Bush, the Atlantic alliance is still as solid as before, and Sino-European relations cannot be compared easily to US–Europe relations. China–US–Europe is not an equidistant triangle. However, it is in the interests of China to promote great power cooperation, not only with the EU, but also with the US. Obviously, at present the strategic calculation is tilted towards the EU, as China categorically supports Germany becoming a permanent member of the United Nations Security Council (while remaining very hesitant regarding the membership of Japan) and it worked together with France to jointly propose a 'Declaration of ASEM Dialogue on Cultures and Civilizations' during the fifth ASEM Summit Meeting held in Hanoi in October 2004 (Song, 2004, p. A7). China seeks to enlarge its freedom of manoeuvre vis-à-vis the US by attracting the European powers through economic benefits, cultural exchanges, and political cooperation.

One outstanding issue in EU–China strategic relations is the EU embargo on arms sales that was imposed on China after the 1989 Tiananmen incident. Almost two decades later it is still a subject of debate among the members of the EU. France and Germany have been enthusiastic in lifting the embargo, as it might facilitate the selling of their arms to China, thus enabling the two countries to affect the regional balance of power in East Asia, especially regarding the cross-straits relations.

This long-outstanding issue has undergone severe criticism from China. During his visit to The Hague in December 2004 for the seventh EU–China Summit, Premier Wen Jiabao claimed that the embargo was political discrimination against China[10] and that it was outdated because it was a legacy of the Cold War. China thinks that it is a matter of principle, and Chinese spokesmen insist that this is an obstacle to the further development of Sino-EU relations. Indeed, the Chinese government emphasizes that, even after the lifting of the embargo, it 'has no intention or the abilities to buy weapons from the EU'.[11] Though optimistic signs appeared during the Summit, the EU decided that lifting the embargo would be postponed until 2005, as human rights conditions in China were not totally satisfactory. In effect, human rights conditions in China have been used frequently as a pretext; the real problem is the serious opposition of the US.

On the one hand, the US has long been assisting Taiwanese forces in order to maintain a strategic equilibrium across the Taiwan Strait, while China could only buy advanced weapons from Russia, apart from accelerating its own research on the high technology used in advanced weapons. China apparently is not satisfied with having only the Russian source to acquire advanced weapons and weapon technology, as these weapons are not necessarily the most advanced nor are they of top quality. China desperately wants to explore other sources for those advanced weapons, and the only source available is, of course, Europe. If the arms embargo was lifted, a China equipped with European weapons would enjoy a strategic superiority, forcing Taiwan to buy more US weapons to maintain an equilibrium. If Taiwan is not financially capable of doing so, it will be caught in a very difficult position. The US insists that resumption of arms sale by the EU to China would certainly disrupt the balance of power in the Asia-Pacific region, but China counter-argues that it is basically the US that is helping Japan and Taiwan to rearm and affects the equilibrium in this region.

On the other hand, the United States is worried that US technology shared with the European counterparts in their military cooperation would be transferred to China through future arms sales from Europe to China. Lifting the embargo would nevertheless facilitate better cooperation between the EU and China, thus enabling the former to export more to China and deriving more economic benefits (Zhang, 2005, p. A3). The dual-use technology can also be exported from Europe to China, thus providing funding for the European consortiums to undertake research on new military technology. What seems to worry the Americans is a scenario in which US soldiers could be killed in the battlefield by European weapons containing American technology.

Under the British presidency of the EU in the second half of 2005, Premier Tony Blair was unwilling to lift the embargo. After the enactment of China's Taiwan-related 'anti-secession law' by the NPC in March 2005, the optimistic tone about lifting the embargo disappeared. Britain and Sweden lobbied their European partners to postpone the decision to lift the sales embargo and both Italy and Belgium have changed their minds, agreeing to postpone the decision.[12] Austria, which assumed the EU Presidency from the British in January 2006, was similarly not interested to discussing the issue (Tkacik, 2005, p. 15). In contrast to her predecessor, the new German Chancellor, Angela Merkel, explicitly declared that it would not be appropriate to lift the embargo if the human rights record in China has not improved.[13]

Though French President Jacques Chirac was keen to lift the embargo, which according to him means the normalization of relationship with China, it does not mean that the EU would then implement a policy to sell arms to China.[14] China seems to believe that, even after the embargo is lifted, it will be unable to acquire state-of-the-art weapons with the most advanced technology; consequently, China could not rely on imported weapons to facilitate defence modernization. In addition, it is reported that in order to dissipate the worries of the US, the EU would design so-called 'behavioural norms' for the military trade, in order to limit the quality and quantity of the arms sales (Zhang, 2005, p. A4). In fact, lifting the embargo should be linked to the EU policy vis-à-vis Taiwan, which would be a major issue in the Common Foreign and Defense Policy (Cabestan, 2004, p. 8). Do the EU and its member countries think solely in terms of economic benefits? Or would they try to figure out the serious consequences in relation to the stability of the East Asian region? This embargo issue is a test of the 'degree' of the EU's independence from the US. But it is also a test of the position of the EU when facing a potential crisis across the Taiwan Strait. It is interesting to note that Japan is also against the EU lifting the embargo.

In any case, no Chinese analysts really believe that the EU would 'normalize' its arms sales to China, especially regarding the advanced technology. It is alleged that 'the EU seems to have a two-handed policy: to lift the embargo and to strengthen the control on arms sale to China. The EU will simply replace "tangible" discrimination with "intangible" discrimination' (Huo, 2005, p. 3). Though China has hopes of a lifting of the embargo, it does not expect Europe to stand besides China in the case of a crisis on the Taiwan issue. Rather the opposite. In a potential crisis across the Strait and Sino-American confrontation, the Chinese calculus maintains that the EU would not alienate itself from the US.

Concluding remarks

In December 2003, the EU passed its first 'Security Strategy Report', which confirmed that China is one of its major strategic partners. The EU and China agree to cooperate on many global issues, including anti-terrorism, non-proliferation of WMD, environmental changes, money laundering, organized crimes and drug trafficking. During the seventh Summit, held in December 2004, the two parties signed a 'Joint Declaration on Non-Proliferation and Arms Control'. Facing up to these challenges in the international arena – even though on strategic issues and foreign policies the two parties are still having dialogues only – paves the way for future cooperation in foreign affairs and security issues. The EU and China are thinking of negotiating a new framework agreement, so as to concretize the goals and plans of Sino-European cooperation over the next 10 to 15 years (Huang, 2004, p. A2). This will become the legal foundation for the realization of the comprehensive strategic partnership.

This analysis of EU–China relations proceeds at three separate levels. On the one hand, the realist approach shows very clearly that China and Europe share a common interest in developing trade and investment. Both of them want to have a more balanced international order. The issue of arms embargo also reflects the importance of interests; strategic and political interests for China, and economic and strategic interests for the EU. On the other hand, the idealist approach determines that China wishes to develop its soft power, and defines and tries to implement what it thinks will be best for the new international political order. China finds similarities in the European approach and is convinced that itself and the EU should be close strategic partners in the realization of such an international order that replaces confrontation by cooperation, puts heavy emphasis on international institutions and international norms, and uses dialogue and mutual interests to settle the conflicts.

However, China is still obsessed by the ideological factor that both Europe and the US are trying to construct a post-Cold War international system based on western values, despite the inevitable reality that they may have divergences over the way to construct such an international order. Globalization only means the expansion of the capitalist mode of production all over the world. So Europe and the US are bound together by a common ideological foundation (Wu, 2005, pp. 1–16). The main approach of the Americans and Europeans towards China is characterized by the following: 'Would not treat China as a major opponent, but appear to be vigilant towards China's development; Hope to integrate China into the international system, but also anxious that the growing influence of China would be detrimental to their interests' (Xiao, 2001, p. 421). In the eyes of some Chinese analysts, the EU is using 'better' methods, such as dialogue and cultural exchanges, but its aim is still to transform or rather, to westernize China. To what extent this point of view is popular and becoming more influential remains to be seen, but it is clear that Chinese leaders are still bound to be affected by their own ideological burden.

Notes

1. Sha Zukang is now the Chinese ambassador to the United Nations in Geneva.
2. 'China Foreign Currency Reserves top US$1 trillion', *Associated Press*, 15 January 2007.
3. See the speech of Hu Jintao, 'China and the New Asian Century', Fortune Global Forum, Beijing, 16 May 2005; *Hong Kong Economic Journal*, 17 May 2005, p. 6.
4. See *Ta Kung Pao*, 9 December 2004, p. A6. By 'comprehensive', it means that the relationship is *tous-azimuth*, multilayered; by strategic, its means the relationship is stable, permanent and global, and that it can go beyond the differences in ideology and social systems.
5. The three categories include cotton pants, knitted shirts, and undershirts made of mixed materials including polyester.
6. See 'Europe's Fable', *Asian Wall Street Journal*, 27 April 2005, p. A11.
7. See the interview of Bo Xilai in *Ta Kung Pao*, 7 May 2005, p. A11.
8. See the editorial of *Hong Kong Economic Journal*, 16 May 2005, p. 1.
9. 'China's EU Policy Paper', see *Renmin Ribao* (People's Daily), 14 October 2003, p. 7.
10. See the speech of Wan Jiabao at The Hague, Netherlands, *Ta Kung Pao*, 9 December 2004, p. A2.
11. The Chinese spokeswoman, Zhang Qiyue replies to journalists, *Ta Kung Pao*, 8 December 2004, p. A2.
12. Reported in *New York Times*, 22 March 2005. See also *Ta Kung Pao*, 23 March 2005, p. 10.
13. See 'In Europe, Hu Faces Trade and Human Rights Issues', *International Herald Tribune*, 10 November 2005, p. 3.
14. See the interview of Jacques Chirac by *Asahi Shimbun*, reported in *Hong Kong Economic Journal*, 24 March 2005, p. 7.

References

Cabestan, Jean-Pierre, 'Behind a Warm Embrace, Serious Questions', *International Herald Tribune*, 14 October 2004, p. 8.
Chen, Zhilong, 'China is Determined to Counter-attack the "Special Protection" of Europe and the United States', *Ta Kung Pao*, 3 June 2005, p. B4.
China Commerce Yearbooks (Beijing, since 2004).
Dai, Bingren, 'Towards Mature, Sound and Stable Sino-EU Relations', *Ouzhou Yanjiu (Chinese Journal of European Studies)*, 23(2) (April 2005), 77, 79, 82.
European Commission, 'Building a Comprehensive Partnership with China', Communication from the Commission, COM (1998) 181 final, 25 March 1998. Brussels: European Commission.
European Commission, 'EU Strategy towards China: Implementation of the 1998 Communication and Future Steps for a more Effective EU Policy', Communication from the Commission to the Council and the European Parliament, COM (2001), 15 May 2001, 1 (Brussels: European Commission, 2001).

European Commission, Commission Working Document, *Country Strategy Paper: China*, IP/02/349, Brussels: European Commission, 2002.

European Commission, 'A Maturing Partnership – Shared Interests and Challenges in EU–China Relations', Commission Policy Paper for Transmission to the Council and the European Parliament, COM (2003) 533 final, 10 September 2003 (Brussels: European Commission).

European Commission, 'EU–China: Closer Partners, Growing Responsibilities', Communication from the Commission to the Council and the European Parliament, COM (2006) 631, final, 24 October 2006 (Brussels: European Commission).

European Commission, Commission Working Document, Accompanying COM (2006) 631 final: Closer Partners, Growing Responsibilities, A policy paper on EU–China trade and investment: Competition and Partnership, COM (2006) 632 final, 24 October 2006 (Brussels: European Commission).

Feng, Zhongping, 'Looking at Sino-European Relations from a Strategic Highground', in *Qiu Shi* (Seeking Truth), (September 2002), pp. 58–60. (This monthly magazine is the party organ published by the Central Committee of the Chinese Communist Party.)

Ge, Qifan, 'China Breaks Through the Space Monopoly of the West', *Ta Kung Pao*, 1 March 2007, p. A28.

Grant, Richard L. (ed.), *The European Union and China: A European Strategy for the Twenty-First Century* (London: Royal Institute of International Affairs, 1995).

Huang, Niansi, 'Europe and China are Receiving the Coming of Honeymoon', *Ta Kung Pao*, 6 May 2004, p. A2.

Huo, Zhengde, 'On Sino-European Strategic Relations', *Guoji Wenti Yanjiu* (International Studies), 106(2) (March 2005), p. 3–4.

International Monetary Fund, *Direction of Trade Statistics* (2006), pp. 133–5.

Johnson, Chalmers, 'No Longer the "Lone" Superpower: Coming to Terms with China', Japan Policy Research Institute Paper, No. 105 (March 2005).

Kristof, Nicholas D., 'North Korea, 6. Bush, 0', *International Herald Tribune*, (27 April 2005), p. 8.

Lu, Zhimin, 'China–Europe Economic Relations and Trade Still Need a Solid Foundation', *Ta Kung Pao*, 1 November 2006, p. A29.

Meng, Honghua (ed.), *Zhongguo: Daguo Jueqi* (*The Rise of Modern China*), Hangzhou: Zhejiang People's Press, 2004, pp. 112, 115–19.

Qiu, Yuanlun, 'The Present and Future of Sino-European Relations', *Shijie Jingji yu Zhengzhi* (*World Economy and Politics*), 10 (2004), 8–16.

Shaplen, Jason T., and Laney, James, 'No Choice but to Deal with Kim Jong Il', *International Herald Tribune*, 27 April 2005, p. 8.

Song, Tianshui, 'Europe and China Should Convene a Conference of the Silk Road', *Ta Kung Pao*, 16 November 2004, p. A7.

Song, Xinling, 'International Political Order and European Union', *Zhongguo Renmin Daxue Xuebao* (Journal of the Renmin University of China), 5 (2001), 24–7.

Su, Fangyi, 'Research on China Policy of the EU in the 90s', in *Wenti yu Yanjiu* (*Issues and Studies*), 41(1) (January/February 2002), 64.

Ting, Wai, 'Situational Dynamics of the Korean Peninsula and the Chinese Security Environment', *Korean Journal of International Studies*, 30(1) (Summer 2003),

99–120. A detailed survey of how the crisis on the Korean Peninsula affects Chinese foreign policies.

Tkacik, John J. Jr., 'Hu Meets a New Europe', *Wall Street Journal-Asia*, 10 November 2005, p. 15.

Wu, Baiyi, 'The Post-Cold War System Change and Sino-EU Relations', in *Ouzhou Yanjiu* (Chinese Journal of European Studies), 5 (October 2005), 1–16.

Xiao, Yuankai, 'The American Factor: the Permanent Influential Factor to Sino-European Relations', in Shunzhu, Wang, *et al.* (eds), *Zou Xiang Xinshiji de Eluosi, Oumeng yu Zhongguo* (*Entering into the New Century's Russia, EU and China*) (Beijing: Contemporary World Press, 2001), p. 421.

Ye, Zicheng, 'Historical and Theoretical Reflections of China's Policy of Multi-polarization', in Shoude Liang, *et al.* (eds), *Xinxingshi yu Xin Guojiguan* (New Situation and New World Views) (Beijing: Central Translation Press, 2004), pp. 1–29.

Yu, Jianhua, 'New Style of Asia–Europe Equal Partner Relationship Facing the New Century', *Shijie Jingji Yanjiu* (*World Economy Studies*), Supplement (2002), 36–9, 44.

Zhang, Shaowei, 'It Will Not be Long Before the EU Lifts the Sanction against China', *Ta Kung Pao*, 27 January 2005, p. A4.

Zhang, Xhaowei, 'Bush's Visit to Europe and Arms Sales Embargo', *Ta Kung Pao*, 2 March 2005, p. A3.

Zhu, Liyu, and Zhang, Xiaojin, 'The Differences between China and Europe in the Views on Human Rights and its Influence on Sino-European Relations', *Guojia Xingzheng Xueyuan Xuebao* (Journal of National Institute of Administration), 4 (2002), 87–90.

9
Taiwan and Europe*

Czeslaw Tubilewicz

Writing more than two decades ago, Reinhard Drifte concluded that 'any discussion of European perspectives concerning Taiwan [...] means speaking about European business interests on the island; political considerations about Taiwan [...] come into play only insofar as these business interests may be threatened by any internal and external political event' (Drifte, 1985, p. 1115). In 1995, Kay Moller wrote of the 'opportunists' and 'cynics' when referring to West European policies on Taiwan (Moller, 1995, pp. 76–7). Seven years later, Moller noted that 'at no time human rights and democracy considerations have visibly affected [German] thinking about Taiwan' (Moller, 1996, p. 722). In 2001, Jean-Pierre Cabestan examined French 'shopkeeper diplomacy' towards Taiwan, while Francoise Mengin claimed in 2002 that in the long term, the Europeans would not oppose the 'one China' policy as their relations with Taiwan were exclusively functional, taking full advantage of Taiwan's economic potential and lacking any political plan with regard to Taiwan's future (Cabestan, 2001; Mengin, 2002, p. 136).

Thus far, the academic analyses of Europe's relations with Taiwan over the past two decades have been remarkably consistent in their conclusions on Europe's Taiwan policy as being focused on the economic, rather than the geostrategic, dimension of relations with the Republic of China on Taiwan (ROC).[1] This chapter will not dispute this shared opinion. Lacking the military capacity to project its 'hard' influence to the Asia Pacific and consumed with the 'in-house' project of economic and political integration, the Europeans did not concern themselves with the

---

* This chapter is a revised version of the article 'Europe in Taiwan's Post-Cold War Foreign Relations', which appeared in *Diplomacy & Statecraft*, 18(2) (June 2007), 415–43.

strategic dimension of the Taiwan problem. They left such geostrategic considerations to the United States (US), which since 1950 had burdened itself with the containment of communist China and, at least until the early 1970s, considered its alliance with Taiwan to be a geostrategic asset. At the same time, the European states pursued non-political relations with Taiwan, which did not violate the 'one China' principle – a foundation of friendship with Asia's regional power, the People's Republic of China (PRC).

Yet, in the process of fostering economic and cultural ties with the rebel island, the Europeans realized the advantages of an institutionalized, if not a political, dialogue with the island, as Taiwan – capitalizing on its economic success and the resulting capacity to dispense economic rewards – tempted the Europeans with promises of economic largesse had they decided to exchange high-level government officials, establish reciprocal offices, sign diplomatic and consular agreements, sell weapons, initiate direct flights or support Taiwanese membership of international organizations. Although Taiwan's greatest triumphs in Europe (namely, the arms deals, diplomatic or consular agreements or gaining support for membership in international organizations) proved either sporadic or short-lived, they demonstrated that the China factor, which often confined the scope and depth of Taiwan's relationships with Europe to the purely non-political realm, did not necessarily restrict the European nations' choices with regards to the Taiwan issue when Taiwan's rewards seemed sufficiently compensating for China's predictable sanctions. More importantly, however, Taiwan – through limited economic diplomacy – successfully established solid foundations for long-term dialogue with all of Europe through *de facto* consular offices, trade bureaus, bilateral committees, parliamentary exchanges and periodical visits by government officials. Thus, while not disputing the existing scholarship on Europe's relations with Taiwan, this chapter will argue that Europe's functional relations with Taiwan, far from being an obstacle to a more comprehensive relationship, facilitated political relations with the island and stimulated Europe's interest in the stability in the Taiwan Strait.

The Cold War divisions

The Cold War divided Europe on the Taiwan question. Most West European states followed the United States' policy of isolating the PRC in the international arena. All Soviet allies in East Central Europe, in turn, stood by PRC and abstained from any contacts with the Republic of China. Governed by social-democratic parties, Switzerland, the Netherlands, Leichtenstein and the Scandinavian states took the middle road: recognizing China in 1950–51, but maintaining non-political relations with Taiwan. American allies in Europe, however – aware of Beijing's effective sovereignty over the Chinese mainland and its power status in Asia – did not wholeheartedly subscribe to the US policy of containing China internationally. Prompted as much by the conviction that China was too important as an Asian power to be ignored as by the desire to challenge the United States, in 1964 the French were the first to break away from the US-led anti-PRC coalition and recognize China (Shin, 2001, pp. 126–8; Erasmus, 1964, pp. 196–7). Taiwan's remaining diplomatic partners in Europe defected to the China camp in the early 1970s, following the Sino-US rapprochement and the PRC's admission to the United Nations in 1971 (Garver, 1997, p. 258).[2] By 1975, the polarization of Europe into the PRC and ROC camps had ended with all states (except the Vatican) siding with Beijing on the question of 'one China'. Given the low degree of political, military and economic interaction with Taiwan prior to de-recognition, West European states chose not to follow the Japanese formula, whereby non-official relations with the ROC were managed by nominally non-governmental organizations. They were also largely unconcerned with Taiwan's political fate.

Responding to increasing international isolation, ROC Premier Chiang Ching-kuo initiated a policy of 'total diplomacy' (*zongti waijiao*) in 1973 to develop substantial ties with states that established diplomatic relations with China, while relying on US support to maintain its claim to internationally recognized statehood (Weng, 1984, p. 465; Yahuda, 1996, pp. 1329–30; Kim, 1994, p. 150). With regards to Europe, 'total diplomacy' focused on expanding economic relations with Western Europe and establishing commercial ties with the 'non-hostile' states in East Central Europe. While economic cooperation with Western Europe did indeed strengthen in the mid-1970s and prompted Britain, France and Belgium to establish trade offices in Taiwan (the first West European bureaus after de-recognition), Taiwan's emphasis on anti-communism as a pillar of its diplomacy prevented it from securing economic rapprochement with communist Europe (*Far Eastern Economic Review*, 22 May 1981; Gao, 1994, p. 20).

In 1988 Taiwan abandoned its hostility towards the Soviet Union's allies (although not the Soviet Union itself), when it allowed direct trading with East Central Europe (*Republic of China Year Book*, 1989, p. 239). When Europe's post-communist states faced the dilemma of pursuing relations with Taiwan at the cost of alienating China for the first time since 1949, they felt reassured by the West Europeans' success at maintaining close relations with Beijing, without sacrificing economic cooperation with Taiwan. Although this achievement owed more to the PRC's relaxed policies regarding Taiwan following the US de-recognition of Taiwan in 1979 and the second Sino-American joint communiqué (1982), which obligated the United States to scale down arms exports to the island, than to the Europeans' diplomatic inventiveness, it substantiated Beijing's tolerance of Taiwan's non-political relations with the wider world. By 1988, 11 West European states considered their advanced level of economic cooperation with Taiwan to justify institutionalization of relations with the island through non-official bureaus dealing with economic, cultural and technical exchanges. Some of these offices functioned as semi-consulates, issuing visas.[3] In 1981, Belgium private firms and their Taiwanese counterparts initiated a bilateral committee to promote economic cooperation. Seven years later, such committees had also been set up with four other European states (Tsai and Ming, 1990, pp. 133–4). Most remarkably, however, Taiwanese growing economic power facilitated the conclusion of the first arms deal with Europe in 1981, when the Netherlands sold two submarines to Taiwan. Ensuing Chinese economic and diplomatic sanctions against the Netherlands, however, reminded Western Europe of the dire consequences of pursuing relations with Taiwan beyond the economic and cultural realm.

Flexible diplomacy

Failing to arrest his country's diplomatic isolation, in 1988 ROC President Lee Teng-hui launched the policy of 'flexible diplomacy' (*tanxing waijiao*) in order to 'strive with greater determination, pragmatism, flexibility, and vision [...] to develop a foreign policy based primarily on substantive relations' (Wu, 1995, p. 31). 'Flexible diplomacy' aimed at: (1) strengthening existing diplomatic ties or gaining new diplomatic allies; (2) maintaining and developing substantive (semi-official) ties with the states that remained loyal to China; and (3) participating or resuming participation in inter-governmental organizations (Hsieh, 1996, p. 76). There was also an economic dimension – namely, diversifying Taiwanese export and import markets in order to render the Taiwanese economy more resilient to the economic cycles in the United States and Japan, Taiwan's major trading partners. Taiwan pursued these foreign policy objectives simultaneously.

Democratization of Taiwanese domestic politics, Taiwan's booming economy, the 4 June events and the end of the Cold War facilitated the execution of 'flexible diplomacy'. The Tiananmen tragedy in particular influenced a shift in international opinion against China and encouraged the perception of Taiwan as a democratic part of the divided China. Taiwan's free market economy contrasted with the economic retrenchment experienced by China in the aftermath of 4 June (Ho, 1992, p. 10; Chi, 1993, pp. 10–12). Due to its international isolation after the Tiananmen event, the PRC's foreign policy focused on regaining respectability in the international community and appeared less effective in isolating Taiwan diplomatically. Finally, the disappearance of the Soviet empire in 1989–91 reduced the perceived significance of the PRC in global geopolitics and encouraged various states to undertake creative approaches to the Taiwan issue (Hsieh, 1996, p. 71).

Seeking new allies

The transition economies' hunger for investments and developmental assistance, and the new democracies' foreign policies, no longer bound by an ideological fraternity with communist China, rendered the European post-communist states' favourably predisposed towards Taiwan. Taiwan calculated that providing the new democracies with economic aid would eventually lead to diplomatic relations.[4] Its first success came in 1989, when Hungary agreed to host an ROC trade office in the hope of gaining substantial foreign aid.[5] In 1991, the Taiwanese announced soft loans (valued at around US$10 million) to Czechoslovakia, Hungary and Poland, and entered into a partnership with the European Bank for Development and Reconstruction (EBRD) to form the Taipei China–EBRD Cooperation Fund, initially holding US$10 million (subsequently expanded), which aimed to assist all post-communist economies. The initial responses from East Central Europe were encouraging. Czechoslovak President Vaclav Havel's wife visited Taipei in 1990, while the Polish President Lech Walesa promised to do so in 1991. Taiwanese officials predicted imminent diplomatic victories in post-communist Europe. Alarmed by the prospects of losing diplomatic ground, in 1991 the PRC resumed high-level political contacts – which had been suspended in 1989 – with Hungary, Poland and Czechoslovakia. Walesa's U-turn about the Taiwan visit symbolized East Central Europe's resolve to adhere to the 'one China principle'. Luckily for Taiwan, the disintegration of the Soviet Union opened a new diplomatic battlefield, where economies were desperate for foreign assistance and China's influence was limited.

Diplomatic communiqués between the PRC and Latvia, Lithuania and Ukraine – vague on the 'one China' policy – raised hopes in Taiwan that some post-Soviet states possibly desired official relations with the ROC and their diplomatic recognition of China was merely intended to facilitate their entry into international organizations (*Renmin Ribao*, 12, 13, 15 September 1991).[6] Latvia – guided by an anti-communist ideology and in need of developmental assistance – was the first to validate these hopes, when it established consular ties with Taiwan in 1992. Economic aid was to cement and upgrade consular ties with Latvia to full diplomatic relations. In addition to around US$60 million in grants, according to Taiwanese media claims, Latvia received US$10 million from Taiwan and was promised US$16 million in soft loans. The loans, however, never arrived, while further aid and investments were conditional upon Latvia's diplomatic recognition of Taiwan. Amid disappointment over the scale of Taiwanese economic assistance and regretting seemingly lost economic opportunities in China, Latvia terminated the consular agreement in 1994 and returned to the China camp (Tubilewicz, 2002, pp. 795–9).

Promises of El Dorado in exchange for diplomatic relations were made to all of the post-communist states, but the rapidly growing Chinese economy and Taiwan's limited generosity towards Latvia discouraged them from pursuing unequivocally pro-Taiwan policies. In 1999, however, the newly-elected centre-right government in Macedonia – ignorant of the larger context of Sino-Taiwanese diplomatic rivalry – took Taiwanese pledges of injecting US$1 billion into the Macedonian economy seriously and extended diplomatic recognition to the ROC. Although the Taiwanese denied a US$1 billion offer, the Macedonians expected massive assistance, which Taiwan ultimately proved either unwilling or unable to provide. In 2001, therefore, Macedonia re-established diplomatic ties with the PRC. Although security factors prevailed in the Macedonian decision to terminate its friendship with Taiwan, perceived insubstantial economic assistance from Taiwan also played a role. Macedonia's disillusionment over the actual scale of Taiwanese aid also undermined Taiwan's scheme to gain diplomatic footholds in other parts of the Balkan region (Tubilewicz, 2004, pp. 796–801).

Sustaining ties with the Vatican

While it failed to maintain consular or diplomatic ties with Europe's new democracies, Taipei was more successful in retaining the Vatican's diplomatic allegiance. And yet this partnership (dating back to the 1950s) also rested on shaky grounds (Chan, 1989, pp. 816–17). As the Vatican grew increasingly aware of the vast potential of converting millions of mainland Chinese into Catholicism, it hoped for a normalization of relations with Beijing through a policy of low-key dialogue which began in the early 1980s (Madsen, 2003, p. 469). In the process of this communication, the Taiwan issue became progressively of less significance to Sino-Vatican diplomatic ties, as the Holy See admitted its readiness to transfer its nunciature from Taipei to Beijing 'not tomorrow, but as soon as the Chinese authorities allow it' (*South China Morning Post*, 22 February 1999). These diplomatic efforts, however, failed due to conflicting agendas. While Beijing insisted on the Holy See's termination of relations with Taiwan as a precondition to diplomatic relations, it also vetoed the Vatican's practice of appointing bishops as constituting interference in China's internal affairs. The Vatican was ready to ditch its diplomatic partnership with Taiwan; however, it was not ready to abdicate its responsibility to lead the Chinese Catholics and protect their religious freedoms (Leung, 2005, pp. 355–7).

Taiwan was concerned over the Vatican's apparent readiness to switch diplomatic sides whenever the opportunity presented itself. Taiwanese leaders travelled to the Vatican to seek assurances over the Vatican's China policy. Although reassured that the Pope would not compromise the interests of the Taiwanese people, Taiwan sought to strengthen its ties with the Vatican by supporting Catholic charity projects and convincing the Vatican officials of the untrustworthiness of the mainland promises regarding religious freedoms (*Central News Agency*, 21 February 1999).[7]

The news of John Paul II's death in 2005 intensified speculation that under new leadership the Vatican would be more willing to find a compromise with China over questions of Taiwan and religious freedom. Hong Kong Bishop Joseph Zen told the media that the Vatican wanted to reopen diplomatic talks with China and was ready to cut its ties with Taiwan (*Agency France-Presse*, 5 April 2005). Unexpectedly, however, the Pope's death strengthened the Vatican's ties with Taiwan, when the Holy See invited ROC President Chen Shui-bian to John Paul II's funeral, which was also attended by US President George W. Bush and other foreign dignitaries. The Vatican's exercise in funeral diplomacy, however, is of no long-term consequence for Taiwan. Given the Holy See's determination to protect the religious freedoms of the Chinese Catholics and to evangelize Chinese masses, the normalization of relations with China remains the Vatican's diplomatic priority.

Strengthening substantive relations

By 1989, Western Europe's substantive partnership with Taiwan consisted of bilateral trade (or pseudo-consular) offices, bilateral economic agreements (including an accord on direct aviation with the Netherlands), and bilateral (private) committees overseeing economic cooperation. Taiwan aimed to inject more officialdom into various contacts with Western Europe through direct communication at the ministerial level, more intergovernmental agreements, intensified interparliamentary exchanges and gaining West European support for its efforts to re-enter international organizations. China's temporary diplomatic and economic problems, resulting from the international isolation after the 4 June tragedy, facilitated Taiwanese 'flexible diplomacy' in Western Europe. France led the way to stronger ties with Taiwan. In 1989, it upgraded its mission in Taipei to the French Institute in Taipei (FIT), analogous to the American Institute in Taiwan, a US *de facto* embassy on the island. A year later, a 'retired' ambassador was appointed to head the FIT. This established a pattern for other European states to follow, appointing foreign ministry personnel to Taipei. The Tiananmen massacre also marked a watershed in Taiwan's relations with the Scandinavian states, which had traditionally shunned contacts with the ROC, but which after 4 June sought friendly ties with democratic Taiwan (Brodsgaard, 1998, p. 143).

Far from relying on the shared beliefs in democratic ideals as the foundation for stronger relations, Taiwan resorted to hard cash to upgrade its relations with Western Europe. In particular, it utilized the Six-Year National Development Plan (1991–96), valued at US$300 billion, by linking the success of international tenders for large infrastructure projects to the degree of friendship between Taiwan and the state where the bidding company came from (Mengin, 2002, p. 148). Eager to win contracts in large infrastructure projects, high-ranking visitors from Western Europe travelled to the island to consolidate friendship. The first cabinet member of any European state to visit Taiwan in a 'private' capacity was the French Minister of Industry and Regional Planning Roger Fauroux in January 1991. Other West European visitors followed, while high-ranking ROC officials were welcomed in Western Europe (Wu, 1995, pp. 32–3; Hsieh, 1996, p. 89; Joei, 1994, p. 319; Mengin, 1997, pp. 236–7). By 1991, 15 European states had established 'private' institutions on Taiwan to handle economic and cultural exchanges (while Taiwan set up offices in 16 West European states) (Hsieh, 1996, p. 89; Shin, 2001, p. 139). Some of these offices (for example, the French, British, German and Spanish) acted as *de facto* embassies or consulates, empowered to issue visas, headed by either retired diplomats or diplomats 'on leave'. Taiwanese offices in Western Europe were allowed to rename themselves to better reflect their status.[8] Taiwan also established direct air services to Austria (1991), Great Britain (March 1993), Germany (July 1993) and France (November 1993).

Taiwan's substantive relations with Western Europe in the early 1990s also included arms deals, with France, Italy, Belgium and Germany selling arms to Taiwan, of which the French sale of Mirage 2000–5 jet fighters (worth US$4 billion) in 1992 was the most widely reported (Hsieh, 1996, p. 90; *Far Eastern Economic Review*, 5 November 1992). The Europeans, however, became increasingly disappointed by the fact that US and Japanese firms were given the thickest slices of the contracts pie while they were stuck with leftovers.[9] By the mid-1990s, following the sale of Mirage fighters, China's economic retribution and the reduction in the number of large Taiwanese contracts, France had re-established warm relations with China. The French reorientation towards Beijing was indicative of the Western Europe's renewed focus on China, then the world's most dynamically developing economy.

The gains of the early 1990s, however, were not lost. In 1995, Italy signed a direct flight accord with Taiwan and in 1996 its office in Taipei began issuing visas. In 1996, German Foreign Minister Klaus Kinkel declared that he had no objections to ministerial-level visits to Taiwan, as long as they dealt with functional matters (Kindermann, 1998, pp. 94–5). The US$10 billion high-speed train project, unveiled in the late 1990s, stimulated a renewed round of ministerial-level visits from Germany and France, whose companies competed for the contract. In 2000, the German Ministry of Foreign Affairs installed the German Institute Taipei, headed by the diplomatic staff 'on duty' (Mengin, 2002, p. 145). West European states welcomed numerous Taiwanese ministers for talks on economic and cultural cooperation, while the visits by Premier Lien Chan to Austria (June 1995), Ireland (January 1997) and Iceland (October 1997) proved that ROC leaders were occasionally welcomed in Europe as well. Taiwan also continued its lobbying efforts in Western Europe via party diplomacy and inter-parliamentary exchanges. By 2002, 14 West European parliaments had established 'Taiwan friendship groups'. The efforts of pro-Taiwanese parliamentarians resulted in numerous resolutions supporting Taiwan's efforts to enter international organizations. However, none of these resolutions were binding.

Building bridges to post-communist Europe

In post-communist East Central Europe, substantive relations with Taiwan were to be created, rather than strengthened. Repeated promises of economic assistance and prospects of advantageous trade with Taiwan proved sufficient to convince the most prosperous post-communist states to exchange representative offices with Taiwan. East Central European offices in Taipei functioned in a manner similar to their West European counterparts. Although ostensibly economic and cultural in nature, they performed consular functions (including the issuing of visas) and were staffed by career diplomats.

Of all the post-communist states, the Czech Republic spearheaded the most dynamic policy with relation to Taiwan. Czech President Vaclav Havel, driven by his anti-communist convictions and his belief in Taiwan's just request for re-entry into the United Nations, engineered a creative strategy that opened channels for high-level official communication with Taipei, without violating the letter of the 'one China' policy. The first signs of the Czech model surfaced in 1990, when Havel's first wife, Olga Havlova, visited Taipei, ignoring Chinese protests. Thereafter, the 'first ladies' diplomacy' became a distinguishable feature of Czech diplomacy, with Havel's second wife, Dagmar, paying a visit to Taipei in 1998 and President Lee's wife, Tseng Wen-fui, and Chen Shui-bian's wife, Wu Shu-chen, reciprocating in 1999 and 2001 respectively. When Taiwan launched a campaign in 1993 to return to the UN, the Czechs (soon joined by the Latvians) expressed their support. In 1995, the Czech Republic arranged a high-profile visit by Vice-President Lien Chan, a few days after President Lee's highly controversial visit to the United States (*Zhongguo Shibao*, 19 June 1995). Taiwanese ministers of foreign affairs, economic affairs and even defence followed Lien Chan. In 2000 the Czech Republic was the second European state (after Britain) to welcome a visit from former ROC President Lee Teng-hui.

Taipei appeared ready to reward the Czechs for their courage to support Taiwan internationally. In 1993, the Czech heavy-industry conglomerate, Skoda, received two sizeable contracts for public works in Taiwan, which coincided with the opening of the Czech office in Taipei (*Gongshang Shibao*, 19 June 1995). After Lien's visit, the Taiwanese promised the Czechs US$100 million in investments in the Taiwan-built Industrial Park. Some Taiwanese investments did indeed arrive in the Czech Republic, but not on the scale promised: a Taiwanese textile company announced its decision to invest US$20 million in the Czech Republic, the first Taiwanese investment in the post-communist economy. The Czech businesses began vocally complaining about President Havel's Taiwan policy destroying their chances of clinching business deals in China's rapidly growing economy, while the Taiwanese investments were very slow in coming. The critics were proven wrong when in the late 1990s–early 2000s, large high-tech Taiwanese companies invested close to US$800 million in the Czech Republic, making Taiwan one of the largest foreign investors in the country.[10] Thus, Taiwanese private business rescued the economic partnership with the Czechs and proved that the pro-Taiwan foreign policy had paid off, although in the manner not originally intended.

By the late 1990s, Taipei's relations with post-communist East Central Europe paralleled their ties with Western Europe. Representative offices were exchanged, economic, cultural and academic cooperation developed, parliamentary exchanges and visits by high-level government officials took place, and agreements over economic and cultural matters were concluded, although none of them in areas desired by Taiwan, such as investment protection. In the process of this substantive communication, Taiwan gained support, ranging from friendly city councillors to academics and journalists who disseminated knowledge about Taiwan as a distinct political, social and economic entity. In addition, these were visits to Taiwan by renowned personalities, such as Walesa and Havel, who – once retired from office – fulfilled their earlier promises of visiting the island.

Taiwan and the European Union (EU)

Given the member states' focus on political and economic ties with China throughout the Cold War, the European Community (EC) unsurprisingly pursued the 'one China' policy and ignored the existence of Taiwan. Surprisingly, however, it also ignored Taiwan's rapidly growing market economy. Visits by the European government officials to Taipei in the early 1990s paved the way for the first ever visit by an EC official to Taiwan, Vice President of the European Commission Martin Bangemann in May 1992. In the short term, his visit, however, neither led to institutionalized relations nor any structured dialogue on economic cooperation between the EC and the ROC (Hsieh, 1996, pp. 90–1).

The EC/EU began playing a greater role in Europe's relations with Taiwan, when Taiwan applied for the accession to the General Agreement on Tariffs and Trade and its successor, the World Trade Organization (WTO). Noting Taiwan's persistent trade surplus with the EU, as well as the US and Japan's preferential access to the Taiwanese market, the member states provided the European Commission with a mandate to support Taiwanese membership and to coordinate the EU's position with the United States, when negotiating with China on Taiwan's accession. The negotiations provided the context for direct consultations between the EU's high-ranking officials and their Taiwanese counterparts. Parallel to these negotiations, since 1996, the Commission has begun developing a multilateral framework for economic cooperation with

Taiwan via the EU-Taiwan industrial roundtables, which brought together industrialists, EU and Taiwanese government officials and the Commission's representatives (Wang, 2001). The EU-Taiwan agreement on WTO accession, signed by the Vice President of the European Commission, Leon Brittan, and the Taiwanese Minister for Economic Affairs, Wang Chih-kang, in July 1998 was the first significant, official agreement inked by the EU and Taiwan (Wang, 1999, p. 109).[11] With Taiwan's entry into the WTO in January 2002, the Commission could argue for the establishment of the EU office in Taipei. Claiming that such an office was instrumental to monitoring Taiwan's compliance with the WTO rules and Taiwan-EU agreements, it disregarded China's opposition and opened the European Economic and Trade Office in Taipei in March 2003. While still formally non-official, the EU's dialogue with Taiwan currently features annual consultations at the vice-ministerial level (alternating between Taipei and Brussels) and exchanges of visits at directorial or ministerial levels. The Taiwanese long-term goal of formalizing relations with the EU through bilateral offices and structured (albeit unofficial) communication has been accomplished.

While the EC and its later reincarnation, the EU – eyeing China's vast market and lacking a mandate from the member states to formulate any proactive policy on Taiwan – shunned Taiwan until the 1990s, the European Parliament (EP) demonstrated a remarkable activism in support of Europe's stronger ties with the island. As early as 1985, the EP adopted a 'Resolution on Trade with Taiwan', which called for improvement of relations with Taiwan (Tsai and Ming, 1990, pp. 135-6). The Association of Friends of Taiwan (or Taiwan Friendship Group), formed in the European Parliament in 1991, sponsored numerous Taiwan-related resolutions in three broad areas.[12] The first supported Taiwan's membership in international organizations, including the WTO, the Asia-Europe Meeting and World Health Organization. On one occasion (resolution passed on 18 July 1996), prompted by China's military intimidation of Taiwan in the spring of 1996, the EP also voiced support for Taiwan's membership of the United Nations. The second category concerned Taiwan's relations with the Union. The Parliament repeatedly urged the European Council to strengthen political relations with the ROC and demanded that the Commission open an EU office in Taipei. The EP also promoted relations with Taiwan via parliamentary exchanges and extending invitations to Taiwanese officials (e.g., Foreign Minister John Chang, who addressed the EP's Committee on Foreign Affairs, Security and Defence Policy in 1997). The third area of the EP's concern focused on the peaceful resolution of the Taiwan problem. This concern was manifested particularly when China staged missile testing in the Taiwan Strait in 1995–96. The EP issued three resolutions from February to July 1996, all calling on the PRC not to carry out any aggressive acts against Taiwan (Kindermann, 1998, pp. 96–100). Thereafter, virtually every resolution regarding relations with China contained a clause stating the EP's demand that China's reunification be accomplished peacefully. The EP also opposed the lifting of the ban on arms sales to China, passing five resolutions on the issue between 2003 and 2005.

Unfortunately for Taiwan, the EP's powers with regard to the EU's external policies are limited to approving international treaties and budgetary matters. In the area of the EU Common Foreign and Security Policy, the EP plays a largely consultative role. Its resolutions must be accepted by the European Council, the EU's decision-making body, in a 'co-decision' framework, before they are passed to the European Commission, the EU's executive body, which will consider turning them into policy. Given the 'one China' policy officially endorsed by the EU and the absence of any EU strategic policy on the Taiwan issue, the Commission and the Council routinely ignored the EP's resolutions on Taiwan, believing that the Taiwan problem should be solved by both of the involved parties (*European Voice*, 23 January 2003). Thus, for example, although the EP's voice on the arms embargo helped the opponents to argue against lifting the ban, the EU's decision in April 2005 to postpone the decision on the embargo resulted from the fear of the US retribution, rather than from the EP's resolutions, or any wider concern for the stability in cross-Strait relations (Saalman and Yuan, 2004).

While unable to gain European Council and Commission support on most of the issues raised in the EP's resolutions, Taiwan gladly notes the Council and Commission's endorsement of the EP's view on the importance of China's peaceful reunification. Witnessing China's rapid military modernization and its increasingly bellicose stand on reunification with Taiwan (most recently manifested in the Anti-Secession Law of March 2005), the Commission moved gradually from merely welcoming 'any steps which can be taken to further the process of peaceful reconciliation' between Beijing and Taipei (*Building a Comprehensive Partnership with China*, 1998) and 'making clear the EU's strong interest in seeing the Taiwan issue resolved peacefully through dialogue' (European Commission, 2003) to articulating more forcefully its 'active interest' in the peace and stability in the Taiwan Strait. In its policy paper on relations with China, issued in October 2006, the European Commission objected strongly to the use of force and any measures amounting to a unilateral change of the status quo (left undefined) in the Taiwan Strait. It voiced support for pragmatic solutions and confidence-building measures on both sides of the divided China and explicitly reserved its right to continue strong economic and trade relations with Taiwan (a point missing in previous policy papers) (European Commission, 2006, p. 11). Given the confines of the 'one China' policy, the shift of emphasis from 'peaceful solution' to 'active interest in peace' is the most explicit expression of the EU's support for the Taiwanese people's freedom to define their future.

Securing economic interests

Since the 1970s, Europe has played an important role in diversifying Taiwan's export and import markets. Taiwan also hoped for European investments in its manufacturing industries and considered the viability of diversifying its investment portfolio to Europe. In order to accomplish its economic objectives, Taipei launched a campaign to turn Europe into one of its major trading partners. According to EU statistics, in the 1990s ROC's trade with the Union more than doubled, as did its trade surplus (see Tables 9.1 and 9.2). The EU remained Taiwan's major trading partner in Europe, buying more than 90 per cent of Taiwan's European exports and supplying the lion's share of Taiwan's imports from Europe. Taiwan's earlier exports to Europe consisted mainly of textile products, garments and shoes. By the late 1990s, technology-intensive products replaced light industrial products. Taiwan's imports from the EU included military equipment and raw materials, factory machinery and steel (Wu, 2005). Despite the rise in trade volume, Europe remained Taiwan's third largest trading partner (after the US and Japan – or fourth, if China and Hong Kong are counted as one entity). The EU's share in Taiwan's total trade peaked in 1998 (16.9 per cent) and began declining thereafter, hitting 12 per cent by 2003, a figure equal to that recorded in the early 1970s. If Europe is taken as a whole (including the post-Soviet states), its share in Taiwan's total foreign trade increased from 6 per cent in 1952 to over 18 per cent in 1998, but it had declined to 12.1 per cent by 2005 (see Table 9.1). Taiwan's entry into the WTO, with the resulting increased market access for European manufacturers of cars, agricultural produce, tobacco and liquor, exerted only a limited impact on the scale of Taiwan's trade with Europe.

Taiwan also benefited from economic cooperation with Europe in terms of attracting European investments. EU investments in Taiwan were small as a percentage of the EU's total outward investments (accounting for 0.34 per cent of all of the EU's foreign direct investments in 2001). By 2005, they stood at a respectable figure of US$13.69 billion (with the Netherlands being by far the largest investor), accounting for

Table 9.1 Taiwan's trade with Europe (including post-Soviet states) (in millions of US dollars)

Period	Total trade	Export	Import	Balance	Share in Taiwan's total trade (in %)
1952	18.4	6.125	12.275	−6.150	6.06
1960	43.095	9.838	33.257	−23.419	9.35
1965	93.954	46.471	47.483	−1.012	9.34
1976	1,926.681	1,091.850	834.831	+257.019	12.22
1980	4,981.936	3,121.193	1,860.743	+1,260.450	12.57
1986	8,010.329	4,774.413	3,235.916	+1,538.497	12.51
1989	19,335.466	10,953.898	8,381.568	+2,572.330	16.31
1990	21,819.268	12,233.431	9,585.837	+2,647.594	17.89
1991	23,949.35	14,001.441	9,947.909	+4,026.532	17.22
1992	26,403.526	13,928.888	12,474.638	+1,454.250	17.20
1993	26,461.802	12,902.013	13,559.789	−657.776	16.32
1994	28,877.221	12,927.365	15,949.856	−3,022.491	16.19
1995	34,426.379	15,725.252	18,701.127	−2,972.875	16
1996	37,088.085	16,944.831	20,143.254	−3,198.432	16.99
1997	40,016.078	18,415.323	21,600.755	−3,185.432	16.92
1998	40,222.497	19,637.458	20,585.039	−947.581	18.69
1999	37,904.886	20,320.476	17,584.410	+2,736.066	16.32
2000	42,726.479	23,713.399	19,013.080	+4,700.319	14.82
2001	34,797.24	19,807.784	14,989.456	+4,818.328	15.12
2002	33,197.527	18,554.021	14,643.506	+3,910.515	13.65
2003	36,692.317	20,452.266	16,240.051	+4,212.215	13.52
2004	44,732.464	23,434.531	21,297.933	+2,136.598	13.08
2005	45,051.158	23,257.335	21,793.823	+1,463.512	12.14

Source: *Taiwan Statistical Data Book 2006* (Taipei: Council for Economic Planning and Development, 2006), http://www.cepd.gov.tw (accessed 11 November 2006).

19.18 per cent of all foreign investments in Taiwan (Ministry of Economic Affairs, 2007). The European Chamber of Commerce in Taipei argued that the ROC government's enforcement of intellectual property rights, revision of 'outdated' industrial regulations, opening of direct links with China and allowing European firms to bid on more government contracts would attract more European investors to Taiwan (*The China Post*, 21 December 2001; *Reuters*, 3 November 2003).

For Europe, trade with Taiwan was neither as profitable nor as important as it was for Taiwan. In terms of its share in the EU's foreign trade, trading with Taiwan never exceeded 2.1 per cent and it dropped to 1.6 per cent by 2003, below the level registered 13 years earlier (see Table 9.2). By 2005, Taiwan was the EU's 14th largest trading partner (down from 9th position in the early 2000s), 9th largest exporter (down

Table 9.2 The EU's trade with Taiwan (in billions of euros from 1 January 1999, in billions of ECU until 31 December 1998)

Period	Total trade	Export	Import	Balance	Share in the EU's external trade (in %)
1990	15.47	5.39	10.08	−4.69	1.8
1991	18.10	6.04	12.06	−6.02	2.1
1992	18.49	6.78	11.71	−4.93	2.1
1993	19.58	8.20	11.38	−3.18	2.1
1994	20.77	9.37	11.40	−2.03	2.0
1995	21.87	10.11	11.76	−1.64	2.0
1996	23.26	9.99	13.27	−3.29	1.9
1997	28.36	12.66	15.70	−3.04	2.0
1998	30.15	12.06	18.09	−6.03	2.1
1999	31.85	11.83	20.02	−8.18	2.1
2000	41.54	14.89	26.65	−11.77	2.1
2001	37.44	13.26	24.18	−10.92	1.9
2002	32.82	11.69	21.13	−9.44	1.7
2003	30.82	10.82	20.00	−9.19	1.6
2004	36.45	12.85	23.6	−10.75	1.8
2005	36.64	12.82	23.82	−11	1.6

Notes: For 1990–2003, the EU refers to EU-15, for 2004–05, the EU refers to EU-25.
Source: Eurostat, (data for 1990–2003), http://epp. eurostat.cec.eu.int (accessed 16 May 2005); *Europe in Figures: Eurostat Yearbook 2005* (data for 2004–05) http://epp. eurostat.ec.europa.eu (accessed 11 November 2006).

from 7th in the late 1990s), 23rd largest importer (down from 19th position in 2004) and 5th trading partner in Asia (after China, Japan, South Korea and India). When it came to politically motivated imports, Taiwan favoured US or Japanese firms, despite the European threats that geostrategic considerations in Taiwan's commercial decisions could damage relations with Europe.[13]

Various European regions promoted their investment attractiveness to Taiwanese businesspeople. ROC investors, however, were concerned about Europe's strict labour regulations and costs, as well as challenging cultural differences, and opted to invest in China and Southeast Asia instead. They also ignored ROC government-sponsored projects, such as the Taiwanese industrial zones in the Czech Republic, Poland and Macedonia. By 2005, Taiwanese overall investments in Europe amounted to US$1.4 billion or over €2 billion (depending on the source of statistics), less than one or 1.5 per cent of its overall outwards foreign direct investment (*Taiwan Statistical Data Book*, 2006, p. 270). Until the late 1990s, 70 to 80 per cent of Taiwanese investments in Europe involving manufacturing projects were located mostly in the UK, where the investment approval process was fast and the labour laws were the most flexible in Europe (*Central News Agency*, 20 March 1998). In the late 1990s, the Czech Republic overtook Britain as Taiwan's favourite investment destination in Europe, accounting for 41 per cent of ROC's total investments in Europe in 2003, compared to 22 per cent for Britain.

Beijing's responses

By 2000, China's trade with the EU had increased fivefold in comparison to 1990. Two years later, China became the EU's second largest trading partner, while in 2004 the EU was China's largest trading partner. At the time, European investments in China reached US$34 billion. Economic considerations, coupled with China's growing international influence, convinced most European states, as well as the EU, of the desirability of toeing to the 'one China' policy. The PRC, however, did not trust the Europeans' self-policing on the Taiwan question and monitored Taiwan's activities on the old continent, intervening when necessary.

Although China accepted Europe's substantive ties with Taiwan, featuring pseudo-consulates, direct flights and ministerial-level meetings, it remained intolerant of Europe's implicit or explicit support for Taiwanese claims to sovereignty, including diplomatic or consular agreements, arms sales to Taiwan, and visits by the ROC president, vice-president, premier, foreign and defence ministers. In each case, Chinese responses involved diplomatic protests, often followed by economic and political sanctions. Thus, for example, China downgraded relations with the Netherlands after the Dutch sale of two submarines to Taiwan in 1980. Following French arms sales to Taiwan in 1992, China's retribution included the exclusion of the French companies from various business deals, closure of the French consulate in Guangzhou, and cancellation of various contracts (*Far Eastern Economic Review*, 27 January 1994, p. 13). When the Czech Republic crossed China over Lien Chan's high-profile visit in 1995, the visit by the PRC State Education Commission was cut short and a planned agreement on student exchange and academic cooperation was delayed (*China Post*, 21 June 1995). Possibly owing to the low level of publicity accorded to Lien Chan's visit by his hosts, the Ukraine escaped with a lighter punishment a year later as the PRC merely postponed a visit by a Chinese government delegation (Chang, 1996, pp. 131–3).

When Latvia and Macedonia mounted the most direct challenge to the 'one China' principle, China resorted to political retributions and preferential policies towards those states neighbouring Latvia and Macedonia, rather than to direct economic sanctions. The steps taken against Latvia included cancellation of the dispatch of the PRC ambassador and the diplomatic isolation of Latvia in the context of Beijing's dialogue with other Baltic states (*Renmin Ribao*, 26 February 1992). China also proffered a small incentive in the form of expansion of Sino-Latvian trade, which until 1995 consistently surpassed the PRC's levels of trade with the remaining Baltic states. In the Macedonian case, the PRC cut off diplomatic ties, halted the implementation of all agreements, recalled its ambassador and vetoed the extension of stay for the UN peacekeeping troops in Macedonia (*Xinhua*, 9 February 1999; *Zhongyang Ribao*, 25–6 February 1999). Yet, it suspended neither soft loans granted before 1999 nor its trading activities with Macedonia. At the same time, the PRC intensified relations with other Balkan states through the exchange of high-level visits, offers of soft loans (US$10 million to Bulgaria and US$500 million to Yugoslavia), non-repayable annual grants (US$72 million to Romania) and humanitarian assistance (US$600,000 to Albania and US$2 million to Yugoslavia).

China's political and economic sanctions served two purposes. First, they were intended to force the reversal of the policy of which they disapproved. Latvia and Macedonia returned to the China camp in 1994 and 2001, respectively. The Dutch promise in 1983 not to authorize any new arms deals with Taiwan paved the way for the restoration of full diplomatic ties with China (Kindermann, 1998, p. 95). In a Sino-French Joint Statement, signed in 1994, the French pledged not to approve any arms sales to Taiwan (*Far Eastern Economic Review*, 27 January 1994, p. 12). The second, possibly even more important, purpose of the PRC's sanctions was to deter other European states from following the 'bad' examples. Thus, most European states learned from the Dutch and French lessons and abstained from arms deals with Taiwan (Drifte, 1985, p. 1118; Jencks, 1994, p. 92; *Far East Economic Review*, 1993, p. 14). Learning from the Czech experience, the Spanish government cancelled Lien Chan's visit at the last minute in 1997, while in the early 2000s, the Swedish, French and Belgian governments refused to grant visas to President Chen Shui-bian.

Nonetheless, the PRC is aware of the danger of the EU developing a more proactive policy on Taiwan either in response to the EP's resolutions or in competition with the United States. China's first ever EU Policy Paper, issued in 2003, reminded the EU that the 'one China' principle was an important 'cornerstone' underpinning China–EU relations and its proper handling by the Union was essential for securing a steady growth of bilateral relations. The paper demanded that the EU prohibit visits by Taiwanese officials and all kinds of political cooperation; should not support Taiwan's accession or participation in any international organizations; and should not sell any military equipment to Taiwan. Only the exchanges of high-level visits and political dialogue with the EU were considered in the paper as more important than the EU's strict adherence to the 'one China' principle in the context of China–EU relations.

Conclusion

In the late 1970s–mid-1980s, East Central Europe entertained no contacts with Taiwan, while the majority of West European states restricted their interaction with the island to purely commercial and cultural cooperation. With the launch of 'flexible diplomacy', reinforced by its economic sweeteners, Taiwan not only upgraded its bilateral relations with Western Europe to semi-official level, featuring representative offices (headed by career diplomats and functioning as *de facto* consulates), direct air links, arms deals, visits at the ministerial or even vice-presidential level, periodical consultative meetings and active cultural, academic and scientific cooperation, but also succeeded in establishing substantive, bilateral relations with the majority of post-communist states in East Central Europe and institutionalizing multilateral cooperation with the EU. Most importantly, it scored two crucial victories when it signed consular and diplomatic agreements with Latvia and Macedonia, respectively. Taiwan also succeeded in maintaining a diplomatic partnership with the Vatican and securing the (short-lived) support of the Czech Republic and Latvia for its bid to re-enter the UN.

It could be argued that Taiwan's most significant achievements in Europe – namely, arms deals, consular/diplomatic accords or support for the membership in intergovernmental organizations – were either sporadic or short-lived and that the Vatican remained in the pool of the ROC's allies because it failed to find a compromise with China on issues unrelated to Taiwan. Even so, to describe Taiwan's diplomacy towards Europe as a failure because it did not live up to the highest expectations is unnecessarily critical. The very fact that the arms deals went ahead, while Latvia and Macedonia acceded to the consular or diplomatic agreements, were laudable achievements, given the dire economic and political consequences for those maverick states' relations with China. Despite Taiwan's limited economic resources and the domestic debates regarding the necessity to fund friendships with the foreign states, as well as Europe's emphasis on cultivating relations with China, a rising economic and political giant, Taiwan's interaction with most European states was surprisingly intense and eventful. Far from being marginalized by the emerging strategic partnership between Europe and China, Taiwan successfully carved its place in Europe's bilateral and multilateral trade and foreign relations. In the process, pro-Taiwan lobbies emerged in the EU and national parliaments, political parties, media and academia that championed Taiwan's closer relations with Europe in the name of shared beliefs in democracy and freedom, rather than merely financial profitability of economic cooperation.

It cannot be denied that European interests in developing closer links with Taiwan were motivated by economic considerations. But it also cannot be denied that Europe – disunited on foreign policy issues and lacking the capacity to project credible power beyond its immediate geographical neighbourhood – was poorly equipped to develop a strategy explicitly reaffirming Taiwan's right to the *de facto* sovereignty. Taiwan's internal disagreements regarding the desirability of the *de jure* independence also conditioned Europe's non-involvement in the intra-Chinese dispute and its continued loyalty to the 'one China' principle. To some extent, the Europeans – championing democracy and human rights world-wide – felt relieved of their duties to defend democratic Taiwan against China's bellicose designs as long as the United States continued its mission to protect Taiwan, albeit no longer as unambiguously as it did until 1980. However, Europe's increasing economic engagement on both sides of the Taiwan Strait enhanced its interest in peace and stability in the region. Moreover, the Europeans, through their elected representatives, became increasingly more appreciative of the achievements of the Taiwanese democracy and explicitly unsupportive of China's plans to subjugate the island militarily. Thus, the emphasis on the functional relationship and the official commitment to the 'one China' policy notwithstanding, Europe – regardless of whether it develops proactive common foreign policy on the Taiwan issue – is more likely than not to stand in Taiwan's defence if and when the PRC decides to complete national reunification against the wishes of the Taiwanese people.

Notes

1. For analytical purposes, in this chapter Europe is divided into two geographical areas: Western Europe and East Central Europe. The former refers to all states west and north of Poland, the Czech and Slovak Republics, Hungary and Slovenia. The latter refers to the former Soviet allies in Europe, including post-Soviet Baltic states, Belarus and Ukraine, but excluding Russia.
2. All East Central European and most West European states supported China's entry into the UN.
3. According to Mengin, in 1985 France became the first European state to issue visas in Taipei (Mengin, 1997, p. 234).
4. Interview with the then Vice Minister of Economic Affairs, Chiang Ping-kun (*Zhongguo Shibao*, 7 June 1991).

5. Taiwanese media speculated that Taipei extended a soft loan of US$100 million to Budapest. In most likelihood, such a loan never took place. The Hungarians managed to sell Taipei buses for about US$43 million.
6. See also Jan Rowinski, 'Politika Chin [ChRL i Taiwanu] wobec Estonii, Litwy i Lotwy. Stosunki wzajemne [1991–1994]' (China's (PRC and Taiwan's) Policy towards Estonia, Lithuania and Latvia. Bilateral Relations [1991–1994]), *Studia i Materialy*, No. 84 (Warsaw: Polski Instytut Spraw Miedzynarodowych, December 1994), pp. 5–6; *Renmin Ribao*, 5 January 1992; *Zili Zaobao*, 27 October 1992.
7. In October 2004, for example, Taipei donated US$100,000 to the Holy See in response to a call by the Pope to assist poor people in Asia (*Central News Agency*, 14 October 2004). In January 2000, Archbishop Paul Cordes, the head of the Vatican's aid agency, toured Taiwan and was awarded a medal of honour by President Lee Teng-hui. Cordes said that his visit was a sign that Vatican–Taiwanese relations were still strong. (*The Associated Press*, 17 January 2000).
8. For example, the Association to Promote Commercial and Tourist Exchanges with Taiwan was renamed the Taipei Representative Office in France; the Free China Information Office in Denmark was renamed the Taipei Economic and Cultural Office and the Taipei Representative Office in 1995.
9. In 1997, for example, the French lost out to the Americans in the bidding for the nuclear power station project. In 2000, Franco-British and German companies were outbid by the Japanese for the construction of a high-speed railway.
10. An interview with the Czech official, Taipei, June 2005.
11. A formal EU–Taiwan WTO agreement was signed in January 1999.
12. Yuchun Lan classified the EP's resolutions on Taiwan in three categories, but according to different criteria than those used in this article: resolutions under consultation procedure, resolutions in response to the annual report of the Commission or the Presidency report on the Common Foreign and Security Policy, and resolutions on members of parliament's own initiative on a topical and urgent subject (Lan, 2004, p. 117).
13. In 2002, for example, state-owned China Airlines chose the Boeing's offer for the purchase of 16 aircraft, valued at US$1.5 billion, despite the fact that Airbus offered more attractive financial terms. A year later, the European Commission warned that China Airlines' purchase of new engines from General Electric, rather than Rolls-Royce plc, could damage Taiwan–EU relations. However, China Airlines did buy seven airbuses in 1999.

References

Brodsgaard, Kjeld Erik, 'The ROC and the United Nations from a Scandinavian Perspective', in Marie-Luise Nath (ed.), *The Republic of China on Taiwan in International Politics* (Frankfurt: Peter Lang, 1998), pp. 131–46.
Building a Comprehensive Partnership with China (25 March 1998). Available at http://ec.europa.eu/comm/external_relations/china/com_98/index.htm (accessed 22 November 2006).

Cabestan, Jean-Pierre, 'France's Taiwan Policy: A Case of Shopkeeper Diplomacy', paper delivered at the international conference, 'The Role of France and Germany in Sino-European Relations', the French Centre for Research on Contemporary China and the Europe–China Centre, Department of Government and International Studies, Hong Kong Baptist University, Hong Kong (22–3 June 2001).

Chan, Gerald, 'Sino-Vatican Diplomatic Relations: Problems and Prospects', *The China Quarterly*, 120 (December 1989), 814–36.

Chang, Ya-chun, 'Beijing's Reaction to Vice-President Lien Chan's Trip to Ukraine', *Issues and Studies*, 32(8) (August 1996), 131–3.

Chi, Su, 'International Relations of the Republic of China during the 1990s', *Issues and Studies*, 29(9) (September 1993), 1–21.

Council for Economic Planning and Development, *Taiwan Statistical Data Book 2004* (Taipei: Council for Economic Planning and Development, 2004).

Drifte, Reinhard, 'European and Soviet Perspectives on Future Responses in Taiwan to International and Regional Developments', *Asian Survey*, 25(11) (November 1985), 1115–22.

Erasmus, Stephen, 'General de Gaulle's Recognition of Peking', *The China Quarterly*, 18 (April–June 1964), 195–200.

European Commission, 'EU Strategy towards China: Implementation of the 1998 Communication and Future Steps for a More Effective EU Policy' (15 May 2003). Available at http://ec.europa.eu/comm/external_relations/china/com01_265.pdf (accessed 22 November 2006).

European Commission, 'EU China: Closer Partners, Growing Responsibilities', 24 October 2006, p. 11. Available at http://ec.europa.eu/comm/external_relations/china/docs/06-10- 24_final_com.pdf (accessed 14 November 2006).

European Economic and Trade Office, *EU–Taiwan Trade Relations*. Available at http://www.deltwn.cec.eu.int/EN/eu_taiwan/eu_taiwantraderelations. htm accessed 15 May 2005.

Gao, Lang, *Zhonghua Mingguo waijiao guanxi zhi yanbian, 1972–1992* (An Evolution of Foreign Relations of the Republic of China) (Taibei: Wunan Tushu, 1994), p. 20.

Garver, John W., *The Sino-American Alliance: Nationalist China and American Cold War Strategy in Asia* (Armonk, NY: M.E. Sharpe, 1997), p. 258.

Ho, Shu-yin, 'Walking the Tightrope: The ROC's Democratization, Diplomacy, and Mainland Policy', *Issues and Studies*, 28(3) (March 1992), 1–20.

Hsieh, Chiao Chiao, 'Pragmatic Diplomacy: Foreign Policy and External Relations', in Peter Ferdinand (ed.), *Take-off for Taiwan* (London: The Royal Institute of International Affairs, 1996), pp. 66–106.

Jencks, Harlan W., 'Taiwan in the International Arms Market', in Robert G. Sutter and William R. Johnson (eds), *Taiwan in World Affairs* (Boulder: Westview Press, 1994), pp. 73–112.

Joei, Bernard T. K., 'Pragmatic Diplomacy in the Republic of China: History and Prospects', in Jason C. Hu (ed.), *Quiet Revolutions on Taiwan, Republic of China* (Taipei: Kwang Hwa Publishing Company, 1994), pp. 297–330.

Kim, Samuel S., 'Taiwan and the International System: The Challenge of Legitimation', in Robert G. Sutter and William R. Johnson (eds), *Taiwan in World Affairs* (Boulder: Westview Press, 1994), pp. 145–90.

Kindermann, Gottfried-Karl, 'The Relations of the ROC with the European Union', in Marie-Luise Nath (ed.), *The Republic of China on Taiwan in International Politics* (Frankfurt: Peter Lang, 1998), pp. 87–118.

Lan, Yuchun, 'The European Parliament and the China–Taiwan Issue: An Empirical Approach', *European Foreign Affairs Review*, 9 (2004), 115–40.

Leung, Beatrice, 'Sino-Vatican Relations at the Century's Turn', *Journal of Contemporary China*, 14(43) (May 2005), 353–70.

Madsen, Richard, 'Catholic Revival during the Reform Era', *The China Quarterly*, 174 (June 2003), 468–87.

Mengin, Francoise, 'Taiwan's Non-Official Diplomacy', *Diplomacy & Statecraft*, 8(1) (March 1997), 228–48.

Mengin, Francoise, 'A Functional Relationship: Political Extensions to Europe–Taiwan Economic Ties', *The China Quarterly*, 169 (March 2002), 136–53.

Ministry of Economic Affairs, Department of Investment Services. Available at http://investintai wan.nat.gov.tw/en/env/stats/fdi_area&ind.html accessed 11 February 2007.

Moller, Kay, 'A New Role for the ROC on Taiwan in the Post-Cold War Era', *Issues and Studies*, 32(2) (February 1995), 67–86.

Moller, Kay, 'Germany and China: A Continental Temptation', *The China Quarterly*, 147 (September 1996), 706–25.

Republic of China Yearbook 1989 (Taipei: Kwang Hua Publishing Co., 1989).

Saalman, Lora, and Yuan, Jing-dong, 'The European Union and the Arms Ban on China', *Centre for Nonproliferation Studies* (July 2004), online edition. Available at www.nti.org accessed 26 April 2005.

Shin, Chueiling, 'Development of ROC–France Relations: The Case of an Isolated State and its Economic Diplomacy', *Issues and Studies*, 37(1) (January/February 2001), 124–59.

Taiwan Statistical Data Book 2006 (Taipei: Council for Economic Planning and Development, 2006).

Tsai, Cheng-Wen, and Ming, Chu-Cheng, 'The Republic of China and Western Europe: Past and Future', in Yu San Wang (ed.), *Foreign Policy of the Republic of China: an Unorthodox Approach* (New York: Praeger, 1990), pp. 123–43.

Tubilewicz, Czeslaw, 'The Baltic States in Taiwan's Post-Cold War "Flexible Diplomacy"', *Europe–Asia Studies*, 54(5) (July 2002), 791–810.

Tubilewicz, Czeslaw, 'Taiwan's "Macedonian Project" 1999–2001', *The China Quarterly*, 179 (September 2004), 782–803.

Wang, Wan-li, 'Taiwan Accession to GATT/WTO: A Case Study in Recent Taiwan–EU Relations', *Tamkang Journal of International Affairs*, 4(2) (1999), 109.

Wang, Wan-li, 'Improved Taiwan–EU Relations will Bring Great Mutual Benefits', *Taipei Journal*, 2 November 2001.

Weng, Byron S. J., 'Taiwan's International Status Today', *The China Quarterly*, 99 (September 1984), 462–80.

Wu, Linjun, 'Does Money Talk?: The ROC Economic Diplomacy', *Issues and Studies*, 31(12) (December 1995), 22–35.

Wu, Rong-I, 'Taiwan–European Relations after WTO Accession'. Available at www.gio.gove.tw accessed 20 May 2005.

Yahuda, Michael, 'The International Standing of the Republic of China on Taiwan', *The China Quarterly*, 148 (December 1996), 1319–39.

10
From an Issue-specific to a Global Partnership: Japan and the European Union

Machiko Hachiya

Introduction

This chapter will try to illustrate the development of relations between Japan and the European Union (EU) from the problem-oriented single issue of trade to a more cooperation-oriented approach across a wider range of activities. In doing so, it will pay particular attention to the deepening and widening of integration in Europe, accompanied by the extending competence of the EU, and Japan's shift in attitude towards evolving European integration.

For almost three decades, the relationship between Japan and the EU was confined to trade, yet its development during these years was significant. To offer just one example: among those countries that provided the EU's imported goods, Japan was ranked 27th in 1957 but by 1988 it had moved to second place.[1]

Such intensification in trade eventually led to cooperation in wider fields, particularly in the context of a changing world system following the ending of the Cold War. In that context, the first Japan–EU Summit in 1991 was a landmark. Japan began to regard the EU as a tough but serious partner in the fields of global issues where the EU was increasingly present either as a representative of, or together with, its member states. It was a difficult process for Japan to acquire the sort of negotiation style necessary for dealing with a multilateral actor. Faced with an inherently multilateral organization like the EU, Japan is beginning to realize the power of 'dual diplomacy', something that both irritates Japan and also obliges it to act more tactically. The agenda in which both Japan and the EU are involved often has global characteristics. It is on those occasions that Japan identifies itself as a more global actor by balancing between national interests and a global role.

In this author's view Japan–EU relations are developing in a global environment within an underpinning institutional framework. This view will be explained, first by chronologically reviewing the development of relations, then by examining two specific cases – the UNFCC-COP 1 of the Kyoto Protocol and the construction site of ITER – and finally by describing how the Japanese government reacted to such a development in relations through organizational reforms. Such fairly recent developments are more evident at the governmental level than at the societal level where closer relations have yet to be satisfactorily enhanced.

Overview of the development of Japan–EU relations

As early as the year following the completion of the Customs Union of the European Communities (EC) in 1968, the Commission of the EC had already obtained a mandate to negotiate with Japan on trade-related issues. The Customs Union also set a common external tariff for European Economic Community (EEC) member states, which encouraged other countries to shift from state-to-state-based bilateral trade agreements to community-based inclusive agreements.

Japan was no exception to this shift. When the common external trade policy was established in 1970, negotiations between Japan and the EC on an inclusive trade agreement were also launched. However, to date, no such agreement has been signed yet because of the safeguard clause that the member states had wanted to include but which Japan rejected. The safeguard clause had already been included in most of the bilateral agreements that Japan had signed individually with the then six EC member states in the 1960s[2] (Ohira, 2002, p. 161). As a fast-growing economy, Japan found the safeguard clause to be discriminatory while the European countries were very suspicious of Japan's overflowing exports. Two attempts at negotiations on an inclusive agreement took place during 1970–71 without success (Ohira, 2002, p. 108).

A textile agreement between Japan and the EC, however, was successfully implemented from 1972–3 and 1976–7. Meanwhile, the office of the Delegation of the Commission of European Communities was opened in Tokyo in 1974.

The failure of an inclusive trade agreement was not in vain; rather, it led to the setting up of a series of regular high-level meetings between the two parties. The first meeting took place in June 1973 in Brussels. Since then, meetings have been held twice a year alternatively between Brussels and Tokyo. High-level meetings eventually covered almost all trade-related matters and served as the only regular and substantial meeting until a regular ministerial meeting was set up in 1984.

Thus, institutional development in dialogue between the two parties can be easily traced as its levels were upgraded from working level to high level to ministerial. However, reinforced institutionalization may suggest a continuation of problems. In fact, the worldwide economic crisis triggered by the first energy crisis in 1973 raised harsh criticism from Europe against Japanese exports. When the so-called Doko Mission, a group of business leaders from major member companies of the Japan Federation of Economic Organizations (Keidanren) led by then President Doko Toshimitsu, visited Europe, they had to confront some very open criticism. It was such a damaging situation for Japan that it recognized that some conciliatory actions would have to be taken. The launch of the Japan/EP interparliamentary meetings was an example of such actions. The first meeting took place in Strasbourg in 1978 with the aim of providing a forum to discuss the mounting trade-related problems between the parliamentary members of the Japanese Diet and the European Parliament (Delegation of the European Union in Tokyo, 2006).[3]

More substantial opportunities for dialogue at the working level were institutionalized in the first half of the 1980s in fields such as fair trade,[4] electronic devices for private industries, industrial cooperation, and post and telecommunications. At the level of civil society, the EU initiated several programmes with a final goal of obtaining increased trade penetration into Japanese society. The Executive Training Programme (ETP) for young European businessmen in 1979 and the Science and Technology Fellowship (STF) for post-doctoral European researchers in 1986 are just two examples among many. Both programmes provided opportunities for young Europeans to spend a few years in Japan to establish more personal relationships in their respective professions.

However, in the 1980s the conflicts over trade not only continued but worsened as the EC's deficit with Japan increased significantly. Against such a background, from 1983 for a period of three years Japan finally decided to impose restrictions on its producers (voluntary export restraints) on ten export items to Europe.

The adoption of the Single European Act in 1985 alerted both Japanese industry and government to the so-called 'Fortress of Europe', which in turn triggered a large increase in direct investment from Japan to EC member states. The single market project also encouraged Japan to make more efforts to abolish the remaining quantitative restrictions (QRs), which were reduced to some 60 items after three non-official meetings held during 1988–89.

Thus, during the 1970s and 1980s relations between Japan and the EU were focused mostly on trade-related problems and their countermeasures. The negotiation frame was shifted gradually from a member state government to the increasing involvement of the Europeank Commission accompanied by the institutionalization of dialogues from working to ministerial levels between Japan and the EU. Although these two decades were coloured by conflicts and suspicions towards each other, it was also a period that saw the intensification of relations at different levels.

The final decade of the twentieth century should be remembered as the most significant era of European integration. It was largely a consequence of the changes in the world system as the Cold War ended. The EC evolved to become the EU in 1993 and partly extended its competence to the political field while clearly identifying itself with more normative values such as democracy, minority rights and the rule of law (*Treaty on European Union*, 1993, Title I, Article F). The Japan–EU relationship also developed into wider fields of cooperation. This was announced explicitly by the Joint Declaration at the occasion of the first Japan–EU Summit meeting in the Hague in July 1991.

The Joint Declaration on Relations between the European Community and its Member States and Japan affirmed the inclusive reinforcement of the bilateral relationship as an equal partnership:

> ...[r]ecalling their increasingly close ties and acknowledging growing worldwide interdependence and, consequently, the need for heightened international cooperation; affirming their common interest in security, peace and the stability of the world; aware of the importance of their deepening dialogue in order to make a joint contribution towards safeguarding peace in the world, setting up a just and stable international order in accordance with the principle and purposes of the United Nations Charter and taking up the global challenges that the international community has to face; ... (European Commission, 1991)

The Joint Declaration further established various forums and dialogues of consultation and cooperation. It was a tendency certainly taking into account the expected enlargement of the EU to 15 members, which has continued subsequently to 25 and now to 27 member countries. Among the results of this reinforced cooperation are the complete abolition of QRs in 1994,[5] the science and technology forum in 1994, expert meetings on deregulation of 192 items in 1994[6] (Ohira, 2002, p. 121), regular summit meetings, and the mutual recognition consultation in 1995.[7] Japan also participated in the Asia–Europe Meeting (ASEM), the first inter-regional forum between Asia and Europe, which started in 1996, and hosted the meeting in 2005.

At the dawn of the new millennium, after ten years of relations under the Joint Declaration, the Japan–EU relationship underwent another substantial development. The tenth Japan–EU Summit in 2001 inaugurated the 'Decade of Japan–Europe Co-operation' and an Action Plan for EU–Japan Cooperation entitled 'Shaping Our Common Future' was drawn up covering the following four objectives: (1) promoting peace and security; (2) strengthening the economic and trade partnership; (3) coping with global and societal challenges; and (4) bringing together people and culture. The implementation of the action plan is reviewed at the annual summit meeting, and the year 2005 was promoted as the 'EU–Japan Year of People to People Exchanges' with nearly 1,000 events registered to participate in the exchange.

Japan–EU relations are evolving from a tentative trade partnership to an equal partnership on global issues. The development of the relationship parallels that of the EU as a regional organization and the integration of Europe. However, when considering Japan's external relations as a whole, it is obvious that Japan's relationship with the United States is still its most important relationship in every aspect, from trade to security. It cannot be denied, moreover, that the Japan–EU relationship has been shaped, to some extent, along the lines of the Japan–US pattern; for example, the Regulatory Reform Dialogue in 1994 was triggered by the commencement of US–Japan SII (Structural Impediments Initiative) talks in 1989.

Nevertheless, there are some good signs that a genuinely equal partnership is developing between Japan and the EU. Both parties successfully managed to participate in the World Trade Organization (WTO) as two of the three major economic powers in the world; sometimes allying against the United States, at other times complaining about each other's actions (Gilson, 2000, p. 150). Despite the conflicts over trade and deregulation, or rather because of the series of negotiations seeking to resolve problems, both parties may have gone through a learning process to act as equal partners, especially in trade-related matters. However, when it comes to issues beyond that of trade, Japan and the EU are still in the process of establishing a global partnership. Their relations outside trade matters at this stage may be called an 'issue-specific alliance'.

The next section will examine how the two parties are learning to work together on specific issues of a global nature.

Issue-specific alliance

The term 'issue-specific alliance' will be applied to an explanation of the relationship between Japan and the EU. The 'issue-specific alliance' takes the form of dual-layered diplomacy for Japan in dealing with the EU. The first layer of diplomacy with the EU member states affects Japan's attitude towards the second layer, which is the EU. It can be concluded that success in the first layer is the key to bringing to fruition this particular form of alliance until Japan learns to act in a multilateral environment.

In an 'issue-specific alliance' form, the EU acts as the principal European negotiator representing its member states with a delegated mandate from them. Therefore, the EU performs as a significant global actor in those particular fields. Yet, to date Japan has been more concerned about the opinions of the member states, even when the EU is granted a mandate. And when it is not, Japan remains rather superficial or slow to commit itself to the EU. Failed cooperation over the landmine issue was a good lesson for both parties. Gilson points out that 'a lack of coordination on both sides without clear-cut framework of project did not produce significant result' (Gilson, 2000, pp. 157–61). Past experiences show that Japan may ally with the EU only through the member states' assurance in a relevant issue – a form of dual-layered diplomacy. For a solid issue-specific alliance, the first layer (of the member states) seems indispensable. In the following section two case studies will be explored to see how Japan and the EU come to terms with each other in the situation of an 'issue-specific alliance'.

The Kyoto Protocol

The Kyoto Protocol of the UN Framework Convention on Climate Change of 1997 at first sight seems to provide a good example of global partnership. However, the negotiation process over the Protocol revealed conflicts and irritation between the two sides. This transpired despite the fact that the EU was a leading actor for ratification and a signatory of the Protocol, while the United States rejected it. These bitter experiences may indicate that Japan and the EU developed their relationship into an 'issue-specific alliance' in the 1990s, but have not yet reached the level of global partnership.

Even when the EU was representing the member states at an international forum, one can observe Japan's irritation towards the EU system, which is by nature multilateral. The negotiating process will be traced through a procedure of the Kyoto Protocol (UNFCC-COP1). In his book, the Japanese chief negotiator of the Kyoto Protocol reviewed in detail the main issues, problems, and negotiation procedures among the main actors involved in the Protocol (Tanabe, 1999).

As is well known, the most difficult matter in reaching agreement about the Protocol was the difference in attitude towards climate change between the groups of developing and developed nations. The Kyoto Protocol was to set up agreed implementation measures including legally-binding target numbers for the developed nations as a follow-up to the previous Berlin mandate which had been derived from the UN Framework Convention. As one may imagine, the most difficult and yet the ultimate task of the Kyoto Protocol was to find a compromise solution acceptable to both groups. However, there was also significant differentiation among the developed nations themselves when it came to concrete figures of emission levels of greenhouse gases.

According to the Japanese chief negotiator, Toshiaki Tanabe, the key players amongst the developed nations were the United States, the EU and Japan. This meant that the success of the Kyoto Conference depended ultimately on reaching an agreement among the three because the problem and responsibility of the target figure was an issue that concerned primarily the developed nations. In light of this understanding, Mr Tanabe confessed that every night he quietly organized a tripartite meeting at a conference hall restaurant, as well as bilateral meetings between the EU and Japan, or the United States and Japan whenever he judged necessary. The frequency of meetings intensified after the ministers arrived in Kyoto. Thus, an extremely intensive communication process took place among the three over a period of less than one week. When the final stage approached, Japanese Prime Minister Hashimoto Ryutaro made direct telephone calls to the heads of states of both the United States and EU member states.

The Japanese chief negotiator explains that a strategy of combining informal tripartite negotiations and summit diplomacy made the Kyoto Conference successful. He also affirms that another decisive factor in the success was a basic consensus among the three to maintain their global competitive power. He goes on to state that even though the EU is often regarded as an environmentally conscious organization, it, ironically, was the most insistent when it came to maintaining competitive power. Although the chief negotiator does not provide an analysis behind the EU's intention, he seems to be making the point that the EU placed its priority on the economic effect of the gas emission reduction, just like other participating nations. Such an attitude could have been a result of a compromise among the EU member states.

He does not hide his irritation towards and even distrust of the EU system of decision-making. At the time of the Kyoto Conference the Presidency was held by Luxembourg. The Japanese chief negotiator observed that the Presidency had not taken the initiative within the EU, but had simply acted as a messenger. While he expresses appreciation in his own way for the individual participants from the EU member states, the EU as a whole was assessed as an inconclusive and incoherent negotiator whether intentionally or unintentionally.

Such a conclusion could have been drawn because of the multilateral decision-making system and its cumbersome procedures, especially in fields where the EU is not granted exclusive competence. Therefore, part of the problem lies on the EU side regardless of with whom or what country it is negotiating. The problem of incoherence was part of the reason behind the draft constitution treaty, which aimed to minimize incoherence not least via the newly-created role of the EU Foreign Minister.[8]

For Japan, the EU as a counterpart apparently provided a learning opportunity when it came to negotiating with a multilateral organization. Japanese negotiators realized that more tactful attention should be paid to even the slightest differences among the EU member states and that, if necessary, they should lobby bilaterally in order to reach a substantial compromise with the member states concerned, which would pave the way for a final compromise at the European level. And yet the words of the EU should always be taken as a reference point, for it is with the EU, represented by the Presidency, that Japan, or any other negotiator, will sit together in order to reach an agreement – whatever the issue may be. Thus, the EU figured itself as a negotiator of a dual-layered system composed of a European level and an individual national level to which equal efforts of lobbying should be paid.

The ITER Project

A similar experience with the EU as a negotiator in dual-layered diplomacy may be observed in the case of the International Thermonuclear Experimental Reactor (ITER), although with a very different pattern of alliance development from the Kyoto Protocol.

ITER is an international project to construct and operate an experimental fusion reactor. Although it is a highly challenging task, the 'final aim is proving the scientific and engineering feasibility of the fusion which is expected to be an ultimate source of energy for human kind' (Ministry of Foreign Affairs of Japan, 2007).

The idea of cooperation over fusion was first proposed at an historic meeting between US President Ronald Reagan and Soviet President Mikhail Gorbachev in Geneva in November 1985. It was the first summit after seven years between the two big powers under a still-divided world. This mega-project for cooperation over fusion was proposed as a compensation following the first summit between Reagan and Gorbachev which had produced little in the way of concrete results. In December 1986, scientists representing the US, the Soviet Union, the EC and Japan met in Vienna, and agreed to work together on the design of an experimental fusion reactor. The project was named ITER. The following is a brief history of the ITER project.

Since 1979, 40 researchers from the four participating parties have been engaged in a 'working group' based in Vienna with the support of the International Atomic Energy Agency (IAEA) on a research project called 'International Next Tokamak Reactor (INTOR)'. Although the researchers were never fully informed about the purpose of the project, they were all hoping to formalize internationally the thermonuclear project (Herman, 1990; Mikado, 1996, pp. 349–52).

The ITER design activities were carried out between 1988 and 2001 at a newly constructed research base in the Max Planck Institute in Garching in Germany. It was agreed that the estimated cost of US$170 million was to be shared equally among the four parties. In 1999, the USA withdrew from the project, but the remaining three parties carried on. Despite its excellence as an energy source, thermonuclear projects have always suffered from a lack of a public understanding because of their unfamiliar nature and huge cost. At any rate, the three remained in collaboration and the design activities were thus completed in 2001.

Following the completion of the reactor design, negotiations were initiated on the joint implementation of ITER, which meant resolving where to build the experimental reactor, how the costs and procurements were to be shared, and how to manage and operate the project. By this time, Canada had joined to make four participating parties: the European Union, Japan, the Russian Federation and Canada. In June 2002, following Cabinet approval, Japan submitted Rokkasho-mura as its candidate for the construction site. The other site offers came from Cadarache of France, Vandellos of Spain, and Clarington of Canada. At this stage, the EU had not singled out its European candidate site.

While negotiations over the site continued, the year 2003 saw a big modification in the participating countries of ITER, ending up with six parties: two additional countries – the United States and China – (re)joined in February, South Korea joined in June, then

Canada withdrew in December. Meanwhile, in December 2003, a ministerial meeting held in Washington finally picked two candidate sites, Cadarache of France/EU and Rokkasho-mura of Japan. Current participating parties were divided in their support. Russia and China supported Cadarache, and the United States and South Korea Rokkasho-mura. Japan and the EU entered into a rivalry over the ITER construction site that continued until June 2005 when the second ministerial meeting was held in Moscow. The six parties finally agreed to Cadarache (Ministry of Foreign Affairs of Japan, 2005).

Japan opted for a position of the 'non-host' after at least three years of officially expressing its initiative to lead the ITER. For Japan, ITER was significant for two distinctive reasons.[9] One was the merit of gaining technological experience for the construction, when the time was right, of a commercial fusion reactor. It has been agreed that ITER will be conducted by compounding machines and equipment from each participant responsible for different aspects of the project. Therefore, a host country of the site will, expectedly, have the advantage of acquiring the outstanding technology, which may allow it to take the lead in the development of a commercial reactor.

The other reason was the fact that ITER, if constructed in Japan, would become the first mega-scale international project to be implemented in Asia. It would contribute to the revitalization of Asia as a whole not only in science and technology, but also in many other aspects as a spillover effect of the project. Naturally, the Japanese government was convinced that Japan would be the natural choice to take the leadership of such a mega-project in Asia.

Why, then, did Japan give way? The outcome was a result of intensive negotiations and the examination of scientific and economic effects in a multilateral as well as a bilateral environment. In February–May 2004 three high-level meetings and one meeting of scientific experts between Japan and the EU were held to discuss the roles to be shared and contents of 'the wider approach' that had been agreed to by the experts of the six parties. A high-level meeting of all the participating parties was held in June 2004, but no agreement was reached. Gradually, the importance of minimizing the merits and demerits between the host and non-host parties was recognized. In April 2005 a ministerial meeting between Japan and the EU agreed on the earliest possible implementation of ITER and an international agreement to be reached before the Group of Eight (G8) Summit in July. By this meeting, Japan seems to have concluded that it should agree to Cadarache with Japan's beneficiary treatment in return (*Le Monde*, 2 May 2005).

Japan explains its position by insisting on the win–win nature of the conclusion (Ministry of Foreign Affairs of Japan, 2005). With 'the Broader Approach' of the project (www.deljpn.ec.europa.eu, 2007),[10] the role-sharing of the host and non-host country had been agreed upon, and Japan opted for a 'quasi-host' position that enabled it, as Japan recognized, to secure its national interest. Japan emphasizes the significance of its shared role in hosting a part of the ITER headquarters function and of its right to recommend the president.

Apart from the diplomatic compromise and rhetorical national interest, the economic aspect is believed to be of greater importance. The current estimated cost of ITER, including the construction and operation costs, is as large as US$12 billion (1,170 billion yen).[11] On top of that, the cost for the site preparation is to be borne by the host country. The final cost may be extremely difficult to estimate, especially with so much uncertainty in regard to the fusion research itself (Mikado, 1996).[12]

The interaction between the Japanese decision and the US attitude remains to be further examined in a wider context. But Europe seems to have been determined to take the leadership of the project – on 23 March 2005 the EU made the decision to begin building the reactor in Cadarache, even without Japan, by the end of that year (Le Monde, 2005). In fact, from the beginning it was France that had maintained a firm position to win the site, and the EU followed France to dress it up as a European outfit.

Once the EU singled out its official candidate site as Cadarache in November 2003, it became a strong negotiator. With the EU being able to stand officially for one site, some member states lobbied for the EU through their own channels. In practice, Japan had to deal with the EU and also with some of the member states. The Japanese project leader has admitted to the impact of the EU's dual negotiation system once an agreement at the European level was established[13] – a process very similar to the case of the Kyoto Protocol.

Japan's decision to opt for a quasi-host position may very well have been drawn from a rational calculation of the direct economic cost versus relative gains. Whatever Japan's expectations may be, it has accepted the EU as a significant partner for a project to which it had committed itself since the initial stage.

Reorganization of Japanese ministries and MoFA

As the two cases discussed above demonstrate, the importance of the EU as a partner for Japan in the global scene is beginning to carry substantial weight. The EU's mandate is no longer limited to trade-related issues but to much wider fields especially when it concerns global tasks and problems. As a matter of fact, almost all the ministries of the Japanese government have a contact window for the EU, and the Ministry of Foreign Affairs (MoFA) acts as a coordinator when more than one ministry is involved.[14] With the increasing number of issues involving the EU, the Japanese government sought to review the organizational structure of MoFA with regard to the EU for higher efficiency. Reorganization was implemented in August 2004.

Obviously, the reorganization of MoFA took place not only because of the changes in Europe. It was part of the long-debated reforms of the Japanese bureaucratic system, which seemed to have become more powerful than politicians and too rigid to meet rapidly changing times. As for MoFA, a series of scandals starting with an article in the *Yomiuri Shimbun* newspaper on New Year's Day 2001[15] made the Japanese public more critical about the ministry. On top of that, a newly-appointed Minister of Foreign Affairs, Mrs Tanaka Makiko, caused a chaotic situation inside MoFA with her unprecedented confrontational attitude toward MoFA officials (Yakushiji, 2003). It is not the purpose of this chapter to go into detail regarding the problems of MoFA, but suffice it to say that the urgent need of reform of MoFA was widely acknowledged as its institutional backwardness had become a target of public criticism. In order to meet the new world system of the post-Cold War era, especially with the growing scenes of global cooperation, Japan stepped forward to join a more multilateral system.

In two bureaus of MoFA, more EU-centred divisions were created. In the European Affairs Bureau, Western Europe Divisions I and II were reorganized as the European Policy Division and the Western Europe Division respectively. The European Policy Division is now responsible for general coordination and diplomatic policy in European regions including Russia, and, of most significance for this presentation, diplomatic and political matters of the EU. Thus, EU matters are now dealt with from within a more comprehensive framework, while bilateral matters are dealt with at the Western Europe Division and Central and South Eastern Europe Division.

The Economic Affairs Bureau reshuffled its six divisions into five, and renamed the International Economic Division I as the Economic Integration Division (EID). The new EID is to assume responsibility for daily contacts with regional integration bodies. In reality, this division is, for the moment, responsible solely for the EU's economic-related policies. Figure 10.1 shows the change of organization in MoFA.

Former organization	Current organization
European Affairs Division	
Western European Division I	European Policy Division
Western European Division II	Western Europe Division
Central and Eastern Europe Division	Central and South Eastern Europe Division
Russian Division	Russian Division
Economic Affairs Division	
International Economic Division I (EU)	Economic Policy Division (OECD, UNCTAD)
International Economic Division II (IMF and others)	International Trade Division (WTO)
International Energy Division	
Developing Area Division (UNCTAD)	Economic Partnership Division (FTA/EPA, ASEM, APEC)
International Organization Division I (WTO)	Economic Security Division
International Organization Division II (OECD)	Economic Integration Division (EU)

Figure 10.1 Organizational reform of the Ministry of Foreign Affairs, Japan
Source: Hiromu Wakabayashi, 'Yoroppa (Europe)' in *Nihon no Gaiko to Kokusai-shakai* (Tokai University Press, 2005) Figure 1, p. 140, MoFA home page. Modified by the author.

The EU as a global partner

The previously mentioned institutional and policy changes demonstrate a clear shift in the Japanese government's attitude towards the EU. Recognizing the growing importance of the EU beyond the economic field, it is treating the EU as a substantial regional actor. This attitude may be understood to underline the perception that while regional cooperation spreads to different parts of the world, the EU may very well remain the front runner, with more advanced institutions and more influence than any other regional body. Hence it becomes important for Japan to establish a close-knit relationship with it that is not limited solely to economic matters.

Although the EU is itself a multilateral organization, Japan was confined to a bilateral relationship rather than a global one with the EU, when the EU's competence was narrow. A reinforced relationship meant widening fields rather than deepening an existing relationship. For the EU, an extension of competence is only possible when the member states mandate it to represent them. Given this inherent nature of the EU, the issues to which the EU is committed often have a strong global aspect, overarching national priorities. As Europe widens and the world is perceived as increasingly globalized, there are more scenes in which the EU is represented as a principal actor to deal with such issues. In other words, when the EU participates, the agenda will be global, and will involve the commitment of a number of countries.

Thus, as Japan reinforces its relations with the EU, it finds itself in a more global setting. The Japan–EU bilateral relationship is being transformed into a global one where the two parties may ally or cooperate amongst many other actors. Japan–EU relations are developing within a sphere of globalization underlain by the increasing mandate of the EU.

Some may consider the Japan–EU relation to be developing in a plurilateral environment, meaning a system where some selected actors among many would perform important roles (Wakabayashi, 2005, p. 138). This author does not concur with this opinion. One of the reasons for not agreeing to a plurilateral environment for Japan and the EU is that the term is often used with a connotation of 'complicated opt-in and opt-out possibilities' (Khor, 2005). The Japan–EU relationship did not develop in an environment based on 'opt-in' or 'opt-out', but as a more institutionalized partnership. Plurilateralism normally refers to influential actors among a large number of participating parties in world politics, regardless of the field of issues. The EU has not yet developed itself as an all-round actor. It still has a limited capacity requiring a mandate from the member states, which does not allow the EU to be present for every issue. However, when it is mandated, issues are very often global and the EU enjoys substantial influence over concerned issues. In such cases, Japan often finds the EU to be an indispensable partner. Therefore, it seems more adequate to call Japan and the EU *global partners* who meet and commit to each other within a fixed frame as an 'issue-specific alliance' in a global environment.

The development of this relationship is coupled with Japan's movement away from timid diplomacy, conducted in the shadow of the United States, towards diplomacy showing signs of a greater degree of self-assuredness. A desire to become a more significant global player can be found in developments such as the pursuit of a permanent post in the United Nations Security Council or the proposal of an 'East Asia Community' as something much more than an abstract concept. For the latter, the only existing reference point could be the EU both as a lesson and a model. In this sense, it is important for Japan to gain a better understanding of the EU, how it functions and why it functions in the way it does. This necessitates a more comprehensive approach towards the EU.

Relations between Japan and the EU at the governmental level are intensifying, with thicker institutionalization accompanying the widening competences of the EU. Those at the societal level, however, still fall short. The Japanese public suffers notably from a lack of understanding of what it is to 'be European' or what life is like in an integrated Europe. The EU is trying to fill in this gap by supporting the activities of local EU associations created in 11 different cities in Japan and by funding EU Institutes to diffuse EU studies.[16]

Being two-thirds of the way through the ten-year long Action Plan, Japanese operations to narrow the gap between the two levels of initiative seem an urgent task for further development of relations with the EU.

Notes

1. Trade (imports and exports) between Japan and the EU remains important. In 2005, Japan was the fifth leading trade partner for the EU; the EU for Japan ranks third after the United States and China. *EUROSTAT* (Comext, Statistical regime 4).
2. It is only an agreement with Italy that did not include any safeguard clause. The rest of the five agreements/protocols included either Quantitative Restrictions (QRs) or Safeguards.
3. Since then, the meeting has been held annually in Japan and Europe alternatively. It now covers wide topics concerning ongoing international affairs as well as Japan–EU bilateral issues.
4. 'Fair trade' is a Japanese version of 'competition policy'.
5. Amendment of the common trade policy and its coming into effect abolished the former Council Regulation which was ruled to be a discriminatory QR against Japan.
6. This was initiated by Japan in order to transform its economic system in the globalizing economic activities. It was innovative for Japan in that it proposed to deregulate its own rules with its own enforcement.
7. The Mutual Recognition Agreement (MRA) was signed in April 2001 in Brussels by the Director General for Trade Mogens Peter Carl and Japan's Ambassador to the EU, Kimura Takayuki. The areas covered by the Agreement

210 *Patterns of Bilateralism*

     are related to telecommunications terminal equipment and radio equipment, electrical products, Good Laboratory Practice (GLP) for chemicals, and Good Manufacturing Practice (GMP) for medicinal products.
8. The ratification procedure of the Constitution Treaty has been slowed down, with many countries postponing it after its rejection by France in May and the Netherlands in June 2005. Two years later, at the Lisbon European Council in October 2007, a revised version of the Constitution Treaty, called the 'Reform Treaty' was approved. The Reform Treaty modified the institutional matters of the previous Constitution Treaty. The leaders of the member states sound relieved to have reached an agreement and expected its acceptance by the European Citizens.
9. For this section, the author owes a great deal to the information kindly provided by Dr Takahiro Hayashi, Project Leader of the Fusion Development Office, Ministry of Education, Culture, Sports, Science and Technology (MEXT).
10. The 'Broader Approach' Agreement was initialed on 21 November 2006 in Brussels, and signed on 5 February 2007 in Tokyo between the Government of Japan and the European Atomic Energy Community represented by the EU Ambassador in Tokyo. This agreement is meant to complement realizing ITER through three individual projects, namely; 1. Engineering Validation and Engineering Design Activities for the International Fusion Materials Irradiation Facility (IFMIF/EVEDA); 2. International Fusion Energy Research Centre (IFERC); and 3. Satellite Tokamak Programme. The EU Ambassador inTokyo emphasizes the significance of the signing as a 'tangible expression of Partnership'.
11. The project has two phases: a construction phase of ten years and an operation phase of 20 years. The estimate for the first phase is about 70 billion yen, and for the second is about 30 billion yen per year.
12. R. Herman's book (translated by Mikado) illustrates the fluctuation of research results; long stagnation and unexpected results almost by coincidence, surprise results for scientists without being sure of the mechanism, and so on. In ITER, it has taken 13 years just to complete a design of an experimental reactor which was first scheduled to be completed in three years.
13. Author's telephone conversation with the project leader on 22 September 2005.
14. In the case of ITER, four ministries and the cabinet office are involved. In addition to the MEXT as a principal actor, the Ministry of Economics, Trade and Industry and the Ministry of Finance participate depending on the agenda of a meeting, and MoFA coordinates the participating ministries, while the Cabinet is informed.
15. It reported an alleged fraud by a MoFA non-career official who was arrested in March. Similar allegations followed, and several officials were actually arrested.
16. An EU Institute is a consortium of three or more universities covering academic and educational programmes as well as out-reach activities. The first one was established in Tokyo in 2003, and the second in Kobe-Osaka area in 2005.

References

Buzan, B., and Waever, O., *Regions and Powers* (Cambridge: Cambridge University Press, 2003).

Cowhey, P.F., and McCubbins, M.D. (eds), *Structure and Policy in Japan and the United States* (New York: Cambridge University Press, 1995).

Curtis, G. L., *The Logic of Japanese Politics* (New York: Columbia University Press, 1999).

European Commission, 'The Joint Declaration on Relations between the European Community and its Member States and Japan', Hague (July 1991).

Fawcette, L., and Hurrell, A. (eds), *Regionalism in World Politics* (New York: Oxford University Press, 1995).

Gilson, J., *Japan and the European Union* (London: Macmillan, 2000).

Herman, R., *Fusion – The Search for Endless Energy* (New York: Cambridge University Press, 1990).

Hoon, J., and Morii, Y. (eds), *Cooperation Experiences in Europe and Asia* (Tokyo: Shinzansha, 2004).

Ikenberry, G. J., and Mastanduno, M. (eds), *International Relations Theory and the Asia-Pacific* (New York: Columbia University Press, 2003).

Jaung, H., and Morii, Y. (eds), *Cooperation Experiences in Europe and Asia* (Tokyo: Shinzansha, 2004).

Khor, M., '"The Future of WTO" Report Contains Controversial Proposals'. Available at http://ased.org/artman/publishi/printer-673.shtml (downloaded in September 2005).

Mattli, W., *The Logic of Regional Integration* (Cambridge: Cambridge University Press, 1999).

Mikado, E., *Kakuyugo no seiji-shi* (Tokyo: Asahi, 1996).

Ministry of Foreign Affairs of Japan, Statement by the Press Secretary, 28 June 2005.

Ministry of Foreign Affairs of Japan. Available at http://mofa.go.jp/policy/s_tech/iter/ (accessed on 20 February 2007).

Ohira, K., 'Nihon-EU Tsusho Keizai Kankei (Trade and Economic Relations between Japan and the EU)', in T. Ueda, (ed.), *21seiki no Oushu to Ajia* (Tokyo: Keiso Shobo, 2002).

Ohtake, H., *Nihonseiji no Tairitujiku* (Tokyo: Chuo Koron, 1999).

Pempel, T.J., *Regime Shift: Comparative Dynamics of the Japanese Political Economy* (Ithaca: Cornell University Press, 1998).

Reiterer, M., *Asia–Europe: Do They Meet?* (Singapore: Asia–Europe Foundation, 2002).

Ruggie, J.G. (ed.), *Multilateralism Matters* (New York: Columbia University Press, 1993).

Schneider, G., and Aspinwall, M. (eds), *The Rules of Integration* (Manchester: Manchester University Press, 2001).

Scharpf, F., *Governing In Europe* (New York: Oxford University Press, 1999).

Sweet, A.S., Sandholtz, W., and Fligstein, N. (eds), *The Institutionalization of Europe* (New York: Oxford University Press, 2001).

Tanabe, T., *Chikyu Ondanka to Kankyo Gaikou* (Tokyo: Jiji Press, 1999).

Taylor, P., *The European Union in the 1990s* (New York: Oxford University Press, 1996).
Tokai Daigaku Kyuyo Gakubu (ed.), *Nihon no Gaiko to Kokusaishakai (Japan's Diplomatic Policies and International Society)* (Kanagawa: Tokai University Press, 2005).
Treaty on European Union, Title I, Article F (1993).
Wakabayashi, H., 'Yoroppa (Europe)', in Tokai Daigaku Kyuyo Gakubu (ed.), *Nihon no Gaiko to Kokusaishakai (Japan's Diplomatic Policies and International Society)* (Kanagawa: Tokai University Press, 2005).
Delegation of the European Commission in Tokyo: http://jpn.cec.eu.int/English/eu-relations/
Government of Japan, Ministry of Foreign Affairs: http://www.mofa.go.jp/policy/energy/
Website: http://www.mofa.go.jp/policy/s_tech/iter/
Yakushiji, K., *Gaimusho* (Tokyo: Iwanami, 2003).

11
The European Union and the Korean Conundrum

Brian Bridges

From the distance of Europe, Korea is a comparatively unknown and apparently obscure part of Asia, especially when compared with its powerful neighbours on the peninsula – China and Japan. Yet South Korea has become a major economic power in its own right, revitalized now after the setbacks of the Asian financial crisis, while the awkward and complex relationship between South and North Korea ensures that the peninsula remains one of the world's 'hot-spots' of geopolitical and strategic interest. Consequently, the commercial successes and attractions of the South and the convoluted and at times fraught interactions between the two Koreas and the four major powers most heavily involved in the peace and security of the peninsula mean that Europeans cannot afford to ignore Korea. This chapter endeavours to outline the extent of the stake for Europeans, economically, politically, and strategically, in the Korean peninsula, analyze how recent trends are impacting on that involvement and discuss how the Europeans might be further involved. In addition, in the context of the continuing debate about the effectiveness and feasibility of the European Union (EU) moving towards a common foreign and security policy (CFSP), the relevance of the Korean case will be discussed.

Korea in Europe's Asian strategy and Europe in the worldview of the Koreas

Sandwiched between its two larger and more attractive neighbours, China and Japan, Korea had largely escaped European interest in the age of imperialism and the brutal Japanese occupation in the first half of the twentieth century helped to ensure that contacts remained minimal. Troops from several West European countries fought in the Korean

War, but it was not until South Korean businessmen and South Korean products began to appear in European markets in the 1980s that Europe began to take Korea more seriously. Even then, South Korea appeared to be little more than a 'clone' of the earlier Japanese economic juggernaut, while the more mysterious North seemed to epitomize the traditional image of a 'hermit kingdom'.

Yet as European self-confidence began to return in the early 1990s with the collapse of communism in Eastern Europe and the creation of the 'single market' in Western Europe, West Europeans became more interested in trying to profit more from the economic dynamism of the Asian Pacific and to overcome the perceived relative weakness of European involvement with that region. This shift in perceptions was shown most clearly in the European Commission's own 1994 policy document, which strongly argued the case for the European Union (EU) to accord a higher priority to Asia and to adopt proactive and better coordinated strategies towards the region (European Commission Communication, 1994). However, there were almost no specific references to either Korea in that document, apart from a note that the Korean peninsula remained an area of dispute that warranted close watching by Europe.

How did Koreans perceive Europe, particularly Western Europe? The Korean experience of external relations historically was conditioned by its interactions with the immediate neighbours, in particular China and Japan, and in the postwar period by the presence and active involvement also of the two superpowers, the United States and the Soviet Union (now Russia). In this context, Europe has certainly seemed very far away and in the postwar period both Western and Eastern Europe were perceived of simply as adjuncts of the respective superpowers. For the South, the West European states provided useful diplomatic back-up to the United States and increasingly important markets for exports, but were still distant partners. President Chun Doo Hwan's visit to four West European countries and the EC headquarters in 1986 was the first such tour ever undertaken by a South Korean president, a testament to the lack of depth – and even novelty – of the South Korean–Western European relationship (Bridges, 1986, p. 76). To the North, which had established close ideological links with East European states, the West Europeans were nothing more than surrogates of the imperialistic United States and apart from establishing diplomatic relations with Portugal and the Nordic countries in the mid-1970s links remained extremely low-key and, in the case of some West European countries, close to non-existent (Winn, 1987, pp. 295–314).

By the early 1990s, therefore, it could be argued that for both the EU and South Korea there were important commercial linkages with each other, but that the relationship as a whole was clearly a secondary one for both sides. In its external relations the EU was preoccupied with other areas of the world and even when it did turn its attention to East Asia it was Japan and China that loomed much larger. The South Koreans also remained preoccupied with the North and with the interactions of the four powers most closely connected to the peninsula. However, the mid-1990s were to see a series of events – the nuclear weapons crisis with the North in 1994, the Asian financial crisis in 1997 and the arrival in 1998 of the new South Korean president Kim Dae-jung committed to a 'sunshine policy' towards the North – which were to make both the Europeans and the two Koreas reassess their policies and their relationships.

The economic challenge

By the mid-1990s South Korea had become an important trading partner of the EU, even though its lack of historical links with Europe and the pervasive power and attraction of the US and Japanese economies meant that the bilateral trade surge did not really begin until the mid-1980s. Contrary to popular European perceptions at the time, South Korea did not consistently maintain a large Japanese-style surplus with the EC/EU, but a plethora of sectoral disputes, bilateral export restraints, piecemeal restrictions and anti-dumping actions nonetheless did emerge during the 1980s, as European producers put pressure on their national governments and the EC to impose some degree of control on imports from the newly-industrializing economies (NIEs), especially South Korea. These European actions, in turn, led Koreans to worry that the developing '1992 process' to create a single European market might further disadvantage Korean producers by creating a protectionist 'fortress' (Lee, 1990, pp. 61–4). From the second half of the 1980s the Europeans had also put increasing emphasis on opening up the fairly heavily protected South Korean market.[1] Access for products of importance to the Europeans, such as cars and whisky, as well as the implementation of fair intellectual property rights protection practices became the stuff of Euro-South Korean commercial talks throughout the late 1980s and early 1990s. Progress was made by the Koreans in opening up their market, specifically by tariff reduction, in adhering to international intellectual property regulations and in reforming and liberalizing the financial market. However, much as has been the case with Japan, while the tariff barriers were being progressively though not totally reduced, the

Europeans found themselves faced with a range of non-tariff barriers, such as the covertly government-inspired campaign against 'conspicuous consumption', which continued to hamper European export growth. The total trade value had risen from US$4.7 billion in 1985 to $31.1 billion in 1995, yet it represented by then only approximately 1 per cent of the EU's total external trade. Therefore, although South Korea was an important export market for some sectors of European industry, it still lagged behind Japan, China and Hong Kong as Asian regional trading partners of the EU. Significantly, however, the trade balance, which had been in South Korea's favour since the mid-1970s, although sometimes only barely so, actually turned in the EU's favour in 1994 (and, indeed, was to remain so until the Asian financial crisis hit). For South Korea, the EU's importance as a trading partner had been slowly but steadily growing, from about 10 per cent of South Korea's total trade in 1985 to 12 per cent in 1995. Clearly, proportionally, Europe was more important to South Korea than vice versa. The other aspect – and one of increasing relative importance compared with trade flows – had been investment flows in both directions. In the 1990s Korean foreign direct investment (FDI) into Western (and Eastern) Europe grew rapidly, so that by 1995 Europe actually attracted a greater flow than did North America (Dent and Randerson, 1996, p. 539).

For the South Koreans, the first half of the 1990s saw an increasing emphasis on what has been described as 'tripolarity' in its external economic relations (Dent, 2002, p. 177), by which is meant the more active South Korean engagement with Europe and developing Asian countries as a conscious means to reduce the high degree of dependence on Japan and the United States as economic partners. As suggested above, the interest in and, to a certain extent, fear of the '1992 process' in Europe also contributed to the heightened status accorded to Europe as a trading and investment partner with which it was important to have good relations.

Despite remaining problems of market access and export surges, by the middle of the 1990s the Europeans were beginning to feel that some balance was being achieved in commercial relations with South Korea. As a result, when the South Koreans approached the EU with two initiatives the Europeans were ready to play ball. One was to establish a Wisemen's Group to consider the broader context of relations; its report in 1995 highlighted the 'significant information and perception gap' between Europeans and Koreans as one of the main reasons for the relative 'underdevelopment' of Euro-Korean relations (*Report of Wisemen's Group*, 1995). The other was to conclude a form of framework agreement somewhat similar to an earlier 1991 EC–Japan agreement. The negotiations from the spring of 1995 to early 1996 were not as easy as might have been expected, for while the South Koreans attached weight to a political declaration, not least because it was seen as reinforcing the South Korean position vis-à-vis North Korea, and preferred a general, rather bland economic and cooperation agreement, the EU, on the other hand, pushed by some member states who felt that the Japanese had been allowed to get away with too many generalities in the corresponding EC–Japanese agreement, argued for more specific commitments to be included in the EU–South Korean agreement. In the end the text of the Framework Agreement for Trade and Cooperation, signed in October 1996, called for closer cooperation in fields such as environment, energy, agro-fisheries, shipping, and science and technology but with an absence of specific provisions (*Korea Herald*, 11 June 1996). Nevertheless, it was a sign of the relationship maturing.

Emerging political contacts

The 1996 EU–South Korean agreement was accompanied by a separate Political Declaration and herein lay the key motivation for the South Koreans in proposing such an agreement. South Korean officials, while wary of the EU interest in issues such as human rights, wanted to secure a strong EU commitment to the South Korean position on inter-Korean relations, especially in the light of the crisis over suspected nuclear weapons development in 1994. The final Declaration was, in fact, carefully worded so as not to specifically target the North, but reference was made to the desire to 'promote peaceful solutions to international or regional conflicts' and to 'enhance policy consultations on international security matters such as arms control and disarmament, non-proliferation and weapons of mass destruction'. The most useful practical result of this Declaration was the provision for annual meetings at the foreign minister level and summit-level meetings between the European Commission President and the South Korean President whenever necessary, but, for a variety of bureaucratic reasons on both sides, coupled with the disruptive impact of economic crisis and political change in South Korea, the Framework Agreement on Trade and Cooperation did not come into force until April 2001 and the first EU–South Korea Summit did not take place until September 2002; a second Summit was held in October 2004.

None of the European states has a formal structured alliance relationship with South Korea, although a senior British officer participates in the UN representation at the Military Armistice Commission. In the two decades after the Korean War, contacts between Europe and the North were almost non-existent. The inability of the North to repay the loans taken out to cover industrial equipment purchases in the early 1970s soured relations and throughout the 1980s trade relations between West European states and the North remained low-key, averaging around $250 million per year. As a result, there was little incentive for those EC countries that had not given diplomatic recognition in the mid-1970s to do so. As Kim Hak-sung (2001, p. 42) has argued, relations 'stagnated, both economically and politically'. The North Korean nuclear crisis and its aftermath in the early 1990s, nonetheless, succeeded in drawing the Europeans more actively into security issues on the Korean peninsula than at any time since the Korean War.

North Korea had become a signatory of the Nuclear Non-proliferation Treaty (NPT) in 1975, but it did not sign the associated safeguard agreement until 1991. However, North Korea's penchant for 'nuclear brinkmanship' by threatening in early 1993 to withdraw completely from the NPT and then stalling on international inspections nearly brought the Korean peninsula to a state of war in mid-1994 (Sigal, 1998, pp. 32–167). Until a framework deal between North Korea and the United States was brokered in October 1994 this crisis remained the primary nuclear proliferation concern in the region. The two UN Security Council states from Europe, Britain and France, together with other EU members, deplored North Korea's actions, but the Europeans were divided over whether or not sanctions should be imposed. Consequently, there was a collective sigh of relief amongst the Europeans when the crisis reached a measure of resolution through the 1994 US–North Korean Framework Agreement. The agreement provides for the provision of two new nuclear power reactors to be built under the auspices of the newly-created Korean Energy Development Organization (KEDO), in return for which North Korea would suspend work on its existing nuclear programme.

Subsequently the Europeans did contribute more actively, lobbying to join KEDO, which had originally been conceived of as a joint US–Japan–South Korea venture, and in September 1997 the EU, through Euratom, began extending financial contributions to KEDO (75 million euros over a period of five years) and gained a seat on its executive council. In joining KEDO, the EU has stressed both the 'high priority' it accords to the NPT regime and its desire to be politically engaged in Northeast Asia (*Agence Europe*, 22 November 1995; *Korea Herald*, 1 August 1997; Drifte, 2002, pp. 160–3). The European role in the 1994 crisis itself was decidedly limited and confined essentially to financial contributions after the dust had settled. Not all of the three lead KEDO countries – United States, Japan and South Korea – were enamoured of a European approach which smacked of trying to buy a way in once the danger had passed and commercial opportunities beckoned.

The cumulative effect of the nuclear weapons crisis, the participation in KEDO and the Political Declaration was that, as noted in one EU report, the 'relative weight of political affairs' in the EU–South Korean relationship had been 'raised'; relations were 'no longer solely dominated by trade' (European Commission Communication, 1998).

The Korean financial crisis

The EU member countries had supported South Korea's application to join the Organization for Economic Cooperation and Development (OECD), the 'club' of advanced economic powers, in part because it was recognition of the reality of the powerful South Korean economy, but also partly because membership would require the South Koreans to take further steps in the liberalization of their domestic market, but entry was to prove a short-lived triumph. The economic situation began to deteriorate visibly in the first half of 1997 and in November 1997 the Kim Young-sam government was forced to take the humiliating step of applying for financial assistance to the International Monetary Fund (IMF) to prop up the economy.

The South Korean crisis was the one that finally seemed to alert the Europeans to the seriousness of what was happening in Asia. Indeed, it was the four largest EU member economies, which were first, ahead of the Japanese and Americans, in offering help to South Korea. The combined total contribution of the EU member states to the rescue package for South Korea in fact amounted to $5.9 billion bilaterally, a figure which was greater than that given by the United States (European Commission Communication, 1998).

As the crisis developed, some Europeans saw some advantage coming to European companies from the forced restructuring taking place in South Korea, for, as the European Commission itself argued, due to the crisis, 'for the first time South Korean politicians, officials and public opinion began to understand that a clean break with the former dirigiste model was urgently needed'. The South Korean government's 'impressive reform agenda' could help to fulfill the EU's 'long-standing market access requests' (European Commission Communication, 1998).

South Korea's financial crisis had a number of significant impacts on its bilateral economic relations with the EU. As far as trade was concerned, the immediate effect was a rapid increase in the trade deficit for the EU. European exports to South Korea shrank by 73 per cent in 1998 alone as local consumers found their purchasing power eroded, companies went bankrupt, unemployment rose, industrial activity declined and 'frugality campaigns' to avoid purchasing seemingly unnecessary (usually foreign) luxury items proliferated, while, at the same time, EU imports from South Korea increased as the depreciated won made Korean products much cheaper and therefore more competitive in the European markets. In the period 1998–2000 South Korean exports to the EU rose annually by double-digit amounts. These rises inevitably brought protests from some of the worst-affected European sectors, such as the dumping complaints filed by European semiconductor manufacturers against Korean memory chip producers in 1998 and sharp exchanges over the South Korean government's bailing out of the bankrupt Daewoo shipyards during 2001–02 (*Korea Herald*, 19 March 1998; *Bulletin Quotidien Europe*, 28 April 2001, 28 June 2002). Nonetheless, the EU felt that keeping its markets open had been helpful in supporting South Korea's recovery (European Council, 1999). The picture for FDI flows was more mixed, as South Korean companies tended to either cut-back or postpone investment projects in Europe rather than closing down existing investments. As for European FDI in the opposite direction, new investment opportunities arose through merger and acquisition activities, encouraged by the strict IMF terms which forced South Korea to relax the limitations on foreign companies seeking to take ownership of Korean companies and, of course, the financially parlous state of those companies (*Korea Newsreview*, 14 March 1998).

While generally the Europeans have been reassured by the recovery of the South Korean economy over the past few years, this does not mean that all commercial disputes have disappeared. Nonetheless, the economic relationship has become a mature and broadly stable one. Indeed, for South Korea, the EU, newly expanded, has become an even more important market, and since 2005 it has been South Korea's third-largest export market after China and the United States, while the EU is also the largest foreign investor in South Korea (*Yonhap News Agency*, 5 July 2005, Lexis-Nexis database). Negotiations for a EU–South Korea Free Trade Agreement (FTA) began in early 2007; this would certainly move the bilateral economic relationship onto a new level, although, like most of Korea's FTA negotiations, it is not expected to be smooth sailing.

Following the sunshine

The EU's relations with North Korea have followed a much less predictable path (Bridges, 2003, pp. 86–107). Kim Dae-jung's arrival in office impacted not only on economic relations with the EU, but also, through his strong belief in trying to bring reconciliation with the North, had an impact on Europe–North Korea relations. Kim's so-called 'sunshine policy' was designed to use cooperation and conciliation as a means of inducing the North to change its policies into a more reformist and conciliatory mode. The Europeans watched with interest Kim's attempts to develop contacts with the North, even though these efforts were not immediately rewarded during his early months in office, and in December 1998 the European Commission held its first-ever round of political talks with North Korea at the senior official level and, in a strong endorsement of Kim Dae-jung's 'sunshine policy', called for a policy to 'actively engage North Korea with the international community'. In July 1999 the Council of Ministers followed this up by proposing that the EU work to maintain stability on the Korean peninsula, press North Korea to behave more responsibly, and review bilateral relations (Drifte, 2002, p. 159).

The EU itself, through the ECHO (European Communities Humanitarian Office) set up in Pyongyang in 1997, and individual EU member governments and non-governmental organizations had become involved to varying degrees in providing humanitarian assistance and food aid to the North from 1995 onwards (Smith, 2005, pp. 183, 213–16), but these steps had not been complemented by any movement in the diplomatic arena. In late 1999, however, the North began to adopt a new strategy, which might be described as a 'diplomatic offensive'. The first breakthrough, in January 2000, came with Italy's decision to recognize North Korea.[2] The North then entered onto a series of talks with other West European states, but the October 2000 ASEM 3 Meeting, coming only a few months after the historic North–South Korean Summit in Pyongyang, provided a convenient context for further European initiatives. Britain and Germany announced that they would begin normalization talks with the North. Even though France held back, citing human rights and nuclear proliferation concerns, Britain formally established diplomatic relations with the North in December 2000, followed in early 2001 by Spain, the Netherlands, Belgium, Germany, Luxembourg and Greece; Ireland agreed in December 2003[3] (Kim, 2001, p. 44).

Finally, in response to a request from North Korea made back in September 2000, the EU itself moved towards establishing diplomatic relations with the North. In early May 2001 a mission of the European troika, Goran Persson, the Swedish Prime Minister and then President of the Council of Ministers, Javier Solana, the EU's High Representative for CFSP, and Chris Patten, the Commissioner for External Relations, visited Pyongyang, met Kim Jong-il and other leaders. They discussed a range of issues, including trade, human rights and nuclear non-proliferation; crucially, the North promised to extend its moratorium on missile testing until 2003. The EU agreed to establish diplomatic relations in mid-May 2001.

For the Europeans, political and strategic motives predominated. Although some European companies had expressed interest in doing business in North Korea, there was no strong lobby from the business sector to establish diplomatic relations and although some business missions have been sent to the North, the number of European investments in the North remains minuscule and the amount of trade similarly very low-level. Although it has been argued that the EU was 'looking to secure an early hold of the market to be in a better position in the mid- and long-term' (Kim, 2001, pp. 53–4), commercial or economic incentives do seem to have been a very secondary concern, for three more important political and strategic reasons can be suggested. First, there was a concern over the North's nuclear and missile programmes and it was felt that talking with the North would be the best way to ensure that these programmes remained frozen. Secondly, there was a perceived need to reinforce Kim Dae-jung's policy positions as a way of ensuring peace and stability on the peninsula. Thirdly, the Europeans were worried about the policy pronouncements of the incoming Bush administration, which had adopted a far more cautious, even suspicious, policy towards the North an the outgoing Clinton administration. While the Bush administration carried out its internal policy review, which implied an interim suspension of all dialogue with the North, the Europeans felt that they could play a useful role in trying to carry forward the momentum of North–South reconciliation and, indirectly, perhaps encourage the Bush administration to resume dialogue with the North. An EU spokesman later claimed that the Bush administration 'encouraged' the EU visit, but he did admit that the Europeans and the Americans did have 'different approaches'[4] (*SCMP*, 5 March 2002).

For the North, a more balanced mixture of economic and political motivations played a part. The North has only very cautiously been opening its doors to foreign investment and trade, and even after the Pyongyang Summit it had remained reluctant to follow anything resembling the Chinese model of economic reform and openness. Rather, the

North would have hoped that in the short run the Europeans would be more forthcoming on food aid and other humanitarian assistance and that in the medium term European companies might be more willing to invest in and trade with it. North Korean officials felt that European companies had not been active enough in their market.[5] In that sense there were much greater expectations of economic benefits on the North Korean side than on the European side.

But there were also important political objectives. Recognition from these European countries and the EU itself will have helped to raise the North's international standing, enabling it to catch up to a certain extent with South Korea, which had leapt ahead in the international recognition stakes a decade or so earlier when the North's former allies in Eastern Europe, the Soviet Union, and even China had recognized the South. The North did not see any major political issues with the Europeans – no territorial problems, no military threats, no historical legacies – of the type that made developing relations with neighbouring great powers, including the United States, more complicated. This helped to make the North feel more 'comfortable' about relations with Europe. But, more importantly, recognition from Western Europe sent a message – the demonstration effect – to the United States and, to a lesser extent, to Japan that they should not be left behind.

The EU mission to the North and the establishment of formal EU–North Korean relations, coupled with individual EU member states' diplomatic recognitions of the North, marked an important change in the nature of European involvement in the Korean peninsula. However, the follow-up was not as fruitful as both sides had hoped.

During the time since the diplomatic breakthrough in EU–North Korean relations, the European side have had three main policy objectives: to provide increased humanitarian aid and develop long-term development programmes to help the suffering North Korean people; to persuade the North not to do anything to contribute to the development and diffusion of weapons of mass destruction; and to encourage peace and stability on the Korean peninsula by fostering dialogue between North and South and between the North and the United States.

On the first objective, since 1997 the European Commission had been consistently providing assistance to North Korea – food and medical aid and agricultural rehabilitation projects – and some European non-governmental organizations as well as ECHO had begun work inside North Korea on supplying such aid directly. The need for a focused and well-established development assistance programme became the main focus of a three-year 'country strategy paper', drawn up at the end of

2001 by the European Commission. This argued for greater access to the more vulnerable groups in North Korean society, improved evaluation and monitoring of assistance programmes, support for effective development projects which do more than just distribute food and medicine, and the creation of training and technical expertise programmes to enable the North to reform its institutional capacity and economic policy making (European Commission n.d., 2002).

Amongst these objectives, the Commission seemed to put particular stress on the last one, arguing that only through reform and greater engagement in the international financial and trading system could North Korea find the way to sustainable economic growth and poverty reduction. Individual European countries had already begun to develop small-scale training courses and scholarship programmes; the Commission's idea was to provide some synergy with slightly more ambitious operations. However, the success of such a policy approach has been dependent on the North's responsiveness and its desire to open and reform. North Korean officials and the media certainly began talking about 'new thinking' during 2001, but the reality of policy change seemed to be lagging behind. However, in the summer of 2002, the North began to announce a series of initiatives, which raised expectations amongst the Europeans that real change was forthcoming.

First, in July 2002, the North announced a number of measures to free up prices and wages, which implied that it was moving towards a semi-market mechanism by raising the prices of previously low-priced or 'free' basic necessities such as rice, while raising wages in return for increased productivity of farm products or industrial goods. North Korean officials were quoted, however, as saying that these measures still 'belong to a command economy' (*Vantage Point*, December 2002, p. 23; Lee, 2002, pp. 357–64).

Then, during the period from September to November 2002, North Korea announced successively the creation of three new special zones, of which one, a 'special administrative region' (SAR) at Sinuiju, at the North Korean–Chinese border, was intriguing for the Europeans, partly because it implied a degree of policy autonomy previously unknown in North Korea (and not available even to the Chinese special economic zones when they were first established in the 1980s) and partly because the man chosen to head this new venture was a very rich Dutch–Chinese businessman called Yang Bin. However, in November 2002 Yang was arrested in China on charges of fraud and corruption and any hopes that he might head the new SAR were over. Despite various rumours that one or another European businessman might be selected in his place, no new head of the SAR has been announced and progress towards the implementation of the new SAR has been minimal (*SCMP*, 28 November 2002).

Finally, in mid-November 2002, the adoption of the euro as the North's preferred foreign currency unit was announced; all dollar-denominated state bank accounts were automatically converted to euro-denominated ones and all foreign exchange transactions were to be carried on in euros from December. This step came as a complete surprise to foreign companies doing business with the North; existing contracts were all cast in US dollars, so that even European companies had problems in making the switch and, in practice, the use of euros has had to be phased in gradually. This move was widely perceived as an anti-American gesture (tensions with the United States were rising at this time) and, to a lesser extent, as a pro-European one (the North would hardly have chosen the yen, the only other feasible foreign currency unit, as relations with Japan had also deteriorated over the issue of kidnapped Japanese). It certainly would make it easier in the medium term for European companies to invest in and trade with the North. However, the move may also have been motivated by a desire to draw out US dollars from the 'underground economy' within North Korea and to help to stimulate the domestic market (Chung, 2003, pp. 24–5).

Nuclear tensions

European expectations that the series of measures introduced in the second half of 2002 might have been symptomatic of a cautious turn towards reform and openness by North Korea were tempered, however, by the emergence of a new crisis over North Korea's nuclear ambitions. After visiting Pyongyang in October 2002, senior US State Department official James Kelly revealed that North Korean officials had admitted to a secret uranium enrichment programme to manufacture nuclear weapons, which the Americans had learnt about some months earlier. The North later objected to Kelly's account, claiming that the North 'was entitled to possess not only nuclear weapons but any type of weapon', but denying that it actually possessed any nuclear weapons (Kelly, 2002; Chong, 2003, pp. 10–13). Tensions steadily escalated over the following months as the North proposed a non-aggression treaty, which the United States rejected, KEDO decided to suspend a pending shipment of heavy oil under the 1994 Agreed Framework, the International Atomic Energy Agency (IAEA) called for the suspension of any North Korean nuclear programmes, the North removed seals and monitoring cameras from its closed nuclear facilities and expelled IAEA inspectors, and then in January 2003 the North announced its withdrawal from the Nuclear Non-proliferation Treaty.

The US and North Korean positions became entrenched. The Bush administration, which was becoming increasingly focused on the Iraq issue in early 2003, argued that it was up to the North to make the first move, by dismantling its nuclear programme in a verifiable manner, after which talks to improve relations could be held. In the meantime, the Americans clearly expected the international community to put diplomatic pressure on the North to respond positively. The North, on the other hand, argued that it is the hostile policy of the Americans that is to blame for this crisis and that only bilateral negotiations could solve the problem, so it was up to the Americans to enter into such talks.

The initial European reaction was to describe the apparent North Korean admission as 'very serious' – to use the words of British Foreign Secretary Jack Straw – and the Danish presidency of the EU called on the North to take immediate steps to comply with its international obligations. However, the European approach was still one of trying to engage the North diplomatically and to find a peaceful solution to the crisis. However, as the crisis became more protracted, the Europeans began to be concerned not just about the North Korean actions but also about US attitudes. Consideration of the correct approach to the North became complicated by the escalating tension between the United States and Iraq and, subsequently, the divisions within the Europeans about how far they should support US military action against Iraq. As an executive board member of KEDO, the EU had been party to the November 2002 decision to suspend the final oil delivery of that year to the North, but generally the Europeans seemed reluctant to support any further sanctions against the North.

The stalemate over the nuclear issue continued, despite the holding firstly of tripartite China–US–North Korea talks and then four rounds of six-party talks (adding South Korea, Japan and Russia) during the period 2003–05. Neither North Korea nor the United States was willing to make the first step, or concession, to allow the talks to make real progress until finally, in September 2005, an ambiguously worded joint statement, which became subject to differing interpretations by both North Korea and the United States, did seem to set some basis for a future framework agreement. However, the follow-up meeting in November 2005, held in the aftermath of US financial sanctions against a bank in Macau accused of laundering illegal North Korean funds, collapsed quickly (Cheon, 2005, pp. 341–59).

In response to this prolonged crisis, the Europeans adopted a two-pronged approach. The first was to float, from time to time, ideas of assisting positively in the resolution of the crisis – if necessary by acting as a mediator. Some European Commission officials suggested that the EU should send another delegation similar to that sent in 2001, but North Korea showed little enthusiasm for this type of approach. Other Europeans – such as, for example, members of the European Parliament – have argued that the EU should even be invited to join formally into the six-power talks (*Guardian*, 5 March 2003; Ford and Kwon, 2005), although none of the six powers has shown anything more than a polite non-committal attitude to that idea.

Underpinning the EU's belief that it could play a role in the resolution of the crisis was the perception that the EU has been 'looked upon favourably' by the North and, moreover, 'it is not the United States' (Hoare, 2003, p. 16; Bellany, 2003, p. 18). It should be noted that while the Europeans have been critical of the North's posturing, they have also demonstrated some frustration at the US approach, in particular its reluctance to talk with the North Koreans, and, in the light of revelations about intelligence errors on Iraq, they also became more sceptical about US revelations of North Korean efforts to cheat on the 'Agreed Framework' by secretly developing highly enriched uranium. For example, in the words of British Foreign Office minister Bill Rammell in mid-2003: 'The talks need to resume and broaden out... The basic choice is North Korea's, but, still, everyone needs to step back' (*Korea Times*, 21 July 2003).

The second approach was for the Europeans to try to demonstrate to the North, through their continued commitment to humanitarian aid and economic restructuring measures, that the answer to the North's economic and energy problems lay with peaceful reform rather than belligerent gestures. In light of the nuclear crisis, the European Council decided not to begin to implement any of the economic development projects envisaged under the earlier country strategy, thereby adopting a stance that Kim Heungchong has described as somewhat similar to South Korea's one of 'conditional linkage' (Kim, 2003, p. 508). However, during the first half of 2005, as the six-party talks failed to revive and North Korea officially stated that it 'possessed' nuclear weapons, the EU's attitudes towards the North hardened somewhat. The EU became more assertive on human rights issues, culminating in the tabling of a resolution denouncing the North's human rights record to the United Nations General Assembly in November 2005, while some member governments, such as Britain, suspended technical cooperation projects and trade promotion activities until after the nuclear issue was settled (*Kyodo News*, 12 October 2005; *Country Profile of Democratic People's Republic of Korea* n.d., 2005; *BBC Monitoring Asia Pacific – Political*, 15 July 2005; text of EU-led UNGA Resolution in *Korea and World Affairs*, Winter 2005, pp. 573–6).

The EU welcomed the September 2005 statement from the six-party talks, so the Europeans were disappointed though not surprised by the subsequent breakdown in the talks. In 2006, however, with talks still suspended, EU–North Korean relations became more tense as first in July North Korea conducted medium- and long-range missile tests and then, in October, it carried out its first nuclear test. Both events were received critically in Europe. High Representative Javier Solana and other officials, as well as the European Parliament, were quick to condemn the nuclear test as a 'threat to global security and stability' and to support the actions at the United Nations that resulted in sanctions against the North (*Bulletin Quotidien*, 10, 12, 18 October 2006). Consequently, even though the six-party talks resumed in December 2006, trade and investment with the North is likely to remain extremely low-key and technical cooperation and aid frozen without renewed progress in solving the nuclear crisis. However, as European Commissioner for External Relations Benita Ferrero-Waldner argued, humanitarian aid would continue, as the North Korean people 'must not be punished further for the folly of its leader' (*Bulletin Quotidien*, 12 October 2006). The EU, therefore, hoped that the more detailed February 2007 agreement amongst the six powers, which set down deadlines and processes for resolving the nuclear and related issues could lead to a new phase of improved relations.

Conclusion

A number of points arise from the above analysis of the recent interactions between the European Union and the Korean peninsula.

The first relates to European priorities. Undoubtedly over the past two decades or so the Korean peninsula has moved from being a region of little direct importance to the Europeans to one in which the Europeans are increasingly involved, both economically and in political-strategic terms. Clearly, the EU member states have developed strong and increasing economic ties with the South and, despite the opening up of diplomatic links with the North, there is little enthusiasm for commercial contacts with the North until it undertakes more serious economic reform and pulls back from its confrontational nuclear stance. However, in the broader context of European policies towards the Asian Pacific region, Korea still does not seem to carry the weight that its economic importance (South Korea) and strategic significance (North Korea) might be expected to require. Despite the attempts of European Commission officials and member governments to focus from time to time on other countries in the region, it is clear that first from the 1970s onwards Japan and, since the mid-1990s, China have been the centrepiece of European perspectives and approaches to the region. As far as Europe is concerned, the Korea peninsula continues to be considered a smaller scene in the Asian panorama.

Secondly, the expansion of the European Union has made little significant impact so far in shifting the nature of the EU's relationships with the Korean peninsula. Although some South Korean companies had previously invested in several of the Central European economies, none of the new member countries can be considered as major trading or investment partners of South Korea. All of the new members had previously established diplomatic relations with North Korea, and some, such as Poland, had long and close relationships, but the most important new dimension brought by the new Central and East European members may well be their experience as transition economies of undertaking economic reforms, which could become a future reference point for North Korea.

Thirdly, the relationship with North Korea as experienced during the two nuclear crises show that European foreign policy is by no means yet a unified one, nor is it clear exactly what role Europe can play in solving this kind of crisis. While the policy differences amongst European member countries are by no means as strident as was seen in the case of the Iraq war, the lack of coordination amongst the Europeans over, for example, recognizing North Korea in 2000–01 was evident. While it might be possible to draw some comfort, as the European Commission President Prodi dryly remarked, that at least only two positions was an improvement on the normal five on most foreign policy issues (*Deutsche Press-Agentur*, 20 October 2000, Lexis-Nexis database), it does suggest that, as in other examples in other parts of the world, the CFSP is not yet a reality.

The Europeans' role in the first nuclear crisis was peripheral and this situation has changed little in the second crisis. Even though the solution to the second crisis seems to be being effected through multilateralism – an approach with which the Europeans have a strong affinity – none of the main protagonists has been actively urging a higher-profile European role in this multilateral exercise. In the almost simultaneous crisis over suspected Iranian nuclear ambitions, the EU, or at least the 'troika' of Britain, France and Germany, has worked closely in the frontline to try to effect a solution (in part, at least, because the United States has left them to do so and other major powers such as Russia and China have also opted to take back-seats). Even though Britain and France became more directly involved in the North Korean crisis when it has been taken to the United Nations Security Council, such as after the missile and nuclear tests in 2006, in general the Europeans will continue to be supporting actors not main players in the final solution to the crisis.

Finally, there is evidently room for improvement in other aspects of the Europe–Korea relationship, such as cultural and educational exchanges and flows of people. Over a decade ago the EU–Korea Wiseman's Group identified the sheer geographical distance, the different cultural backgrounds, the lack of close historical ties, and the postwar preoccupation of both sides with immediate neighbours and the United States as having all contributed to a sense of benign neglect. Knowledge of each other may have grown since then, but there is still much more to do. In recent years, the outflow of Korean popular culture has dramatically changed the image of South Korea amongst Asian neighbouring countries and people; while the TV dramas and films may not have the same resonance amongst European audiences, they do nonetheless demonstrate how perceptions can change – and in a positive direction.

Notes

1. Typical of European views was the complaint in 1988 by the then British Chancellor of the Exchequer Nigel Lawson about South Korea's 'very controlled and un-open' economy, *Korea Herald*, 20 May 1988.
2. An Italian diplomat stated that the primary Italian objective had been 'the chance to help North Korea open up', but for the North the possibilities of greater humanitarian aid – Italy gave over $5 million in such aid during the year 2000 – and the leverage it achieved for coaxing other states into following the Italian example were no doubt more important (*South China Morning Post*, 17 January 2001).
3. For French objections, see comments by French President Jacques Chirac, in *South China Morning Post*, 26 March 2001.
4. The fact that the activist Swedish government, which historically had long-standing links with the North, held the EU Presidency in the first half of 2001 probably also contributed to putting momentum behind the EU initiative (Drifte, 2002, p. 166; Smith, 2005, p. 214).
5. Interview with North Korean Foreign Ministry official, Pyongyang, June 2002.

References

Bellany, Ian, 'Kindness to Korea', *The World Today* (April 2003), pp. 17–18.
Bridges, Brian, *Korea and the West* (London: Routledge and Kegan Paul, 1986).
Bridges, Brian, 'Western Europe and North Korea: New Openings and Old Problems', *East Asia*, 20(3) (2003), 86–107.
Cheon, Seongwhun, 'North Korea; Nuclear Crisis: Current Status and Past Lessons', *Korea and World Affairs* (Fall 2005), 341–59.
Chong, Bong-uk, 'Another Nuclear Crisis', *Vantage Point* (January 2003), 10–3.
Chung, Yun-ho, 'North Korea's Banning of Dollar Usage', *Vantage Point* (March 2003), 22–5.
Country Profile of Democratic People's Republic of Korea. Available at https://www.uktradeimnvest.gov.uk/ukti/appmanager/ukti (accessed 3 October 2005).
Dent, Christopher, *The Foreign Economic Policies of Singapore, South Korea and Taiwan* (Cheltenham: Edward Elgar, 2002).
Dent, Christopher, and Randerson, Claire, 'Korean foreign direct investment in Europe: the determining forces', *Pacific Review*, 9(4) (1996), 531–52.
Drifte, Reinhard, 'The European Union and North Korea', in Tsuneo, Akaha (ed.), *The Future of North Korea* (London: Routledge, 2002), pp. 155–70.
European Commission, *Country Strategy Paper 2001-04: EC-Democratic People's Republic of Korea*, n.d. Available at http://europe.eu.int/comm/external_relations/w8/2.htm (accessed 26 February 2002).
European Commission Communication, *Towards a New Asia Strategy*, COM (94) 314 (13 July 1994). Brussels: European Commission.
European Commission Communication, *European Union Policy towards the Republic of Korea* (9 December 1998). Available at www.europa.eu.int.
European Council, *Council Conclusions on Korea Peninsula* (23 July 1999). Available at http://europa.eu.int/comm/dg01/koreacon.htm (accessed 26 September 1999).
Ford, Glyn, and Kwon, Soyoung, 'Pyongyang Under EU's wing', *Japan Times* (17 March 2005), www.japantimes.co.jp/cgi-bin/geted.pl15?eo200050317al.htm (accessed 18 March 2005).
Hoare, James, 'North Korea: Suspicious and Cautious', *The World Today* (April 2003), pp. 15–16.
Kelly, James, 'Why North Korea must act first for better relations with the US', *South China Morning Post*, 19 December 2002.
Kim, Hak-sung, 'EU Involvement in the Korean Question: Background and Implications', *East Asia Review*, 13(2) (Summer 2001), 39–56.
Kim, Heung-chong, 'Inter-Korean relations and the roles of the US and of the EU', *Asia Europe Journal*, 1 (2003), 503–9.
Kyodo News (12 October 2005). Available at http://home.kyodo.co.jp/modules/fstStory/index.php?storyid+207785 (accessed 12 October 2005).
Lee, Chae Woong, 'The EC 1992: Trade Policy Implications for Korea', *Korea and World Affairs* (Spring 1990), 54–66.
Lee, Jung-chul, 'The Implications of North Korea's Reform Program and Its Effects on State Capacity', *Korea and World Affairs* (Fall 2002), 357–64.
Report of the Wisemen's Group on EU–Korean Relations (27 October 1995).
Sigal, Leon, *Disarming Strangers: Nuclear Diplomacy with North Korea* (Princeton: Princeton University Press, 1998).

Smith, Hazel, *Hungry for Peace: International Security, Humanitarian Assistance, and Social Change in North Korea* (Washington: United States Institute of Peace Press, 2005).

Winn, Gregory F.T., 'Sohak: North Korea's Joint Venture with Western Europe', in Jae Kyu, Park, Byung Chul, Koh, and Tae-hwan, Kwak (eds), *The Foreign relations of North Korea: New Perspectives* (Boulder, CO: Westview Press, 1987), pp. 295–314.

12
India–EU Relations: Building a Strategic Partnership

Ummu Salma Bava

The European Union (EU) emerged as a larger political actor in 1992 after the Treaty of Maastricht and it has tried to fashion for itself a Common Foreign and Security Policy (CFSP) and also develop a Common Security and Defence Policy (CSDP). These efforts by the EU at further institutionalization and attempts to forge a common political voice are part of a series of endeavours aimed at shaping and strengthening its political identity. The EU is no longer merely a trading entity and regards itself increasingly as an important and significant political player at the global level. The process of creating a new identity in the EU is taking place at multiple levels – economic, political, strategic and legal.

The EU's engagement with Asia as a region and the individual country partners within it is intensifying. One only has to look at the EU's 'Asia Strategy'. As China and India emerge as the future centres of globalization and the new drivers of world economic growth, the eagerness of the EU to engage with both is evident in its efforts to upgrade the nature of the political relationship. The EU has set for itself the task to 'follow a forward-looking policy of engagement with Asia, both in the region and globally' (Commission of the European Communities, 2001).

Clearly the EU is giving a new value to its relationship with India. But it is critical to ask how India views these new developments. India has significant potential and is recognized as one of the emerging powers in the global order. It therefore needs both a vision and a strategy to realize this potential so that it can engage dynamically with other players in the international community. This chapter explores how India–EU relations are changing and what new driving forces are leading to this strategic partnership. It examines where cooperation is possible and what challenges there will be in the near future.

In talking about building multilateralism in the EU–Asia relationship, two issues stand out. First, who are the actors, and secondly, what kind of multilateralism is being constructed? Therefore, this chapter also briefly explores the strategic partnership between India and the EU in the context of building new multilateralism and contrasts the elements of that relationship with India's new strategic partnership with the USA.

The EU as an actor in international politics

One could argue that the EU has emerged through its various developments to become a composite actor and is imbued with all the attributes of an actor in international politics. A 'minimal behavioural definition of an actor would be an entity that is capable of formulating purposes and making decisions, and thus engaging in some form of purposive action' (Bretherton and Vogler, 1999, p. 20). Categorizing actors in world politics is not easy, as is well reflected in the international relations literature (Young, 1972; Keohane and Nye, 1973, p. 380; Rosenau, 1990, p. 119; Ruggie, 1993, p. 172). Piening argues that the EU 'may not be a superpower, but it is certainly a global power in the sense that its actions – and indeed its very existence – have come to have a significant effect far beyond its borders, both by default and intention' (Piening, 1997, p. 196).

European integration is a process that involves more than just economics; it is also about organizing Europe in such ways that the great conflicts of the past do not recur in the future. The apparent linearity which stretches from the Single European Act of 1986 through to the 2004 draft constitution belies the changes taking place below, as what has emerged in the process is an institutional system of extraordinary complexity. It is difficult to put a label on this new entity; is it a superstate, a supranational body or a post-modern state? In the process of this political development 'the EU also challenges as how we conceptualize democracy, authority and legitimacy in contemporary politics' (Laffan, 1999, p. 330). At one level of analysis it is all this and more, for in policy-making terms one definitely sees multi-level governance and an even more significant development is the progressive growth of the EU as a political entity.

The EU is enhancing its capacity as an international actor in several spheres. Increasingly, it aims to position itself as a common security actor in the new Europe and, consequently, the role of the Union in shaping member states' foreign policies will assume greater importance. The new constitution, which still awaits ratification from all of the member states, has been on a slippery slope especially since the 'no' vote it received in France and Netherlands – two of the founding member states – but increasing the EU's capacity to meet external challenges remains central (Bava, 2003).

Given the focus of this volume on EU–Asia relations, one is immediately challenged to define the contours of Asia, as this impinges on the different kinds of actors engaging each other in this region. There is South Asia, Central Asia, Southeast Asia, Northeast Asia, and Austral-Asia. If the EU is a post-modern polity then its dialogue partners in Asia range from individual countries like China, Japan, India, and South Korea to regional organizations such as the Association of South-East Asian Nations (ASEAN) and the South Asian Association for Regional Cooperation (SAARC). In other words this Asia–Europe relationship has all the elements of both bilateral and multilateral relations. It is not a simple 1 × 1 matrix, but a complex set of relationships, each with its own unique characteristics influenced by the political, economic and security compulsions of the region and the country in particular.

India–EU relations

'The corner stone of the EU–India relationship lies in trade and investment'. This statement by Pascal Lamy, the European Union Trade Commissioner, in 2003 underscores the nature of the relationship.[1] After all, the EU is India's largest trading partner. But the EU that India has engaged since 1963 is not a static entity. From its modest beginnings in the 1950s, the one-time European Economic Community (EEC) has grown into the EU of today which is one of the leading global economic players. The EU accounts for 40 per cent of global trade and 50 per cent of world outward foreign direct investment (FDI) and receives 24 per cent of inward FDI. It is the largest provider of Official Development Assistance (ODA) and humanitarian assistance in the world.

India and the EU are the largest democracies in the world. The ties between India and the EU, or rather the individual member states of the EU, go back centuries. Although diplomatic relations with the then EEC were established in 1963, the economic and political relationship developed rather slowly given the poor performance of the Indian economy, in the 1970s the Indian economy became even more inward-looking. Although there was a systematic upgrading of the relations between the European Community (EC) and India, however, until the 1990s there was no significant 'value added' in this partnership. For the EC, strategically, India was not an important regional player. It was the events of 1990–91, with the end of the Cold War and the dramatic changes in international politics, that also brought newer players to centre stage. While domestic economic compulsions forced India to adopt a new economic policy, the transformed geopolitics also made the EU interested to take a more proactive policy towards Asia as a region. In 2004, at the Hague, the India–EU Strategic Partnership was launched, thereby elevating the level of the existing relationship. This immediately raised questions about what kind of future could be envisaged for this relationship. It is within this economic and political context that this chapter examines the implications of the EU–India Strategic Partnership.

India–EU political relations

As already mentioned, India's relations with the EU date back to 1963 when it established diplomatic relations with the then EEC. A brief overview in the way this relationship has evolved is crucial to the understanding of what lies ahead on the political road (see Table 12.1). Today India–EU relations cover key areas such as political relations, trade and investment, economic and development cooperation as well as cultural exchanges.

Although trade has been the driver of this relationship since 1963, this overview shows unequivocally that India–EU political relations have also grown steadily. 'The deepening of the political partnership is embedded in a strong institutional architecture. Annual ministerial meetings and summits are the most visible feature of the ongoing political dialogue between the EU and India. Senior officials and experts also regularly meet on issues of common concern such as terrorism. Political relations are also strengthened by the regular exchange of visits between EU and Indian parliamentarians' (Delegation of the European Commission to India, 2007).

For India, therefore, the strengthening of political relations has been linked to the EU's emergence as a larger political actor at the global level in the 1990s. The process of creating a new identity in the EU is taking place at multiple levels: economic, political, strategic and legal (Bava, 2003). Post-1992 Maastricht Treaty it is important to ask whether 'Europe is heading in the direction of becoming a new center of power' (Kupchan, 2003, p. 210). Kupchan writes that Europe has great geopolitical ambition and it is using 'integration as a way to acquire power and project geopolitical ambition for Europe as a whole' (Kupchan, 2003, p. 211). In other words this contrasts to Europe's earlier endeavour to use integration as a mechanism to escape its past. In December 2003 the EU adopted the

Table 12.1 Overview of the major developments in India–EU relations (1963–2007)

Year	Main events
1963	Establishment of diplomatic relations.
1971	The EEC introduces the general tariff preferences for 91 developing countries, including India under the Generalized System of Preferences (GSP) scheme. India and the EEC signed the Commercial Co-operation Agreement in 1973.
1981	India and the EEC sign a five-year Commercial and Economic Co-operation agreement (16 November).
1983	EC Delegation in India established at New Delhi.
1985	Commercial and Economic Co-operation Agreement is signed between the EEC and India.
1988	EC–India Joint Commission meeting (March).
1993	EC and India sign Joint Political Statement, simultaneously, with the Co-operation Agreement on Partnership and Development (December).
1994	Commission presents the EU's proactive policy towards Asia in a communication: 'Towards a new strategy for Asia' (13 July). EC–India Co-operation agreement on Partnership and Development comes into force.
1996	Commission adopts the communication on EU–India Enhanced Partnership.
1999	European Parliament endorses the Commission's Communication on 'EU–India Enhanced Partnership'.
1999	Decision to launch an EU–India Round Table is formally adopted.
2000	The first-ever India–EU Summit, Lisbon, Portugal (28 June).
2001	Second India–EU Summit, New Delhi (23 November).
2002	The European Commission presents the Country Strategy Paper 2002–06 for India, which charts the course for development and economic co-operation between India and the European Commission. Some €225 million to be made available for that five-year period for development and economic cooperation.
2002	Third India–EU Summit, Copenhagen, Denmark (10 October).
2003	Fourth India–EU Summit, New Delhi, India (29 November).
2004	Proposal by the Commission on an EU–India Strategic Partnership (June), Indian Response Paper (August), Conclusions of the Council (October) and Recommendations of the European Parliament (October).
2004	Fifth India–EU Summit, The Hague, Netherlands (8 November). *Launch of the EU–India Strategic Partnership*
2005	Sixth India–EU Summit, New Delhi, India (7 September). *Adoption of India–EU Joint Action Plan*
2006	Seventh India–EU Summit, Helsinki, Finland (13 October). *Review of Implementation of the Joint Action Plan*

European Security Strategy in which it states, 'As a union of 25 states with over 450 million people producing a quarter of the world's Gross National Product (GNP), the European Union is inevitably a global player... it should be ready to share in the responsibility for global security and in building a better world.' It is against this backdrop that one should analyse the new initiatives by the Union to enhance the level of partnership with India.

India–EU economic relations

As stated above, it is trade that drives the India–EU relationship. For a long time the EU was India's largest economic partner, accounting for over 25 per cent of its total trade (1997–98) and also bringing in around 20 per cent (2005) of its total inward FDI. The trade volume had grown from €4.4 billion in 1980 to €28.4 billion in 2003. The products traded between India and the EU consist of agricultural products, chemical and minerals, engineering goods, gems and jewellery, leather products, metal and steel; textile, clothing and shoes and wood and paper. In 2002, textiles, clothing and shoes accounted for 36 per cent of the total Indian exports followed by chemical and minerals at 13 per cent, whereas Indian imports from the EU in the same year were led by engineering goods at 37 per cent and gems and jewellery accounting for 34 per cent.

However, even to the casual eye the commodity composition of the exports by India to the EU attest to the predominance of traditional items. The fact that textiles, clothing, shoes, gems and jewellery, along with leather products, total 55 per cent of the exports underscores the low added-value nature of the goods list. Thus, modernizing and expanding production in the existing sectors is critical to increasing the trade volume and the value of the traded goods. A matter of concern for policy makers on both sides was the issue of expanding trade and this was addressed by the private sectors from both sides that conducted Joint Sectoral Studies. Eight sectoral studies have been conducted with respect to food processing, mechanical engineering, information technology, telecommunications, energy and power, textiles, biotechnology and financial services. These new sectors highlight the shift from traditional to scientific areas and the entry of India into these fields. Recommendations were made to increase trade and investment in certain industries on both sides and some working groups were also constituted to examine the suggestion for future policy.

At the Business Summit held at the time of the third EU–India Summit in Copenhagen in October 2003, it was decided to set a bilateral trade target between EU and India of €35 billion by 2005 and €50 billion by 2008. In 2003, the total trade between EU and India registered a growth of 6.36 per cent, but in 2004 this total trade increased from €28.4 billion in 2003 to €33.2 billion in 2004, registering a growth of 16.9 per cent. Thus, given the strong growth trends that have been observed since the decade of the 1990s in the bilateral trade relations, the 2008 target figures are achievable. However, there are other trends at work, since over the period 2001–06 trade between India and the EU as a share of total Indian trade has been declining and the fastest-growing trading partner is Asia and the ASEAN region combined together (see Tables 12.2, 12.3 and 12.4).

Seen from the EU perspective, however, these figures tell a very different story. In 2004 EU imports from India accounted for just 1.6 per cent

Table 12.2 India's exports in % share with different regions of the world (April–March 2001–06)

Region	2005–06	2004–05	2003–04	2002–03	2001–02	2000–01
1 Europe	24.06	23.55	24.54	24.16	24.78	25.94
EU Countries (25)	22.34	21.69	22.62	22.47	23.13	23.98
2 Africa	5.44	5.05	4.82	4.66	4.93	4.09
3 America	20.61	20.10	20.98	24.45	22.95	24.65
North America	17.73	17.52	19.19	21.99	20.76	22.43
4 Asia & ASEAN	48.46	49.50	47.60	44.39	40.19	38.69
5 CIS & Baltics	1.20	1.31	1.62	1.75	2.22	2.35
6 Unspecified Region	0.24	0.49	0.44	0.59	4.93	4.29
Total	100.00	100.00	100.00	100.00	100.00	100.00

Source: Department of Commerce, Government of India.

Table 12.3 India's imports in % share with different regions of the world (April–March 2001–06)

Region	2005–06	2004–05	2003–04	2002–03	2001–02	2000–01
1 Europe	21.17	22.98	24.04	24.98	26.54	27.55
EU Countries (25)	16.04	17.14	19.18	20.81	20.59	21.00
2 Africa	2.72	3.01	3.50	4.70	4.11	3.21
3 America	7.78	8.82	8.9	9.86	9.11	7.89
North America	6.09	6.97	7.37	8.16	7.16	6.48
4 Asia & ASEAN	35.22	36.19	35.36	30.11	31.43	28.61
5 CIS & Baltics	2.03	1.76	1.61	1.37	1.43	1.36
6 Unspecified Region	31.09	27.25	26.59	28.97	27.38	31.38
Total	100.00	100.00	100.00	100.00	100.00	100.00

Source: Department of Commerce, Government of India.

240 Patterns of Bilateralism

Table 12.4 India's trade with major trading partners (exports & imports)

(a) *India's exports % growth change of total with some main countries (April–March 2001–06)*

	% change in growth to previous year					
	2005–06	2004–05	2003–04	2002–03	2001–02	2000–01
EU	26.66	25.44	21.91	16.89	−4.10	10.09
US	24.97	19.81	5.45	27.98	−7.98	10.17
UAE	16.94	43.36	54.04	33.54	−3.50	24.19
China	19.68	90.04	49.59	107.52	14.88	53.81
Hong Kong	20.73	13.18	24.82	10.44	−10.07	5.65
Singapore	39.22	88.28	49.47	46.21	12.93	28.70
Japan	15.54	24.09	−8.30	23.41	−15.11	5.70
Bangladesh	0.08	−6.30	48.02	17.34	14.80	37.23

Source: Department of Commerce, Government of India.

(b) *India's exports % share of total with some main countries (April–March 2001–06)*

	% share of total exports					
	2005–06	2004–05	2003–04	2002–03	2001–02	2000–01
EU	22.34	21.69	22.62	22.47	23.13	23.98
US	16.75	16.48	18.00	20.67	20.76	20.96
UAE	8.36	8.80	8.03	6.31	5.69	5.86
China	6.54	6.72	4.63	3.75	2.17	1.88
Hong Kong	4.34	4.42	5.11	4.96	5.40	5.97
Singapore	5.42	4.79	3.33	2.70	2.22	1.95
Japan	2.39	2.54	2.68	3.54	3.45	4.04
Bangladesh	1.59	1.95	2.73	2.23	2.29	1.98

Source: Department of Commerce, Government of India.

of its total global imports and its exports to India are only 1.8 per cent of its global exports (see Table 12.5). India attracts only 0.3 per cent of the EU's worldwide investments. Thus the challenge for India in its trade and investment relations with the EU, up to this recent round of EU enlargement, was focused on enhancing the list of goods being traded and the volume of trade and investment it drew from the Union.

In this context, it is interesting to make a comparative examination of India's trade with its major trading partners and to determine the trends. In India's exports, it is the EU followed by the US that are positioned in the first and second positions respectively, while in imports the

Table 12.4 (Continued)

(c) India's imports % growth change of total with some main countries (April–March 2001–06)

	% change in growth to previous year					
	2005–06	2004–05	2003–04	2002–03	2001–02	2000–01
EU	19.49	27.51	17.30	20.75	0.84	−5.47
US	11.09	39.06	13.31	41.08	10.91	−20.32
UAE	−7.09	125.31	115.24	4.58	40.06	−72.01
China	51.30	75.12	45.17	37.11	36.44	15.99
Hong Kong	25.28	15.91	53.48	33.44	−12.97	2.40
Singapore	21.83	27.14	45.34	10.02	−9.02	−6.59
Japan	9.81	21.27	45.27	−14.45	17.13	−27.73
Bangladesh	100.03	−23.52	25.10	4.96	−19.98	−5.48

Source: Department of Commerce, Government of India.

(d) India's imports % share of total with some main countries (April–March 2001–06)

	% share of total imports					
	2005–06	2004–05	2003–04	2002–03	2001–02	2000–01
EU	16.04	17.14	19.18	20.81	20.59	21.00
US	5.46	6.28	6.44	7.24	6.13	5.68
UAE	3.03	4.16	2.64	1.56	1.78	1.31
China	7.54	6.36	5.19	4.55	3.96	2.99
Hong Kong	1.52	1.55	1.91	1.58	1.42	1.68
Singapore	2.27	2.38	2.67	2.34	2.54	2.87
Japan	2.49	2.90	3.41	2.99	4.17	3.67
Bangladesh	0.08	0.05	0.10	0.10	0.11	0.15

Source: Department of Commerce, Government of India.

EU leads, followed by China and the US. India's trade with China shows the most rapidly expanding bilateral trade relationship. The EU's major trade relations are indisputably with the US, but the second position in terms of its imports is occupied by China at a healthy 12.3 per cent compared to a dismal 1.6 per cent of the EU's imports coming from India in 2004. These figures underscore not only the dynamic nature of the Chinese economy, but also the Chinese ability to capitalize on its trade relations with the EU, an issue which both India and the EU seriously need to address in order to take the necessary policy measures which will enhance the volume of trade.

Table 12.5 EU's trade with major trading partners (% share)

(a) EU's exports (in million euros)

	2004	share %	2003	share %	2002	share %	2001	share %
US	223,912	24.3	220,718	22.57	237,080	24.0	239,902	24.36
Switzerland	74,960	7.79	71,243	8.11	72,636	8.07	76,390	8.56
China	48,039	5.0	40,091	4.10	33,822	3.42	30,099	3.05
Russia	45,664	4.74	37,086	4.22	34,275	3.81	31,370	3.51
Japan	43,067	4.5	40,088	4.09	41,507	4.20	44,920	4.56
India*	17,013	1.8	14,235	1.45	12,867	1.30	12,281	1.24

Note: *India's rank is fourteenth.
Source: Eurostat.

(b) EU's imports (in million euros)

	2004	share %	2003	share %	2002	share %	2001	share %
US	157,443	15.3	151,217	15.28	172,690	17.57	195,627	19.02
China	126,737	12.3	95,549	9.65	81,504	8.29	75,914	7.38
Russia	80,539	7.8	67,779	7.21	61,908	6.57	62,976	6.40
Japan	73,536	7.2	66,817	6.75	68,114	6.93	76,308	7.42
Switzerland	61,409	5.9	58,796	6.25	61,411	6.52	63,356	6.44
India*	16,233	1.6	13,354	1.34	12,984	1.32	12,816	1.24

Notes: *India's rank is thirteenth.
Source: Eurostat.

The new European Union and India

On 1 May 2004 the EU space suddenly grew, with a jump in population from 380 million to 450 million and with it has come a new and expanding market. This was the result of the EU's fifth round of enlargement that brought in ten new member states from Central and Eastern Europe (CEE): Cyprus, the Czech Republic, Estonia, Hungary, Latvia, Lithuania, Malta, Poland, Slovakia and Slovenia. While the new member states added 20 per cent to the population of the EU, their combined economic contribution was only around 4.8 per cent to the total gross domestic product (GDP) of the Union. This enlargement is unlike the previous ones and brings into the EU relatively poorer countries with greater regional disparities.

Although previous enlargements had also brought in countries with economic levels below the EU's previous economic levels, this time there will be a greater multiplier effect because of more members and because of a greater surge in population that will impact on the overall economic profile of the Union. Each enlargement has added and modified the identity of the Union (Baun, 1999, pp. 269–89). In the case of the United Kingdom (UK), Ireland and Denmark in 1973, UK and Ireland valued their transatlantic ties and on other issues UK and Denmark did not fully accept the political goals of European integration. The 1980s enlargement brought in a distinctly Southern and Mediterranean profile and these countries were relatively poorer and based on agriculture. The admission of Greece brought with it attendant problems with Turkey. The 1995 enlargement (Austria, Finland and Sweden) brought in countries which, while being net contributors to the budget, showed a preference for free trade and had strong social democratic traditions (Bava, 2006). The Eastern enlargement of 2004 has made the EU more agricultural and has pulled the overall per capita GDP down by 16 per cent (Commission of the European Communities, 1997, pp. 109–10). On the other hand it brought in economies with different levels of development and different economic structures. In January 2007 Bulgaria and Romania joined the EU taking the number to 27 and further adding to the diversity of the Union in terms of politics, issues, identities and culture.

From an Indian perspective, EU enlargement offers new opportunities for enhancing trade relations, but there are also other impediments. Enlargement has enhanced the EU's strength and voice at the level of global trade and this will be more acutely felt at the top – in the World Trade Organization (WTO) talks. In the economic sector the impact of enlargement needs to be examined in three areas: effect on industrial and agricultural trade, on services and on FDI. In the case of developing countries like India, agriculture will assume even more importance in relations with the EU.

Enlargement brings opportunities – one large common market with a common tariff. Some of the new members previously had higher tariffs which have come down to a uniform 4 per cent. From an investment perspective it also provides greater security for Indian companies and investors in the new member states due to their compliance with EU law. With their entry into the EU, the ten Central and East European (CEE) countries, which shared many common trade concerns, such as market access and non-tariff barriers with India at the world level, have lost this commonality of interest with India. This has in turn made the European Union stronger as it now represents a larger interest group. The new EU states are also likely to offer competition to India on offshore outsourcing. In some countries like, Hungary the level of skill is very high, although the sector needs to be better organized.

The dominant fear in the EU has been that there would be a major shift in manufacturing, with some industries being relocated to the cheaper East-China and India which have the twin advantages of cheaper labour costs and lower social costs. Rigid labour market regulations, high social costs and growing regulatory burdens on industry in the EU have raised alarm bells that they are witnessing a process of 'de-industrialization' across the EU.

The extension of the euro zone is also taking place steadily. The 12 new members will also adopt the euro as their currency in the future. However, unlike Denmark, Sweden and the UK, these countries do not have the right to opt out of the single currency. Poland and Hungary could be early entrants, provided they fulfil the economic criteria of a high degree of price stability, sound fiscal conditions, stable exchange rates and converged long-term interest rates. These new countries offer more potential for growth and thus offer better investment opportunities.

So the enlargement has taken place, but is the Indian government and business ready with strategies and action plans to convert these challenges into prospects and also exploit the opportunities? How is India engaging with a new Europe? More importantly, as enlargement will have economic implications at the global level, is India able to focus on developing negotiation strategies within the WTO framework? In 1992, when the European Single Market came into being, the notion of 'Fortress Europe' gained currency. The question to ask today after the EU's eastern enlargement is whether this notion will become a reality.

Some efforts have begun already to understand the larger economic implications of the enlargement process on India and especially on its exports. In a study carried out by the Indian Institute of Foreign Trade (IIFT) in New Delhi, the objective was explicitly to

> analyse the implications of the enlarged EU on Indian exports to the EU, use of Article XXIV (6) of GATT, which can be invoked in case tariffs are raised by the acceding countries and framing a negotiating strategy to seek compensation for products of export interest to India where the tariffs are likely to be hiked once the accession comes into effect.

It is interesting that the study found that on the whole the impact on India would be positive. The reason being that the common external tariff of the EU was much lower than the prevailing tariffs in the ten acceding countries, except in the case of a few products like textiles, organic chemicals and leather products.

India is concerned about whether or not non-tariff barriers (NTB) will affect its exports adversely, given the EU's stringent sanitary and phytosanitary conditions. These standards constitute non-tariff barriers and will be extended to the 12 new member states as well. In the past the EU had invoked these standards in the case of the export of agricultural produce from India. The other area of concern is textiles, which, along with clothing and shoes, constitutes around 36 per cent of Indian exports to the EU and is the core of India's trade. Around 23 per cent of India's total trade with the EU attracts NTBs with the highest being on carpets (86.2 per cent), textiles and clothing (65.85 per cent) and leather (31.35 per cent) (Nataraj and Sahoo, 2004). In a study by the Federation of Indian Chambers of Commerce and Industry (FICCI), it was observed that both Poland and the Czech Republic in particular were India's main competitors in 46 of the top 100 export items, especially in items such as auto components, synthetic yarn, footwear and leather products. Another area of concern is the implications of the removal of the Multi-fibre Agreement as that may lead to a higher imposition of tariffs.

The Indian Commerce Ministry is gearing up to help Indian exporters face up to the new challenges and convert them into opportunities. The new members enjoy a tariff advantage of over 4.6 per cent over India in the exports to the rest of Europe. A multi-pronged approach is needed to address the trade issues. The Commerce Ministry has proposed different strategies for Indian exporters to meet the challenge.

India should explore newer areas that show greater promise in the new member states and look for major technological collaborations, especially in knowledge-driven areas such as information technology, biotechnology and pharmaceuticals. As Indian tariffs are falling, the potential for enhancing the volumes of two-way trade is tremendous. In the pharmaceutical sector India today offers state-of-the-art and cost-effective medical and research facilities and has highly-trained scientific manpower. On a positive note the EU has also been a key source of technology transfer to India. In the period August 1991 to December 2004 more than 3,600 technical collaborations, accounting for about 38 per cent of the total technical collaboration, were approved by the Indian government. Germany, UK and Italy were the leading countries from the EU-25 that had enhanced technical collaboration with India.

EU–India investment flows have grown significantly, as the available figures indicate. From a mere US$78 million in 1991 it expanded to about US$4 billion in 2003–04. However, the new member states could present serious investment competition for third countries and this could also have implications for India. The new members are more likely to attract greater EU investment in their area and as a result India would receive less EU investment. Two important reasons for this shift, at least in the short term, are, first, the geographical proximity of the new members and the seamless market that has opened to EU investors, and, secondly, the comparative cheaper labour costs in the CEE countries, which is where the Indian market has also enjoyed an advantage in the past. There is a strong possibility that other countries exporting to the EU would be affected by the trade and investment diversion that will take place within this enlarged Union. In the long term, however, the second advantage would be diluted considerably as the living standards of the CEE countries grow and their economies come to be on a par with the old EU.

Even before the accession of the new states took place in 2004, the restructuring of a few industries in some old member states (especially close to the border with the incoming members) was undertaken. Major industries 'such as cars, machinery, textiles, consumer electronics and food processing have been working to create international production networks (IPNs) through trade and investment in mostly low/medium value added products in the Candidate Countries' (Noë, 2002, p. 9). For India to contend with this kind of competition, it would have to expand its trade and also aim to secure better market access to the EU. Here it needs to work hard on its brand image and be a consistent and quality player. These two aspects are critical to the long-term success of Indian business abroad and the ability to retain and expand its market base. The new member states' attractiveness as a good investment area began in 1994 when the EU committed itself to an eastern enlargement and grew as the CEE countries began the process of accession to the EU. Thus investor confidence grew and post accession the inevitability of investment flows increasing in the new member countries is a foregone conclusion.

In comparing the economies of the United States and the EU, recent figures clearly substantiate the view that the EU has fallen behind in all three major areas: GDP growth, productivity and income levels. The EU 15's unemployment rate for 2003 stood at 9.1 per cent and for the EU 27 in February 2007 was 7.3 per cent. By comparison the US had 6 per cent and 4.5 per cent for the corresponding periods. On the other hand the GDP increase for the same period stood at 0.9 per cent for the EU 25 and 3.1 per cent for the United States. Under these circumstances the eastern enlargement has had a multiple impact on the European economy: on the one hand it has increased the heterogeneity of the economy and on the other there has been a decline in the per capita income and productivity. This will widen further the performance gap between the United States and the EU. In a Global Competitiveness Report by the World Economic Forum (2004) the United States came in at second among 80 countries[2] while the EU was lagging behind. These types of concern had already prompted the EU to launch the 'Lisbon Strategy' with the declared objective to catch up in the intense competition with the United States by bringing Europe on to a growth path and establish a knowledge society. This ten-year strategy was adopted in March 2000 with the stated aim 'to make the EU the world's most dynamic and competitive economy and commitment to bring about economic, social and environmental renewal in the EU' (Commission of the European Communities, 2000).

Thus the incentive for India is to engage both the United States and the EU given their different economic potential and capabilities. The areas or sectors where good collaboration between India and the EU is possible are in power generation and distribution, ports, highways and agri-produce, banking and insurance and advanced medical care. These were also the areas flagged at a Roundtable organized by the FICCI in April 2005.[3] The challenge for India is to also initiate and sustain the reforms in these sectors and put in place the regulatory structure. Merely highlighting potential areas for investment and technological cooperation will not appeal to the European investor without the requisite legal infrastructure in place. On the Indian side procedural and processing delays have pushed away many a foreign investor and have even become a potent instrument of negative publicity. The FDI receipts of a country are directly linked to the nature, speed and sustainable economic reforms of a country and this applies equally to India if it wants to enhance the level of its economic partnership with the EU.

As the euro grows steadily stronger against the dollar, its impact on international trade and as a reserve currency also becomes increasingly significant. In 2002 the Head of the Delegation of the European Commission in India observed at a seminar that the euro would have an important role to play in transforming trade and investment relations between EU and India because a substantial part of India's trade with EU countries was currently invoiced in US dollars. Indian firms and business would also face growing competition from East European countries as many of them are becoming anchored to the euro and also switching to euro-invoicing. The euro thus provides a singular opportunity to Indian firms to increase their external competitiveness. Indian business would have to also address issues such as changing their legal instruments for new contracts to be drawn in euros, organizational restructuring in cash handling systems. The decision in 2005 of the Reserve Bank of India to designate the euro as the second intervention currency was an important step in giving a further boost to EU–India commercial relations.

India–EU relations: building a strategic partnership

Many studies and reports are talking about the twenty-first century being the Asian Century, dominated by the two main players – China and India – who are also emerging as the key drivers of the international economy. The EU's engagement with Asia as a region and with the individual country partners within Asia is intensifying. When considering the EU's Asia strategy it is clear that the EU's relationship with China also assumes significance for India.

The step-by-step upgrading of the India–EU political and economic relationship to summit level in June 2000 in Lisbon could be viewed as signalling the EU's intention to enhance its relations with India. The subsequent launch of the India–EU Strategic Partnership in 2004 was the recognition by the EU of India as a regional power that was gradually exerting a growing influence on many international issues. In fact, in the post-nuclear testing period since May 1998, it has become clear that India meant to pursue a new kind of foreign policy that would be both more pragmatic and assertive. At one level the Nehruvian discourse of foreign policy was injected with a massive dose of *realpolitik* as India added more firepower to its hitherto normative positions (Raja Mohan, 2003). That the EU should call India an equal partner affirms India's rise to a new status. India aspires to be both a regional and a global power. To that extent one can identify that India is redefining its national interest, especially its policies to its immediate contiguous neighbours and then expanding to areas both east and west and moving beyond the commercial interests to address political-security interests.

A further endorsement of the growing significance of India in regional and global politics came when the 2003 European Security Strategy identified India as one of the six countries to be a strategic partner to the EU. The India–EU Strategic Partnership is the sixth in line of such partnerships that the EU has forged; the earlier ones being with the United States, Canada, Russia, Japan and China. The EU wants to bring its relationship with India to 'the same parity, density and quality' as with the other Strategic Partners. A senior European Commission source told one newspaper that 'In doing this we are recognizing that India is gaining in real importance for the EU. Before we looked more to China, and saw India rather as a leader in the developing world. Now it's an equal partner'. The communication by the EU on 16 June 2004 proposing an EU–India Strategic Partnership draws upon the approach outlined in High Representative Javier Solana's paper of December 2003 entitled 'A Secure Europe in a Better World'. In this paper he identified India as a key partner with which the EU should develop strategic relations.

Clearly, the EU is already giving a new value to its relations with India. But it is critical to ask how India views these new developments. The Indian government's response to the EU–India Strategic Partnership emphasized that 'Europe is an important political and strategic actor influencing international power equations, affecting major international political and economic developments. The EU–India dialogue reveals a strong identity of views on the strategic priorities and issues of vital importance to both sides' (Delegation of the European Commission to India, 2005). Both India and the EU advocate multilateralism in international relations and both are open to dialogue on multilateral issues such as counterterrorism, disarmament and climate change. The largest democracies in the world share common values and beliefs that make them 'natural partners as well as factors of stability in the present world order' (Delegation of the European Commission to India, 2005). The India–EU Strategic Partnership Joint Action Plan endorses the view that both share 'a common commitment to democracy, pluralism, human rights and the rule of law, to an independent judiciary and media' and wish to foster a rule-based international order (Delegation of the European Commission to India, 2005).

The India–EU Strategic Partnership Joint Action Plan committed itself to the following areas (Delegation of the European Commission to India, 2005):

- Strengthening dialogue and consultation mechanisms;
- Deepening political dialogue and cooperation;
- Bringing together people and cultures;
- Enhancing economic policy dialogue and cooperation;
- Developing trade and investment.

In the area of *Political Dialogue and Cooperation*, the Action Plan has listed a very ambitious agenda. It emphasizes the pluralism and diversity that both India and the EU share. It promotes the idea of dialogue on Regional Cooperation in the EU and in SAARC and also supports democracy and human rights. It endorses effective multilateralism; and envisages that India and the EU will 'work together at the International

Level within a UN Framework on Peacekeeping, Peace-Building and Post-Conflict Assistance'. It further emphasizes that both will work collectively on disarmament and the non-proliferation of WMD and have a Security Dialogue. It also identifies that India and the EU would cooperate on fight against terrorism and organized crime, both of which make their respective areas very vulnerable to the new emerging threats.

In the area of *Economic Policy Dialogue and Cooperation* sectoral cooperation has been identified and emphasizes Industrial Policy, Science and Technology, Finance and Monetary Affairs, Environment, Clean Development and Climate Change, Energy, Information and, Communication Technologies, Transport, Space Technology, Pharmaceuticals and Biotechnology, Agriculture, Employment and Social Policy. It outlines how business and development cooperation can be further enhanced.

India has significant potential and is recognized as one of the emerging powers in the global order. India therefore needs both a vision and a strategy to realize this potential so that it can engage dynamically with other players in the international community. India has to synergize the economic and political aspects of its relationship with the EU to enhance the potential of this partnership. India needs a sustained growth rate, such as that which currently (in 2007) stands at 9 per cent, and a strong economic performance, together with the requisite reform of the economy, in order to improve the trade relations with the EU. However, India needs different kinds of partnerships at the global level. The EU is not a hegemon and it is no counterweight to the United States. India needs to engage the EU more as they 'are in fact natural partners', to quote European Commission President Romano Prodi in a speech he gave in India in 2004. The Indian government response was that

> with the EU's emergence as a major geopolitical and economic force in the new world order, it is opportune that India's approach towards the issue of shaping our relations with the EU in the coming years, should be formalized, so that a coordinated and mutually reinforcing strategy can be evolved

As India builds partnerships it needs to go beyond the economic aspects to enhancing the political and strategic value of the relationship with the EU.

An assessment of the India–EU Strategic Partnership draws immediate comparison with the India–US Strategic Partnership which was also launched a few years ago. The visit of the Indian Prime Minister Dr Manmohan Singh to Washington in July 2005 enhanced India–US bilateral ties and paved the way for the visit of US President George Bush to India and the historic 'nuclear deal' which endorsed civilian nuclear cooperation between the two states.

These developments are truly remarkable given that, as Nicholas Burns, Under Secretary for Political Affairs, remarked, 'successive Administrations in Washington and Delhi approached each other alternately with episodic engagement on the one hand, but with wariness and even downright opposition on the other' (Burns, 2005). In fact, the 1998 nuclear test by India had further exacerbated relations and India 'was not seen in Washington as an essential and cooperative part of the solution to many major international problems. Rather, India was viewed as one of the problems, outside the Non-Proliferation Treaty (NPT) and an obstacle to US non-proliferation efforts internationally' (Burns, 2005).

In the light of these past American sentiments about India, the India–US bilateral relation has indeed grown by leaps and bounds in recent years with both countries now endorsing the view that 'the successful transformation of the US–India relationship will have a decisive and positive influence on the future international system as it evolves in this new century' (White House Press Release, 2006). The US–India Joint Statement of March 2006 focused on five key areas:

- Economic Prosperity and Trade;
- Energy Security and Clean Environment;
- Innovation and Knowledge Economy;
- Global Safety and Security;
- Deepening Democracy and Meeting International Challenges.

> Both our countries are linked by a deep commitment to freedom and democracy; a celebration of national diversity, human creativity and innovation; a quest to expand prosperity and economic opportunity worldwide; and a desire to increase mutual security against the common threats posed by intolerance, terrorism, and the spread of weapons of mass destruction. (White House Press Release, 2006)

So where are the differences in these two strategic partnerships? The answer lies in the way in which these two partnerships situate themselves in the emerging geopolitics. While the India–EU partnership talks about a rules-based order, the India–US partnership endorses security aspects. The striking distinction in approach is self-evident and these differences are even more apparent in the area of civil nuclear energy. While the EU is unable to take a strong stand about India's new nuclear status, the

India–US partnership not only recognizes this new reality but has gone ahead in an unprecedented way to endorse civilian nuclear cooperation. This cooperation seeks to end the technology drought that India has faced since 1998 and also recognizes its claims of being a responsible nuclear actor. Singularly, the new approach by the US where it has singled out India for a special treatment in which it chooses to so engage India corroborates the changing geopolitical reality of the region and the world.

India's pre-eminent role in South Asia may be contested by its neighbour Pakistan but it cannot be denied. India is the largest country in the region, sharing a border with six other neighbours who all together constitute the South Asian Association for Regional Cooperation (SAARC). The SAARC countries are Bangladesh, Bhutan, India, the Maldives, Nepal, Pakistan, and Sri Lanka. Recently the SAARC had its first expansion with the inclusion of Afghanistan as the eighth member; a significant step which seeks to further integrate Afghanistan and also realigns the entire region. However, the process of regionalism in Western Europe and in South Asia is very different. South Asia is beset by numerous bilateral conflicts, with the most intense and long-standing conflict being between India and Pakistan, which has also cast its shadow on the regional organization. The absence of the kind of internal and external factors and impulses in South Asia that facilitated the regional process in Western Europe and the divergence in the security perceptions of the SAARC members have prevented it from emerging as a medium of successful regional integration. In its 1994 EU Asia Strategy, the EU decided to 'deepen and extend its dialogue with Asian countries and regional groupings'. The contact between the EU and SAARC was established by a memorandum of understanding on administrative cooperation in 1996. However, cooperation between both has been limited due to the weakness of SAARC as a regional organization. Thus within South Asia the countries prefer to conduct their relations bilaterally with the EU. The EU–India Strategic partnership recognizes the existing power constellation in South Asia and will have no impact on the EU–SAARC relationship.

In contrast to India, China established diplomatic relations with the EEC in May 1975. Though a late starter compared to India, its trade volumes and political relations have surpassed EU–India relations, clearly underscoring the importance attached by each to the economic and political aspects of their relationship. China has been more prepared to deal with the impact of enlargement on its trade relations. It even started negotiations before the process of enlargement to ask for compensation, as the ten new member states would have to scrap their individual bilateral trade agreements. China wanted to offset the probable trade loss by negotiating for either lower tariffs or higher quotas in different commodity areas. China strode ahead of India in the launch of the Strategic Partnership, which was initiated in 2003 and initialled in March 2004. Although the EU is China's third largest trading partner, behind Japan and the United States, their trade volume surpasses that of India–EU trade. Chinese exports to the EU for 2003 were recorded at US$250 billion, in contrast to India's exports to the EU of around $50 billion. China has a head start compared to India and is already participating in many joint technology projects, including the European Galileo satellite navigation programme. One writer called the China–EU relationship a 'new emerging axis' (Shambaugh, 2004); the potential of the relationship definitely endorses such a caption. So can India–EU relations be another axis?

The India–EU Strategic Partnership launched in 2004 has the potential to develop into an important axis. But is the India–EU Strategic Partnership Action Plan a wish list that is long on ideas and short on implementation? The main reason for such a perception is the parallel developments in the India–US Strategic partnership that was launched in 2005. As discussed above, the differences between these two strategic partnerships could not be more obvious. In the case of India and the US it is a one-to-one relationship between the global hegemon and an emerging India (Bava, 2006). Although the EU is an undisputed global economic actor, it does not yet have the commensurate political or military strength. Its inability to articulate a common foreign policy position and the strong bilateral positions articulated by individual member states have also diminished its credibility as a critical security player. These factors demonstrate that the EU's appeal for endorsing a normative global structure is attractive only to the extent it can enforce it, which in practice has been fairly limited. Thus the India–EU partnership has the potential, but due to the EU's lack of cohesiveness as an actor it fails to capture the political imagination of how these two could restructure global politics.

Post-Cold War there is a new fluidity in power alignments and a reconfiguration of the political, security and economic environment. With the emergence of new realities and new opportunities, India seeks to promote its national interest such that it can enhance its influence and secure its political and economic objectives. What has caught the world's attention is that India's economic power is progressively increasing and this dynamism is also reflected in its political engagements. It is no longer a country on the sidelines of global economic development, but is now emerging as one of the principal economic drivers of the region. As India aspires to a new role, the new kind of realism in its foreign policy has to be guided by its existing political and economic capabilities. But, undoubtedly, it is this 'new' India with which the EU wants to engage intensively.

Notes

1. Pascal Lamy at Luncheon meeting at CII, New Delhi, 14 March 2003.
2. India stood 48th in terms of global competitiveness in 2002.
3. Address by Ms Bhaswati Mukherjee, Joint Secretary (Europe-I), Roundtable on India and New Europe: Emerging Perspectives, FICCI, New Delhi, 28 April 2004.

References

Baun, M., 'Enlargement', in L. Cram, D. Dinan and N. Nugent (eds), *Developments in the European Union* (London: Macmillan, 1999).
Bava, U.S., *West German Realpolitik, Unification, EU and European Security, 1949–95* (New Delhi: Kanishka, 2001).
Bava, U.S., 'European Integration and European Identity', at an international seminar on Multiculturalism in India and Europe organized by Jawaharlal Nehru University European Union Studies Programme, Maison des Sciences de l'Homme, EU Commission, Fundacao Oriente and DAAD, New Delhi, Unpublished paper (2003).
Bava, U.S., 'European Integration and the Challenges of Institutional Reform', in R.K. Jain, H. Elsenhans and A. Narang (eds), *The European Union in World Politics* (New Delhi: Radiant, 2006).
Bava, U.S., 'India – An Emerging Power in International Security?', in A.C. Vaz, *Intermediate States, Regional Leadership and Security: India, Brazil and South Africa* (Brasilia: University of Brasilia, 2006).
Bretherton, C., and Vogler, J., *The European Union as Global Actor* (London: Routledge, 1999).
Burns, N., *The U.S. and India: The New Strategic Partnership*, Under Secretary for Political Affairs Remarks to the Asia Society, New York City, 18 October 2005).
Commission of the European Communities, *Agenda 2000: For A Stronger and Wider Union*, Bulletin of the European Union, Brussels, Supplement 5/97 (1997), pp. 109–10.
Commission of the European Communities, *Lisbon Agenda* (2000). Accessed at http://ec.europa.eu/growthandjobs/key/index_en.htm.
Commission of the European Communities, *Europe and Asia: A Strategic Framework for Enhanced Partnerships* (Brussels: European Commission, 2001).
Cram, L., Dinan, D., and Nugent, N. (eds), *Developments in the European Union* (London: Macmillan, 1999).

Delegation of the European Commission to India, *The India–EU Strategic Partnership: Joint Action Plan*, New Delhi, 7 September 2005. Available at www.delind.cec.eu.int/en/political_dialogue/summits/sixth/joint_action_plan.pdf.

Delegation of the European Commission to India, *EU–India Political Dialogue*, New Delhi (2007). Available at http://www.delind.cec.eu.int/en/political_dialogue/introduction.htm.

Keohane, R.O., and Nye, J.S. (eds), *Transnational Relations and World Politics* (Cambridge, MA: Harvard University Press, 1973).

Kupchan, C., 'The Rise of Europe, America's Changing Internationalism and the End of US Primacy', *Political Science Quarterly*, 18(2) (2003).

Laffan, B., 'Democracy and the European Union', in L. Cram, D. Dinan and N. Nugent (eds), *Developments in the European Union* (London: Macmillan, 1999).

Nataraj, G., and Sahoo, P., 'Enlargement of EU – Effects on India's Trade', *Economic and Political Weekly*, 8 May 2004.

Noë, Willem, European Commission, DG Economic and Financial Affairs, National Europe Centre Paper No. 8, Australian National University, 12 March 2002.

Piening, C., *Global Europe: The European Union in World Affairs* (London: Lynne Rienner, 1997).

Raja Mohan, C., *Crossing the Rubicon: The Shaping of India's New Foreign Policy* (New Delhi: Viking, 2003).

Rosenau, J.N., *Turbulence in World Politics: a Theory of Change and Continuity* (New York: Harvester and Wheatsheaf, 1990).

Rosenau, J.N., Davies, V., and East, M.A. (eds), *The Analysis of International Politics* (New York: Free Press, 1972).

Ruggie, J.G., 'Territoriality and Beyond: Problematizing Modernity in International Relations', *International Organization*, 47(1) (1993), 139–74.

Shambaugh, David, 'China and Europe: The Emerging Axis', *Current History* (September 2004), 243–8.

US Department of State, *US–India Civilian Nuclear Cooperation*, Washington, DC (22 July 2005). Available at www.state.gov/r/pa/prs/ps/2005/49969.htm.

White House Press Release, US Department of State, *US–India Joint Statement*, New Delhi (2 March 2006).

Young, O.R., 'The Actors in World Politics', in J.N. Rosenau, V. Davies and M.A. East (eds), *The Analysis of International Politics* (New York: Free Press, 1972).

Index of Names

Abraham, I. 115, 120
Acharya, A. 41, 45
Allen, D. 50, 64
Angenendt, S. 103, 104, 105, 108, 114, 116, 117, 119
Aron, R. 9, 22
Aspinwall, M. 211
Avila, J.L. 40, 45, 78, 81

Balme, R. 15, 17, 20
Batistella, G. 103, 104, 117, 118, 119
Baun, M. 243, 254
Bava, U.S. 16, 20, 235, 236, 243, 253, 254
Bellany, I. 227, 231
Benton, G. 108, 109, 120
Bergsten, F. 71, 45, 81
Berkofsky, A. 43, 45
Bobrow, D.B. 32, 45
Boisseau du Rocher, S. 39, 45
Bretherton, C. 234, 254
Bridges, B. 11, 16, 17, 22, 144, 214, 221, 231
Brodsgaard, K.E. 179, 192
Burns, N. 251, 254
Buzan, B. 211

Cabestan, J.P. 167, 169, 172, 193
Camroux, D. 4, 22, 30, 45
Chan G. 138–44, 177, 193
Chang Ya-chun, 188, 193
Chen Zhilong 156–69
Cheon Seongwhun 226, 231
Chi Su 176, 193
Cholewinski, R. 116, 119
Chong Bong-uk 225, 231
Christiansen, F. 112, 119
Chung Yun-ho, 225, 231
Cox, R. 9, 22
Cram, L. 254, 255
Curtis, G. 211

Dai Bingren 157, 159, 169
Davies, V. 255

de Schoutheete, P. 49, 65
Deighton, A. 51, 65
Dejean de la Batie, H. 39, 45, 131, 134, 136, 144
Dent, C. 11, 22, 216, 231
Dinan, D. 254, 255
Dolowitz, D. 89, 101
Douw, L. 15, 21
Drifte, R. 172, 189, 193, 218, 221, 230, 231
Dupont, A. 108, 119

East, M.A. 255
Erasmus, S. 174, 193
Eshuis, R. 113, 119
Estanislao, J. 92

Fagot Aviel, J. 9, 23
Fawcette, L. 211
Feng Zhongping 150, 170
Fligstein, N. 211
Fogarty, E. 95, 96, 101
Ford, Glyn 227, 231
Fort, B. 39, 45
Freeman D. 130, 144

Gao Lang 174, 193
Garver, J.W. 174, 193
Ge Qifan 155, 170
Geddes, A. 115, 119
Geense, P. 112, 119
Gill, B. 35, 45
Gilpin, R. 9, 22
Gilson, J. 4, 11, 18, 22, 23, 30, 45, 199, 200, 211
Godement, F. 2, 8, 14, 18, 22, 136, 137, 144
Goldstein, J. 6, 22
Gosset, D. 126, 144
Grant, R.L. 160, 170
Gregory, J.S. 2, 22
Griese, O. 128, 144
Guglielmo, R. 116, 119
Guiraudon, V. 115, 119

Index of Names

Hachiya, M. 16, 19
Hall, P.A. 89, 99, 101
Hänggi, H. 28, 31, 45
Herman, R. 203, 211
Hernandez, C.G. 103, 105, 114, 116, 119
Hill, C. 47, 65
Ho Shu-yin 176, 193
Hoare, J. 227, 231
Hobson, J.M. 2, 23
Hoon, J. 211
Howorth, J. 51, 65
Hsieh Chiao Chiao 175, 176, 179, 180, 182, 193
Huang Niansi 168, 170
Huang, Y. 35, 45
Huo Zhengde 161, 167, 170
Hurrell, A. 211

Ikenherry, J.G. 29, 45, 211

Jaung, H. 211
Jencks, H.W. 189, 193
Joei, Bernard T.K. 179, 193
Johnson, C. 150, 151, 170

Kelly, J. 225, 231
Keohane, R.O. 234, 255
Khor, M. 208, 211
Kim, Hak-sung 218, 221, 222, 231
Kim, Heung-Chong 4, 15, 20, 82, 227, 231
Kim, Samuel, S. 174, 193
Kindermann, G.K. 180, 184, 189, 194
Kraft, H.J. 93, 101
Krause, J. 95, 101
Kristof, N.D. 146, 170
Kruse, I. 103, 104, 116, 119
Kugler, J. 9, 23
Kull, S. 5, 23
Kupchan, C. 236, 255
Kwon Soyoung 227, 231

Laffan, B. 234, 255
Lan Yuchun 192, 194
Laney, J. 146, 170
Langenhove, L. van 59, 65

Larat, F. 18, 23
Lazcko, F. 114, 120
Lechervy, C. 4, 22, 30, 45
Lee Chae Woong 215, 231
Lee Jung-chul 224, 231
Lemke, D. 9, 23
Leonard, M. 61, 65
Leung, B. 178, 194
Li, Minghuan, 107, 113, 120
Lim, P. 78, 82
Lim, Timothy C. 115, 120
Lu Zhimin 157, 170
Luhulima, C.P.F. 84, 101

Madsen, R. 178, 194
Mantaha, Z. 11, 23
Marcus, G.E. 115, 120
Marsh, D. 89, 101
Martens, E. 112, 121
Mastanduno, M. 29, 45, 211
Mattli, W. 211
Maull, H.W. 11, 23, 28, 45
McCubbins, M.D. 211
Meng Honghua 148, 150, 170
Mengin, F. 172, 179, 180, 191, 194
Mikado, E. 203, 205, 211
Ming Chu-Cheng 175, 183, 194
Moller K. 127, 144, 172, 194
Moore, M. 115, 120
Morgenthau, H. 9, 23
Morii, Y. 211
Muldoon, J. 9, 23
Müller-Brandeck-Bocquet, G. 50, 65

Nataraj, G. 245, 255
Nischalke, T.I. 91, 101
Noë, W. 246, 255
Nugent, N. 254, 255
Nuttall, S. 49, 53, 54, 65
Nye, J.S. 234, 255

Ohira, K. 196, 198, 211
Organski, A.F.K. 9, 23
Orren, H.E. 105, 108, 116, 117, 119

Park, S.H. 4, 15, 20, 82, 74, 78, 79, 82
Pelkmans, J. 70, 82

Pels, T. 112, 119
Pempel, T.J. 36 45, 211
Pieke, F.N. 106, 108, 109, 111, 120
Piening, C. 234, 255
Polanyi, K. 104, 120
Preston, P. 11, 23

Qiu Yuanlun 152, 153, 164, 170

Raja Mohan, C. 248, 255
Redding, G. 113, 120
Regelsberger, E. 55, 65
Reitano, R. 9, 23
Reiterer, M. 211
Robles, A.C, Jr. 85, 102
Roloff, R. 31, 45
Rosenau, J.N. 234, 255
Rueland, J. 85, 87, 102
Ruggie, J.G. 211, 234, 255
Rüland, J. 31, 45

Saalman, L. 184, 194
Sabatier, P.A. 88, 89, 102
Sahoo, P. 245, 255
Sandholtz, W. 211
Santos Neves, M. 144
Sasse, G. 116, 120
Scharping, T. 106, 120
Schendel, W. van 115, 120
Schneider, G. 211
Scollay, R. 79, 82
Segal, G. 11, 23, 28, 29 45, 46, 115, 120
Shambaugh, D. 137, 144, 253, 255
Shao Cheng Tang 137, 144
Shaplen, J.T. 146, 170
Sharp, F. 211
Shichor, Y. 106, 120
Shin Chueiling 174, 179, 194
Shin, Don-Ik 115, 120
Shinkai, H. 70, 82
Sigal, L. 218, 231
Simon, S.W. 94, 102
Singh, D. 115, 120
Skeldon, R. 105, 121
Smith, H. 221, 230, 232
Smith, Karen E. 15, 17
Smith, M.E. 47, 65

Söderbaum, F. 59, 65
Solana, J. 50, 61, 65
Song Tianshui 165, 170
Song Xinling 153, 170
Stålgren, P. 59, 65
Stone, D. 99, 102
Strange, S. 11, 23
Stubbs, R. 33, 46
Su Fangyi 159, 170
Sullivan, Earl 9, 23
Suu Kyi, Aung San 59, 60
Sweet, A.S. 211

Takashi, S. 32, 46
Tanabe, T. 201, 211
Tanaka, A. 36, 46
Tanaka, T. 11, 23
Tay, S.S.C. 92, 102
Taylor, P. 212
Thielemann, E. 116, 120
Ting Wai 16, 17, 20, 146
Tkacik, J.J. Jr. 166, 170
Tsai Cheng-Wen 175, 183, 194
Tubilewicz, C. 16, 19, 115, 120, 177, 194

van den Muijzenberg, O. 106, 107, 108, 121
Vogel, E.Z. 36, 46
Vogels, Ria 112, 121
Vogler, J. 234, 254

Waever, O. 211
Wakabayashi, H. 207, 208, 212
Waltz, K. 9, 23
Wanandi, J. 11, 23, 28, 45, 91, 102
Wang Wan-li 183, 194
Waters, T.W. 116, 119
Weng Byron, S.J. 174, 194
Wiessala, G. 11, 23, 61, 65
Winn, G.F.T. 214, 232
Wu Baiyi 168, 170
Wu Linjun 175, 179, 194
Wu Rong-I 185, 194

Xiang, Biao 106, 121
Xiao Yuankai 168, 171

Yahuda, M. 174, 194
Yakushiji, K. 206, 212
Ye Zicheng 164, 165, 171
Yeo Lay Hwee 4, 11, 15, 18, 23, 102
Young, O.R. 234, 255
Yu Jianhua 159, 171

Yuan Jing-dong 184, 194
Yuan, M. 36, 46

Zhang Shaowei 166, 167, 171
Zhang Xiaojin 162, 171
Zhu Liyu 162, 171

Index of Subjects

Aceh 34, 55–6
ACP (African, Caribbean and Pacific countries) 69, 74, 85, 95
actor, 'actorness' (EU as a global actor): 59, 62, 207–9, 234–5
ADB (Asian Development Bank) 37
Afghanistan 34, 44, 55–8, 85, 252
Africa 52, 55–56, 69
AIDS (Acquired Immune Deficiency Syndrome), 139
Albania (and Taiwan), 189
alliance 36–7, 200
AMED (Asia–Middle East Dialogue) 95
see also Middle East
Amsterdam Treaty 33, 50, 51
Andean Pact 95
APEC (Asia-Pacific Economic Cooperation Forum) 30–2, 37–8, 43, 71–2, 78, 80
Arab League 95
arms embargo (EU–China) 33, 34, 136–8, 165–7
arms sales 33, 166, 167, 180, 188, 190
ASEAN (Association of South-East Asian Nations) 1, 4, 10–12, 14, 15, 17–19, 34–5, 40–3, 54–63, 70, 71, 74, 76, 78, 83–100, 148, 149, 235, 239
   ASEAN+3 (ASEAN and China, Japan and South Korea) 18, 33, 43
   ASEAN–EC Joint Study Group 84
   ASEAN–EC Ministerial Meeting (AEMM) 84–87
   ASEAN–EU Cooperation Agreement 84, 85
   ASEAN–EU Eminent Persons Group 87
   ASEAN–ISIS (ASEAN–Institute of Strategic and International Studies) 93, 94

ASEAN Charter 93, 97, 98
ASEAN Committee 98
ASEAN Council 98
ASEAN Declaration 91
ASEAN Economic Community 93
ASEAN Foreign Ministers Meeting 86
ASEAN Free Trade Area (AFTA) 86, 87, 91, 99
ASEAN Investment Area (AIA) 86, 87, 91
ASEAN Ministerial Meeting 98
ASEAN Programme for Regional Integration Support (APRIS) 92
ASEAN Regional Forum (ARF) 11, 17, 39, 43, 86, 93, 94, 95
ASEAN Secretariat-General 92, 97, 98
ASEAN Security Community 93
ASEAN Summit 42, 96, 98
ASEAN Way 90, 91, 97
ASEM (Asia–Europe Meeting) 1, 4, 7, 9, 11–15, 18–20, 27, 30–33, 43, 57, 59, 60, 63, 67, 70–80, 88, 95, 96, 127, 183, 199, 207, 221
ASEM Summit 30, 32, 60, 70
ASEM Trust Fund 78
Asia 1–24, 27–44, 48, 52–63, 66–7, 70–80, 87, 95–6
   Central Asia 36, 56, 141, 147, 163, 235
   East Asia 15, 27, 33, 67, 70–80, 138, 215
   Northeast Asia 1, 11, 73, 75
   South Asia 1, 4, 18, 29, 73, 74, 76, 147, 235, 252
   Southeast Asia 1, 3, 11, 27, 29, 34–39, 67, 73–5, 83, 87, 93, 99–100, 187, 235
Asian financial crisis (1997) 4, 18, 31–7, 75–80, 88, 91–4, 100
Asian Miracle 28, 30, 35

Asia-Pacific region 6, 16, 27, 28, 31, 32, 35, 38, 72, 87, 94, 95, 166, 229
  see also APEC
Asian Strategy (of EU)
  see NAS, New Asia Strategy
Asian Tigers 73
Atlantic Alliance 165
Australasia 75–6, 235
Australia 31, 36, 60, 62, 69, 84, 94
Austria 71, 166, 180, 243

Balkans 14, 58, 189
Baltic States 189
Bangkok 4, 27, 30, 32, 70
Bangladesh 252
Beijing 140, 145, 146, 147, 154, 155, 163
Belgium, and China 130, 166
  and Korea 221
  and Taiwan 174,175,180
Benelux 35
Berlin Wall 85, 127
Bhutan 252
bilateral relations 11–14, 19–20
Blair, Tony 51, 166
Bo Xilai 156
Brazil 60
Britain
  see United Kingdom
Brittan, Leon 183
Brusselization 50, 52, 54
  see also integration of foreign policy
Brussels 43, 50, 52, 54, 196
Bulgaria 189
Burma 3, 42, 55, 56, 59, 60, 85
  see also Myanmar
Bush, George 4, 137, 222, 226, 250

Cadarache 203–5
Cambodia 34, 55, 59, 60, 85, 88, 99
  see also Kampuchea
Canada 60, 62, 69, 84, 94
Canada (and India) 248
Canada (and Japan) 203,204
Cancun meeting (2003) 22
Catholicism 177, 178
Chang, John 183

Chen Shui-bian 178,181,189
Chiang Ching-kuo 174
Chile 30
China (People's Republic of China)
  and India 233, 235, 240–4, 248, 252–3
  and Japan 203–4
  and Korea 213–16, 220, 223–4, 226, 229–30
  and Taiwan 145, 148, 162, 167, 173–7, 184, 188–91
  Anti-Secession Law 166
  Arms Embargo 136–8
  Cultural Revolution 126
  development of the European Union policy 126–9
  economic relations with the EU 71–5, 129–2, 151–8
  exchange rate (RMB) 131
  Four Modernizations Policy 126
  hard power 125, 140
  human rights, political dialogue with the EU 132–5, 162–7
  Ministry of Commerce 132, 155
  Ministry of Foreign Affairs 147
  multilateralism 140–1
  National People's Congress (NPC) 137, 161, 166
  New International Order 149
  One China Policy 172, 176, 181–5, 188, 191
  Opium War 163
  People's Liberation Army (PLA) 155
  People's Supreme Court 135
  Sino-US relations 134, 135, 174
  Sino-Vatican relations 178
  State Education Commission 188
  Tiananmen incident 61, 71, 127, 133, 150, 165, 175
  westernization 158–62
  Xingjian province 147
China–USA–Europe 165
China–US–North Korea talks 226
Chirac Jacques 133, 167
Chun Doo Hwan 214
Clarington 203
climate change 200
  see also Kyoto Protocol, UNFCCC
Clinton administration 29, 32, 222

Index of Subjects 263

Cold War 3, 9, 14–17, 27–8, 31, 36, 49, 54–8, 86, 94, 145–7, 162, 165, 173, 175, 182, 195, 198, 206, 236
colonialism 27, 41, 66
constructivism 7, 43, 116
cooperation and development 34, 37, 69, 74, 84–85, 95, 132, 158, 235
  see also ADB, ODA, LDC, Lomé, International Aid, World Bank, WHO
Copenhagen Summit Meetings 78
Council of Europe 18
CSCAP (Council for Security Cooperation in the Asia-Pacific) 94
CSCE (Conference on Security and Cooperation in Europe) 95
Cuba 69
Cyprus 242
Czech Republic 176, 181, 187, 188, 190, 242

Dagmar 181
Delors, Jacques 126
decolonization 3, 86
Deng Xiaoping 126, 136
Denmark (and India) 237, 243, 244
Denmark (and China) 128, 133
Dien Bien Phu 3
Dili 59
Doha 40
Doko, Toshimitsu 197

EAEC (East Asian Economic Caucus) 31
East Asia Community, 209
East Asian Community of ASEAN 60
East Asian Summit 18, 22, 43
Eastern and Central Europe (and Taiwan) 173, 174, 176, 180–2, 190
Eastern and Central Europe (and Korea) 214, 216, 223
Eastern and Central Europe (and India) 242, 243, 246
Eastern Turkistan Movement 147
EC (European Community) 48, 49, 53, 54, 57, 59, 67, 84, 85, 86, 94, 95, 126, 127, 182, 183, 187, 196, 197, 198, 203, 235, 237
ECHO (European Communities Humanitarian Office) 34, 221, 223
ECSC (European Coal and Steel Community) 90
EEA (European Economic Area) 69, 76
EEC (European Economic Community) 83, 84, 90, 196, 235, 236, 237, 252
EFEX (European Financial Expertise Network) 78
EFTA (European Free Trade Association) 62, 69, 74
energy security 41
environment 9–16, 37, 40, 86–7, 90, 96, 115, 155, 157, 160, 167, 200–8, 217, 247–53
EPC (European Political Cooperation) 48, 49, 55, 57
epistemic community 92–3
Estonia 242
EU (European Union)
  CAP (Common Agricultural Policy) 71
  CFSP (Common Foreign and Security Policy) 6, 17, 18, 47–62, 95, 127, 184, 213, 222, 229, 233
  Constitutional Treaty 22, 33, 34, 44, 52, 202
  Council of the European Union 41, 49, 51, 55, 58–61, 127, 129, 136, 183–6, 220, 227
  Customs Union 67, 196
  ESDP (European Security and Defense Policy) 52–62, 167
  EU–ASEAN dialogue 19, 83–100
  EU–Japanese Joint Declaration (1991), 19
  EU–Korea Wiseman's Group 229
  EU–Mercosur partnership 95
  Euro-Mediterranean partnership 95
  European Commission 28–32, 39–41, 49, 67, 72–3, 74–9, 127–40, 182–5, 157–62, 198, 214–29, 236–50

EU (European Union) – *continued*
  European External Action Service 53, 62
  European Initiative on Democracy and Human Rights (EIDHR) 139
  European Parliament 41, 52, 53, 127, 135, 183, 184, 189, 197, 227, 228
  European Security Strategy 55, 57, 236, 248
  EU–South Korea Free Trade Agreement (FTA) 220, 217
  External Relations Commissioner 53, 58
  Petersberg Tasks 50, 52, 53
  Presidency 135
  Troika 127, 222
  High Representative 50, 53, 62
  see also Amsterdam Treaty, Maastricht Treaty, Nice Treaty, Single European Act, Single European Market
Euratom (European Atomic Energy Community) 140
European Bank for Reconstruction and Development (EBRD) 176
European Chamber of Commerce, 186
EUROSTAT 76
EVSL (Early Voluntary Sectoral Liberalization) 78

Fauroux, Roger 179
FDI (Foreign Direct Investment) 35, 77, 130, 139, 151–4, 185, 216, 220, 235, 237–8, 243, 245–6
FEALAC (Forum for East Asia and Latin America Cooperation) 95
Ferrero-Waldner, Benita 128, 228
Finland 71, 237, 243
Fischer, Joshka 135
'Fortress Europe' 31, 71, 81, 116
France 3, 5, 12, 14, 17, 19, 22, 30, 34, 41, 50, 51, 87
  and China 130, 136, 137, 138, 161, 165
  and India 235
  and Japan 203, 204, 205
  and Korea 218, 221, 230
  French Institute in Taipei (FIT) 179

Galileo (system of satellite navigation) 128, 154, 253
Gam 34
GATT (General Agreement on Tariffs and Trade) 67, 127, 182, 244
GCC (Gulf Cooperation Council) 95
Geneva (Conference) 3
German Ministry of Foreign Affairs 180
Germany 5, 12, 14, 30, 50, 87
  and China 130, 134, 137, 161, 165
  and Korea 221, 230
  and Taiwan 180
Giannella, Annalisa 137
Goebbels, Joseph 29
Gorbachev, Mikhail 203
Great Britain
  see United Kingdom
Greece 221, 243
Group of Eight (G8) 9, 204
GSP (Generalized System of Preferences) 41, 69
Guangzhou 188

Hanoi 60
Hashimoto, Ryutaro 201
Havel, Vaclav 176, 181, 182
Havlova, Olga 181
Helsinki (European Council) 51, 52
Holy See 178
Hong Kong 3, 7, 18, 22, 73, 128, 130, 178, 185, 216
Hu Jintao 148
Human Development Index 7
human rights 10–15, 20, 29, 32, 41, 43, 55–63, 86–7, 132–5, 159–67, 172, 191, 217, 221–2, 240
  see also UNHRC
humanitarian aid 23, 27, 28, 34, 37, 39, 40, 50, 134, 221–3
Hungary 176, 242, 243, 244

IAEA (International Atomic Energy Agency) 203, 225, 226
ICCPR (International Covenant for Civil and Political Rights) 129, 161, 162

Index of Subjects   265

Iceland   62
ICSECR (International Covenant for Social, Economic and Cultural Rights)   161
idealism   145–50, 167–8
IMF (International Monetary Fund)   28, 37, 219, 220
imperialism   213
India   3–5, 12–20, 36, 40–41, 44, 57–62, 84, 99
　and China   147
　and Taiwan   187
　EU–India Summit   238
　EU–SAARC relationship   252
　India–EU Strategic Partnership   236, 248, 249, 250, 253
　India–US Strategic Partnership   250
　Indian Chambers of Commerce and Industry (FICCI)   245, 247
　Indian Institute of Foreign Trade (IIFT)   244
　Reserve Bank of India   248
Indian Ocean   34
Indochine   3
Indonesia   3–5, 30, 55, 56, 59, 83
Intellectual Property Rights (IPR)   13, 129, 131, 186, 215
INTOR (International Next Tokamak Reactor)   203
integration of foreign policies   16–17
Interdependence Theory   7
international aid   139, 177, 189
inter-regional dialogue   70, 95–6, 99–100
　see also AMED, ASEM, FEALAC, TEP
Iran   50, 138
Iraq   8, 17, 33, 37, 50, 225, 227, 229
Ireland   221
ITER (International Thermonuclear Experimental Reactor)   16, 196, 202–5
Italy   5, 87
　and China   130, 136, 166
　and Korea   221
　and Taiwan   180

Japan   2–20, 27, 30–1, 34–6, 39, 41–2, 44, 57–63, 67, 69–72, 75–5, 84, 94
　and China   137–9, 151–4, 163, 165
　and India   235, 240–2, 248, 253
　and Korea   146, 213–19, 223, 225–6, 229
　and Taiwan   174–5, 180, 182, 185, 187
　arms sales   166–7
　Diet   197
　Federation of Economic Organizations (Keidanren)   197
　Kyoto Protocol   200–2
　Ministry of Foreign Affairs   202–7
　relations with EU   195–200
Jenkins, Roy   126
Jiang Zemin   32
John Paul II   178
JUSCANZ (Japan, US, Canada, Australia and New Zealand)   61

Kampuchea   85
　see also Cambodia
Karlsruhe   87
Kashmir   8, 14
Kim Dae-jung   215, 221, 222
Kim Jong Il   146, 222
Kim Young-sam   219, 221
Kinkel, Klaus   180
Kohl, Helmut   30, 133
Korea
　EU strategy   67, 74, 213–15, 217–19
　Korean Energy Development Organization (KEDO)   39, 56, 218, 219, 225, 226
　Korean financial crisis   219–20
　North Korea   37, 39, 43, 57, 58, 69
　North Korea and the EU   221–5
　North Korea and China   134, 138, 146–7
　North Korean refugees (China), 134
　nuclear crisis   218, 225–8
　see also Six-Party Talks
　South Korea   36, 42, 57, 60, 63, 69, 70, 71, 73, 75, 76, 84
　South Korea and China   146
　South Korea and Japan   203, 204
　South Korea and India   235
　South Korea and Taiwan   187
　Sunshine policy   221

Korean Peninsula (political relations) 3–19, 36, 39, 44, 58, 146, 164, 213–14, 218, 221, 223, 228–30
Korean War 38, 218
Kosovo 161
Kuala Lumpur 42, 84, 96
Kupchan 236
Kyoto Protocol (UNFCC-COP1) 8, 16, 196, 200–202, 205

Laeken (European Council) 52
Lamy, Pascal 235
Laos 59, 60, 88, 99
Latin American countries 56, 69, 85, 100
  see also MERCOSUR
Latvia 176–7, 181, 188–90, 242
LDC (Least Developed Countries) 74
  see also Lomé Convention
liberalism and neo-liberalism 7, 114
League of Arab States 43
Lee Kwan Yew 30
Lee Teng-hui 175, 181
Leonard, Mark 61
Liechtenstein 62, 174
Lien Chan 180, 181, 188, 189
Lithuania 176, 242
Lomé Convention 54, 85
London 78
Luxembourg 221

Maastricht Treaty 28–32, 49–50, 55, 127, 233, 236
Macau 3, 128, 226
Macedonia 177, 187–190
Malaysia 3, 18, 19, 22, 83, 86
Maldives 252
Malta 242
Mandelson, Peter 155
Manila 18
Market Economy Status (MES) 131, 157–8
Max Planck Institute 203
Mediterranean countries 55, 56, 58, 69, 71
MERCOSUR 42, 69
Merkel, Angela 166
MFN (most favoured nation) 69, 85

Middle East 37, 52, 56, 58, 95, 100, 141
migration 104, 107–8, 115–16, 118
  Chinese to Europe 105–14
  other Asians to Europe 105–7, 111–12
  Authorized Destination Status 155
missile tests 222, 228
modernism and post-modernism 8, 40
Mohammad, Mahathir 31, 86
Moscow 148
Multi-Fibre Agreement 245
multilateralism 5–10, 16–18, 47, 57, 61, 63, 79–80, 94, 98, 140–1, 149–50, 164, 229
multilayered relations 20–1, 59
multipolarity 5–10
Musharaff, President 147
Muslim States 147
Myanmar 21, 42, 43, 55, 59, 88, 99, 136
  see also Burma

NAFTA (North American Free Trade Area) 30, 42, 75, 76, 77
NAS (New Asia Strategy) 67, 70, 73, 74, 75, 80, 87
NATO (North Atlantic Treaty Organization) 44, 49, 50, 51
Nepal 57, 252
Netherlands (The) 3, 22, 35, 40
  and China 128, 130, 138
  and Korea 221
  and Taiwan 174, 175, 179, 185, 188
New World Order 49
New York 62
New Zealand 60, 62, 69, 84
Nice Treaty 33, 52
non-intervention 97
Non-Tariff Barriers (NTB) 245
Nordic countries 214
Norway 7, 62
nuclear
  1994 crisis 217–18
  2002 crisis 57, 225–8

nuclear – *continued*
  Non-proliferation Treaty (NPT) 218, 226, 251
  research (EU–China) 140
  test (North Korea) 228
  uranium enrichment 225, 227
  see also Six-Party Talks, ITER, INTOR

OAU (Organization of African Unity) 43
ODA (Official Development Assistance) 34, 235
OECD 69, 74
OSCE (Conference for Security and Cooperation in Europe) 18

Pakistan 18, 57, 146–7, 252
Partnership and Cooperation Agreement (PCA) 132, 158
Patten, Chris 222
peace-keeping 34, 39, 40, 50, 55
Pearl River Delta 130
Persson, Goran 222
Philippines 3–5, 83
Poland 5
  and India 242, 244, 245
  and Taiwan 176, 187
political economy 10–14
policy learning 88–90, 98–100
policy networks 140
policy variations 11–14, 20–1
Polo, Marco 66
Portugal 3, 30, 41, 59, 87, 214
Prodi, Romano 229
protectionism 39
public opinion 4
Pyongyang 221, 222, 225

Rammell, Bill 227
Reagan, Ronald 203
realism and neo-realism 6, 114, 125, 140, 145–50, 167–8
Red Cross, 134
regionalism, regional integration 17–19, 29, 33, 95, 149
  see also APEC, ASEAN, EU, NAFTA, MERCOSUR, SAARC, Shanghai Cooperation Organisation
Rice, Condoleezza 137

Rokkasho-mura 203, 204
Romania 189
Roosevelt, Theodore 27
Russia 5, 55, 58, 60, 84
  and China 136, 138, 141, 157, 163, 166
  and Japan 203, 204, 206, 207
  and Korea 214, 226, 230
  see also Soviet Union

SAARC (South Asian Association for Regional Cooperation) 59, 60, 235, 249, 252
Scandinavian countries 174, 179
Seattle 32
Second World War 9, 27, 29, 31, 32, 66, 71, 79
security 55, 57, 86–100, 236, 248
  see also arms embargo, arms sales, Korea, nuclear, peace-keeping, September 11, Six-party talks, Taiwan, terrorism, Timor Leste, WMD
Seoul 78
September 11 (2001) 37, 128
Shanghai 38
Shanghai Cooperation Organization 43, 163
Singapore 3, 4, 7, 19, 30, 42, 73, 83, 86
Singh, Manmohan 250
Single European Act 197, 234
Single European Market 49, 66, 71, 72, 80, 126, 127
Six-party talks 146, 164, 226–8
  see also Korea
Slovakia 242
Soames, Christopher 126
soft power 29, 40–1, 43–4, 115, 125, 158–62
Solana, Javier 50, 61, 222, 228
South Korea
  see under Korea
Soviet Union 9, 27, 55, 85
  and China 126
  and Korea 214, 223
  and Taiwan 174, 176
  see also Russia

Spain   5, 189, 203, 221
Special Administrative Region (SAR)   224, 225
Sri Lanka   252
stability (of international relations)   5–10
Straw, Jack   225
Sudan   136
Suharto   32
Sweden   17, 71, 166, 243–4
Switzerland   62, 76, 174

Taiwan (Republic of China, ROC)   3, 12, 14, 16, 18–19, 36, 37, 73, 137, 145, 148, 162, 166, 167, 176–86
 and East and Central Europe,   176–80
 and Vatican,   177–8
 and Western Europe   178–80
 democratization   175
 economic diplomacy   172–3, 179, 181, 182
 economic interests   185–8
 EU–Taiwan relations   182–5
 flexible diplomacy   175–6, 179, 190
 Taipei China–EBRD Cooperation Fund   176
 Taiwan Strait   8, 14, 173, 184, 191
 total diplomacy   174
Tanaka, Makiko   206
Transatlantic Economic Partnership (TEP)   70
Transatlantic Free Trade Area (TAFTA)   69
Taliban (Afghanistan)   147
Tanabe, Toshiaki   201
terrorism   4, 5, 10, 14, 21, 36–8, 57–8, 104, 147, 167, 236, 240, 250, 251
textile exports   131–2, 155–6, 196, 234, 244–6
Thailand   40, 42, 57, 83
Timor   3, 30
Timor Leste (East Timor)   7, 34, 41, 56, 58–60, 71, 85–7
Tokyo   196, 197

trade
 EU–China   129–39, 151–3
 EU–India   236–8
 EU–Japan   195
 EU–Taiwan   185–8
 liberalization   29
 Quantitative Restrictions (QRs)   197, 198
 Trade Barriers Regulation (TBR)   77
 USA–China   126, 131, 151–6
 see also textile exports, GATT, Uruguay Round, WTO, protectionism
Tseng Wen-fui,   181
Tsunami (December 2004)   37
Turkey   5, 7, 243

Uighur separatist movement   147
UK (the United Kingdom)   3, 5, 11, 19, 20, 50, 51, 34, 41, 87, 174, 180, 181, 188
 and China   130, 134, 136, 137, 161, 166
 and India   243
 and Korea   218, 221, 227, 230
 and Taiwan,   174, 180, 181, 188
Ukraine   55, 58, 60, 176, 188
UN (the United Nations)   8, 9, 12, 14, 22, 28, 53, 57, 61, 62, 85, 135, 148, 149
 and Japan   198, 200
 and Korea   227, 228, 230
 and Taiwan   174, 181, 183, 189, 190
UN Framework Convention on Climate Change (UNFCCC)   200, 201
 see also Kyoto Protocol
UN General Assembly Resolution   85, 227, 228
UN High Commissioner for Human Rights   134
UNHRC (United Nations' Human Rights Commission)   127, 128, 133, 135, 136, 159
UN Human Rights Council   135
UN Human Rights Covenants   134
UN Security Council   3, 127, 132, 148, 165, 209, 218, 230

UNCTAD   77
UNDP   7
unipolarity   5–10, 21–2, 125, 141, 145, 158, 164
Uruguay Round   71, 72, 73, 155
USA (United States of America)   1–24, 27–44, 49, 58–62, 66–79, 84, 86, 94
  and Eastern Turkistan   147
  and India   234, 240–2, 246, 252–3
  and Japan   148, 150, 163, 199–208
  and Korea   214–30
  and Kosovo   161
  and Pakistan   147
  and Taiwan   166, 173–91
  neo-conservatives   146, 149
  war on terror   4
US Arms Embargo on China   136–8, 162, 166–7
USA–China trade   126, 131, 151–6
US Congress   137
US–Japan alliance   148, 150, 163
US–North Korean Agreed Framework   146
Uzbekistan   56

Vandellos   203
Vatican   14, 18, 177–8, 190
  see also Holy See

Vietnam   3, 37, 55, 70, 85
Vietnam War   3, 38

Walesa, Lech   176, 182
Wang Chih-kang   183
war on terror   4
Washington   37
Wei Jinsheng   128
Wen Jiabao   154, 165
Westphalian system,   8
WEU (Western European Union)   18, 50, 51
WMD (weapons of mass destruction)   57, 138, 162, 163, 167, 250
World Bank   37, 73
World Health Organization (WHO)   183
World Trade Organization (WTO)   8, 9, 10, 12, 13, 22, 40, 67, 69, 74, 155, 156, 182, 183, 185, 199, 207, 243, 244

Yang Bin   224
Yangon   42
Yangtze River Delta   130
Yugoslavia   189

Zen, Joseph   178